ARNE & CARLOS

FAVORITE DESIGNS

Greatest Hits & New Inspirations

Photography: Ragnar Hartvig

TRAFALGAR SQUARE
North Pomfret, Vermont

First published in the United States of
America in 2018 by
Trafalgar Square Books
North Pomfret, Vermont 05053

Originally published in Norwegian as
Arne & Carlos: Favoritter.

Copyright © 2017 Cappelen Damm AS
English translation © 2018 Trafalgar
Square Books

ISBN: 978-1-57076-881-1

Library of Congress Control Number:
2017963086

Photography: Ragnar Hartvig
Stylist: Ingrid Skaansar
Design and Layout: Ingrid Skjæraasen
**Photos, pages 150, 154-155 and
160-161:** Hans Christian Barth
Styling: Patra Knoblauch
Hair and Makeup: Heiko Palach
Photo, page 9: Børre Høstland,
National Museum
Models: Caroline Schrödl/Mega and
Jonathan Hannestad/Modelwerk
Translation: Carol Huebscher
Rhoades

Printed in China

10 9 8 7 6 5 4 3 2 1

Contents

Foreword **7**

In the Playroom **11**

Easter at
Our House **53**

Out in Our Garden **95**

In the Wardrobe **147**

Christmas at
the Cabin **197**

Techniques **258**

Abbreviations **264**

Foreword

The best up to now—and a little more!

This year, we are celebrating 15 years as the design team ARNE & CARLOS. We've had quite a fantastic trip so far! From the day we decided to try and establish ourselves in the fashion industry up to today, we can look back on an unbelievable international career. We've published ten books in sixteen languages and enjoyed many other exciting projects, ranging from collaborations with the avant-garde Japanese fashion brand Comme des Garçons on designs from wine serviettes and wine packaging, to self-patterning sock yarns for the German yarn company Regia. We've been privileged to have the opportunity travel around the world, making many wonderful and inspiring new friends; we've told our stories and listened to theirs.

Many people wonder where our ideas come from, and we tend to answer that most of them come when we're at home. We do derive a lot of inspiration from places we visit and people we meet! But it's here at our house in Tonsåsen, Norway, that products and designs are developed. When you have an old house that needs maintenance or refurbishing, and you do much of the work yourself, you can clear your head and think things through while you take down a wall or build a new one. It's not always so easy to differentiate between what your job is and what is private. Much of what might otherwise be private can easily become part of our books. It often happens like that when one does creative work! Sometimes we think it's rather remarkable that this has become our job, and even if a lot of work is involved, we are lucky that we can make a go of it. But one can't just be fortunate or lucky—one must work hard.

We started small, with some simple gingham fabric that we bought on sale, a lot of courage, and a clear vision of what we wanted to do and how we could establish ourselves as designers. Dolly Parton and an old record player with the accompanying vinyl records were our first source of inspiration. The year was 2002. That was when our personal universe was conceived and began to take shape. At the beginning, we didn't even realize we were creating our own world out of all these things we love; we didn't know how it would end up

7

developing, step by step, through our work. After we created our company, these sources of inspiration took on their own life and found a secure home in our little universe. Today we believe that many of our most enthusiastic readers think of the world of Arne & Carlos as a colorful and productive place filled with creativity and the joy of handcrafting.

Our garden is especially important and has a central place in our universe, with flowers, birds, and insects as continual sources of inspiration. We love to be creative through play and are very much inspired by our childhoods, so dolls and dollhouses often figure in our books. Handcrafts are ever-present in our house, especially knitting, crochet, and embroidery. And we are very happy in our joint Nordic handcraft traditions. We often look at old patterns and techniques and try to bring out the best in them, to give them a modern twist and make them relevant for today's public. The Christmas balls are a shining example of how we've transformed traditional motifs and used them in new ways—and not just for the sake of creating something exciting and new, but also to develop our cultural heritage and make these lovely traditions come alive for a new generation.

In this book, we've collected our favorite designs and some of the projects that have been the most successful. *55 Christmas Balls to Knit* launched our knitting world careers in 2010. Those balls have taken us around the world, and we've knitted several hundred of them! Every year, when fall arrives, we take them out again. Sometimes we knit old designs from the book, but we're always developing new designs, further enriching the concept.

The knitted dolls continue in the best of health. And if any of our designs may be said to live their own lives, it's definitely the knitted dolls! The dolls are still gaining new members of their little family, and it is totally fantastic to see how different each can be. We love the notion that we don't only make patterns people can knit from, but we also inspire

people to develop their own creativity! By that we mean that *Knitted Dolls* is the book most often mentioned to us as the one that first inspired someone to try developing their own ideas and designs, instead of always following patterns. You can knit the dolls by sticking only to our exact instructions, but there's no limit to the possibilities you can pursue if you want to, and it's easy to change little things about the dolls to make them your own. This is the biggest compliment we can receive!

As we mentioned earlier, the garden is our most important source of inspiration, and the primrose throw was the first design we made for the book *Knit-and-Crochet Garden*. We crocheted 525 flowers with various types of yarn, each in a different color combination! This is perhaps one of the best collaborative projects we have had—particularly towards the end, when one of us sat and crocheted all the flowers together while the other followed, weaving in all the ends until the throw was completely finished.

We have also taken some of our favorites from *Norwegian Knits with a Twist*, but this time we decided to add some projects from our collaboration with the German company Schachenmayr. Combining old traditions in new garments is one of our most important mantras when we work with design.

Last, but not least, slippers and socks had to be included because it's so nice to wear colorful and warm foot coverings when you want to be cozy at home.

Looking back on everything we've produced during the past fifteen years, choosing some of the items we think are best, placing them in a completely new context, and giving them a new twist has been a very exciting project.

This is our story.
Come on in!

ARNE & CARLOS

Dolly Parton, an old record player, and a vinyl record collection were our first sources of inspiration. That was back in 2002.

DOLLY PARTON-KOLLEKSJONEN
Vår/sommar 2002

Arne & Carlos hentar inspirasjon frå
Dolly Parton, musikken hennar og
det livet ho lever. Kombinas...
humor, kitsch og forseggjor...
set stemninga for kollek...

Imagine you're a kid again, and walk into a house full of surprises. A house stuffed with rare items and toys, where it's totally okay to be messy, to take out everything and put it wherever you want it, with no one telling you to clean up after yourself! A house with many antique dressers, large chests, and old wardrobes, all full of hand-knitted clothes, dolls, and other exciting things—things that have been sitting there, quietly put away, but get to come out and play when you visit. Everything you could ever want to make you happy!

In the Playroom

PLAY WITH ME

Slippers

with motifs from an old scrapbook

We found this pattern idea in a calendar with drawings of costumes from various nations, including those of Native Americans. We sketched it out in 2007 but never used it. This slipper pattern proves that you should never discard old design ideas! You never know when they might come in handy.

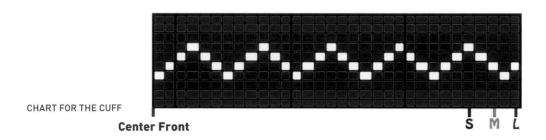

CHART FOR THE CUFF

Center Front

S M L

With Brown and short circular or dpn, CO 56 (60, 64) sts. Join, being careful not to twist cast-on row. The rnd begins at center back of the slipper; pm for beginning of rnd. The cast-on row = the first row of the chart. Don't forget to knit by alternating two strands of the color when working single-color rounds. Knit around following the chart, beginning at the marker for your size. After completing the 9 charted rounds, continue with 2 strands of Red. Divide the sts to work the heel: Use the center back 28 (30, 32) sts for the heel and leave the rem 28 (30, 32) sts on a holder for the instep.

HEEL
Row 1: K14 (15, 16), knitting last st with both strands; turn.
Row 2: Sl 1, p27 (29, 31), purling last st with both strands; turn.
Work another 11 rows back and forth in St st over the 28 (30, 32) heel sts, always slipping the first st.

HEEL TURN
Row 14: P13 (15, 17), p2tog, p1 with both strands; turn.
Row 15: K3 (5, 7), k2tog, k1 with both strands; turn.
Rows 16-23: Continue the same way, working back and forth in St st and shaping, with 1 more st before the decrease on each row (the decrease joins the sts before/after the gap).

LEVEL OF DIFFICULTY
Advanced

MATERIALS
Yarn:
CYCA #4 (worsted/afghan/aran),
Rauma Vamsegarn (100% wool,
91 yd/83 m / 50 g)
Yarn Colors and Amounts:
Brown V64, 100 g
Red V18, 100 g
Green V45, 50 g
Light Blue V50, 50 g
White V01, 50 g
Bright Yellow V25: 50 g
Needles: U.S. size 8-10 / 5-6 mm:
16 in / 40 cm circular and set of 5
dpn
Recommended Gauge: 14-16 sts =
4 in / 10 cm

NOTE: Alternate two strands of
yarn on every stitch throughout (as
for two-end or Fair Isle knitting).

Slippers with Motifs from an Old Scrapbook

FOOT CHART

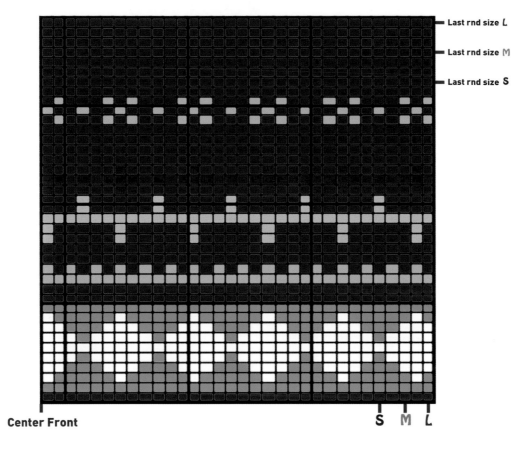

Last rnd size **L**

Last rnd size **M**

Last rnd size **S**

Center Front

S M L

Row 24: P12 (14, 16), p2tog, p1 with both strands; turn.

Row 25: K13 (15, 17), k2tog with both strands; turn. (This row ends with k2tog and not k1 as previously).

Row 26: P13 (15, 17), p2tog, p1 with both strands; turn.

FOOT

Set-up Rnd: Ssk, k6 (7, 8). Pm at center of sole, k7 (8, 9), pick up and knit 7 sts evenly spaced across one side of the heel flap, k28 (30, 32) across instep, pick up and knit 7 sts evenly spaced across other side of heel flap and k7 (8, 9) on sole. The beginning of the rnd is at center of sole.

Foot: Knit 33 (36, 39) rnds on the 56 (60, 64) sts of foot.

TOE SHAPING

Divide the sts onto 4 dpn with 14 (15, 16) sts on

each needle. With Brown, shape toe as follows, with 8 sts decreased on each decrease rnd.

Rnd 1 (decrease rnd): At beginning of each needle: K1, k2tog. At end of each needle: K2tog, k1.

Rnd 2: Knit.

Repeat Rnds 1-2 until 16 (20, 16) sts rem. Cut yarn and draw end through remaining sts. Pull tight and weave in all ends neatly on WS.

Gently steam press slippers before felting.

FELTING

Use a wool-safe liquid soap. For 2.2 lb / 1 kg knitted fabric, you should use about 6 tablespoons / 100 ml soap. Set the water temperature for the machine at 104-140°F / 40-60°C (the temperature options vary from machine to machine). Start at the lower temperature and check the degree of felting occasionally.

Sock Yarn Teddy Bear

This is one of our most popular designs. Originally, we made the bear Såve for our book *Norwegian Knits with a Twist*. The idea was to use Setesdal patterns in a new way, on items other than sweaters.

Sock Yarn Teddy Bear

We've revised the pattern for the teddy bear, because the old bear was knitted with one strand and omitted some stitches needed to balance the motifs. You can say that this is an updated version of our teddy bear—Såve, version 2.0. We like how the colorways now match on both legs, arms, and ears. To achieve this effect, it's important to follow the row sequence in the instructions when knitting the parts of the body. On our old bear, you began with the legs and then worked the stomach. On our new Såve bear, you first work one leg, one arm, and one ear. Then you unwind the yarn ball until you find the beginning of the same color sequence as for the beginning of the first leg, and then you can knit the second leg, arm, and ear. After that, you work the stomach from the unwound yarn, and that way you'll use up most of the yarn in the ball.

LEVEL OF DIFFICULTY
Advanced

MATERIALS
Yarn:
CYCA #1 (fingering), Schachenmayr Regia Design Line by Arne & Carlos, 4-ply (75% wool, 25% nylon, 459 yd/420 m / 100 g), 100 g.
Yarn Colors:
We have designed 21 color combinations of sock yarn for Regia Design Line by Arne & Carlos, so there is bound to be a colorway for every taste! You'll also need some single-color white yarn for the face and black yarn for the nose and mouth.
White 02080
Black 02066
Other Materials: Fiberfill or carded wool batts for stuffing; 2 safety pins
Needles: U.S. size 1.5 / 2.5 mm: 16 in / 40 cm circular and set of 5 dpn
Gauge: 30 sts and 42 rnds = 4 x 4 in / 10 x 10 cm
The exact number of stitches per 4 in / 10 cm is not as important here as that the knitting be firm enough so the filling won't show through the knit fabric when Såve is knitted and filled.

Knitting Tips
We recommend that you knit the pieces in this sequence if you want the right and left sides of the teddy to match: 1st leg, 1st arm, 1st ear; 2nd leg, 2nd arm, 2nd ear. Sew any holes from the cast-on rows closed, and then join the pieces as described in the instructions.

Sock Yarn Teddy Bear

LEG

Unwind the yarn to find a point in the color sequence that will be easy to match for the next leg.
NOTE: See page 259 for increase method.

With dpn, CO 12 sts. Divide sts evenly onto 4 dpn = 3 sts per needle. Join.
Rnd 1: K12.
Rnd 2: (K2, inc 1, k1) around = 16 sts.
Rnd 3: K16.
Rnd 4: (K1, inc 1, k2, inc 1, k1) around
Rnd 5: K24.
Rnd 6: (K1, inc 1, k4, inc 1, k1) around.
Rnd 7: K32.
Rnd 8: (K1, inc 1, k6, inc 1, k1) around.
Rnds 9-12: K40.
Rnd 13: K1, inc 1, k38, inc 1, k1.
Rnds 14-17: K42.
Rnd 18: K1, inc 1, k40, inc 1, k1.
Rnds 19-22: K44.
Rnd 23: K1, inc 1, k42, inc 1, k1.
Rnds 24-35 (= 12 rnds): K46.
Rnd 36: K1, inc 1, k44, inc 1, k1.
Rnd 37: K48.
Rnd 38: K1, inc 1, k46, inc 1, k1.
Rnd 39: K50.
Rnd 40: K1, inc, k48, inc 1, k1.
Rnds 41-43: K52.
Rnd 44: BO 5 sts, k42 (including the last st from bind-off), BO 5 sts. Divide rem sts onto 2 dpn with 21 sts on each needle.
Place the leg sts on a holder or circular needle.

ARM

Unwind the yarn to find a point in the color sequence that will be easy to match for the next arm. With dpn, CO 12 sts. Divide sts evenly onto 4 dpn = 3 sts per needle. Join.
Rnd 1: K12.
Rnd 2: (K2, inc 1, k1) around = 16 sts.
Rnd 3: K16.
Rnd 4: (K1, inc 1, k2, inc 1, k1) around.

Rnd 5: K24.
Rnd 6: (K1, inc 1, k4, inc 1, k1) around.
Rnds 7-9: K32.
Rnd 10: K1, inc 1, k30, inc 1, k1.
Rnds 11-13: K34.
Rnd 14: K1, inc 1, k32, inc 1, k1.
Rnds 15-17: K36.
Rnd 18: K1, inc 1, k34, inc 1, k1.
Rnds 19-21: K38.
Rnd 22: K1, inc 1, k36, inc 1, k1.
Rnds 23-25: K40.
Rnd 26: K1, inc 1, k38, inc 1, k1.
Rnds 27-43 (= 17 rnds): K42.
Rnd 44: BO 5 sts, k32 (including the last st from bind-off), BO 5 sts. Divide rem sts onto 2 dpn with 16 sts on each needle.

EAR

Unwind the yarn to find a point in the color sequence that will be easy to match for the next ear. With dpn, CO 12 sts. Divide sts evenly onto 4 dpn = 3 sts per needle. Join.
Rnd 1: K12.
Rnd 2: (K1, inc 1, k1, inc 1, k1) around = 20 sts.
Rnd 3: K20.
Rnd 4: (K1, inc 1, k3, inc 1, k1) around.
Rnd 5: K28.
Rnd 6: (K1, inc 1, k5, inc 1, k1) around.
Rnd 7: K36.
Rnd 8: (K1, inc 1, k7, inc 1, k1) around.
Rnd 9: K44.
Rnd 10: (K1, inc 1, k9, inc 1, k1) around.
Rnd 11: K52.
Rnd 12: (K1, inc 1, k11, inc 1, k1) around.
Rnds 13-23: K60.
Rnd 24: (K1, k2tog, k9, k2tog, k1) around.
Rnd 25: K52.
Rnd 26: (K1, k2tog, k7, k2tog, k1) around.
Rnd 27: K44.
BO knitwise and sew the hole at the cast-on together.

Now work the second leg, arm, and ear the same way, matching the color sequences. Use the beginning yarn end to close the holes at the cast-on for each piece.

STOMACH
Now join the legs: hold the legs with the bound-off edges against each other, in towards the center, and attach inner legs with safety pins. Place sts on circular = 84 sts. Work the stomach with the yarn you wound for it until you get to the starting point for the second leg.
Begin on one side of one leg.
Rnds 1-26: Knit.
Rnd 27: (BO 5 sts, k32 (including last st from bind-off), BO 5 sts) 2 times.
Place the sts of the front and back on separate needles with 32 sts on each needle. Seam the groin.

CHEST
Now join the arms to the body. Hold one of the arms with the bound-off edge to the corresponding edge on the body and attach the pieces with safety pins.
Attach the other arm on opposite side of body the same way.
Work each arm with two dpn until the shaping allows you to place the arms onto one circular. Shape raglan as follows:
Begin with the 1st row on body for the front of the teddy.
Rnd 1: K128.
Rnd 2: K128.
Rnd 3: (K1, k2tog, k26, k2tog, k1) around.
Rnd 4: K120.
Rnd 5: (K1, k2tog, k24, k2tog, k1) around.
Rnd 6: K112.
Rnd 7: (K1, k2tog, k22, k2tog, k1) around.
Rnd 8: K104.
Rnd 9: (K1, k2tog, k20, k2tog, k1) around.
Rnd 10: K96.
Rnd 11: (K1, k2tog, k18, k2tog, k1) around.

Rnd 12: K88.
Rnd 13: (K1, k2tog, k16, k2tog, k1) around.
Rnd 14: K80.
Rnd 15: (K1, k2tog, k14, k2tog, k1) around.
Rnd 16: K72.
Rnd 17: (K1, k2tog, k12, k2tog, k1) around.
Rnd 18: K64.

Remove the safety pins and seam the underarms. Weave in yarns on WS.

Rnd 19: (K1, k2tog, k10, k2tog, k1) around.
Rnd 20: K56.
Rnd 21: (K1, k2tog, k8, k2tog, k1) around.
Rnd 22: K48.

Begin filling the bear with fiberfill or wool.

Rnd 23: (K1, k2tog, k6, k2tog, k1) around.
Rnd 24: K40.
Rnd 25: (K1, k2tog, k4, k2tog, k1) around.
Rnd 26: K32.

HEAD
Rnd 1: K32.
Rnd 2: K32.
Rnd 3: (K1, inc 1, k6, inc 1, k1) around.
Rnd 4: K40.
Rnd 5: (K1, inc 1, k8, inc 1, k1) around.
Rnd 6: K48.
Rnd 7: (K1, inc 1, k10, inc 1, k1) around.
Rnd 8: K56.

Next, make the opening for the snout. Place the sts from Ndl 1 (front) onto a holder while you work back and forth over the rem 42 sts.

Row 9: P42.
Row 10: (K1, inc 1, k12, inc 1, k1) across.
Row 11: P48.
Row 12: (K1, inc 1, k14, inc 1, k1) across.
Row 13: P54.

Row 14: (K1, inc 1, k16, inc 1, k1) across.
Row 15: P60.
Row 16: (K1, inc 1, k18, inc 1, k1) across.
Row 17: P66.
Row 18: (K1, inc 1, k20, inc 1, k1) across.
Row 19: P72.
Row 20: (K1, inc 1, k22, inc 1, k1) across.
Row 21: P78.
Row 22: (K1, inc 1, k24, inc 1, k1) across.
Row 23: P84.
Now arrange the sts onto 4 dpn as follows:
Row 24: Work across Ndls 2-4: (K1, inc 1, k26, inc 1, k1) on each needle. CO 30 new sts on a new Ndl 1 over the gap for the snout.
Rnd 25: K120.
Rnd 26: (K1, inc 1, k28, inc 1, k1) around.
Rnds 27-35 (= 9 rnds): K128.
Rnd 36: (K1, k2tog, k26, k2tog, k1) around.
Rnd 37: K120.
Rnd 38: (K1, k2tog, k24, k2tog, k1) around.
Rnd 39: K112.
Rnd 40: (K1, k2tog, k22, k2tog, k1) around.
Rnd 41: K104.
Rnd 42: (K1, k2tog, k20, k2tog, k1) around.
Rnd 43: K96.
Rnd 44: (K1, k2tog, k18, k2tog, k1) around.
Rnd 45: K88.
Rnd 46: (K1, k2tog, k16, k2tog, k1) around.
Rnd 47: K80.
Rnd 48: (K1, k2tog, k14, k2tog, k1) around.
Rnd 49: K72.
Rnd 50: (K1, k2tog, k12, k2tog, k1) around.
Rnd 51: K64.
Rnd 52: (K1, k2tog, k10, k2tog, k1) around.
Rnd 53: K56.
Rnd 54: (K1, k2tog, k8, k2tog, k1) around.
Rnd 55: K48.
Rnd 56: (K1, k2tog, k6, k2tog, k1) around.
Rnd 57: K40.
Rnd 58: (K1, k2tog, k4, k2tog, k1) around.
Rnd 59: K32.
Rnd 60: (K1, k2tog, k2, k2tog, k1) around.
Rnd 61: K24.

Rnd 62: (K1, k2tog, k2tog, k1) around.
Rnd 63: K16.
Rnd 64: (K1, k2tog, k1) around.

Cut yarn and draw end through rem 12 sts; tighten yarn and use end to close the hole at top of head. Weave in all ends neatly on WS.
Before you knit the snout, fill the body with fiberfill or wool.
If you want to reinforce the neck, roll a piece of cotton fabric and push it down into the chest to anchor it, allowing it to extend halfway up into the head (see photo to right). Cushion all around the fabric with fiberfill or wool.

SNOUT
With one dpn, pick up and knit 30 sts around the snout opening. Place the snout's bottom edge 14 sts from the holder on another dpn. With a separate dpn for each side, pick up and knit 16 sts on each side of the snout. Now divide all the sts onto 4 dpn with 19 sts on each.

Rnd 1: K76.
Rnd 2: (K1, k2tog, k13, k2tog, k1) around.
Rnd 3: K68.
Rnd 4: (K1, k2tog, k11, k2tog, k1) around.
Rnd 5: K60.
Weave in the yarn ends before you continue knitting.
Rnd 6: (K1, k2tog, k9, k2tog, k1) around.
Rnd 7: K52.
Rnd 8: (K1, k2tog, k7, k2tog, k1) around.
Rnd 9: K44.
Rnd 10: (K1, k2tog, k5, k2tog, k1) around.
Rnd 11: K36.
Rnd 12: (K1, k2tog, k3, k2tog, k1) around.
Rnd 13: K28.
Rnd 14: (K1, k2tog, k1, k2tog, k1) around.
Rnd 15: K20.
Rnd 16: (K1, k2tog, k2) around.
Rnd 17: K16.

Rnd 18: (K1, k2tog, k1) around.

Cut yarn and draw end through rem 12 sts. Fill the head with fiberfill or wool through the hole in the snout. Sew the hole closed and weave in ends.

Lay the ears flat and then round them at the base, with the front towards the snout. Sew the ears securely to the head on the sides of the opening. With black yarn, embroider on the mouth, nose, and eyes.

Knit a few rounds. If you're afraid the head will be floppy, you can fix that now. We used a piece of cotton fabric, folded it in half, and rolled it into a "sausage," which we doubled over. The fabric should extend a little way into the chest and halfway up into the head. Fill the lower neck with fiberfill or wool and finish by filling the head behind the fabric.

The stitches around the snout have been picked up and the first round has been knitted.

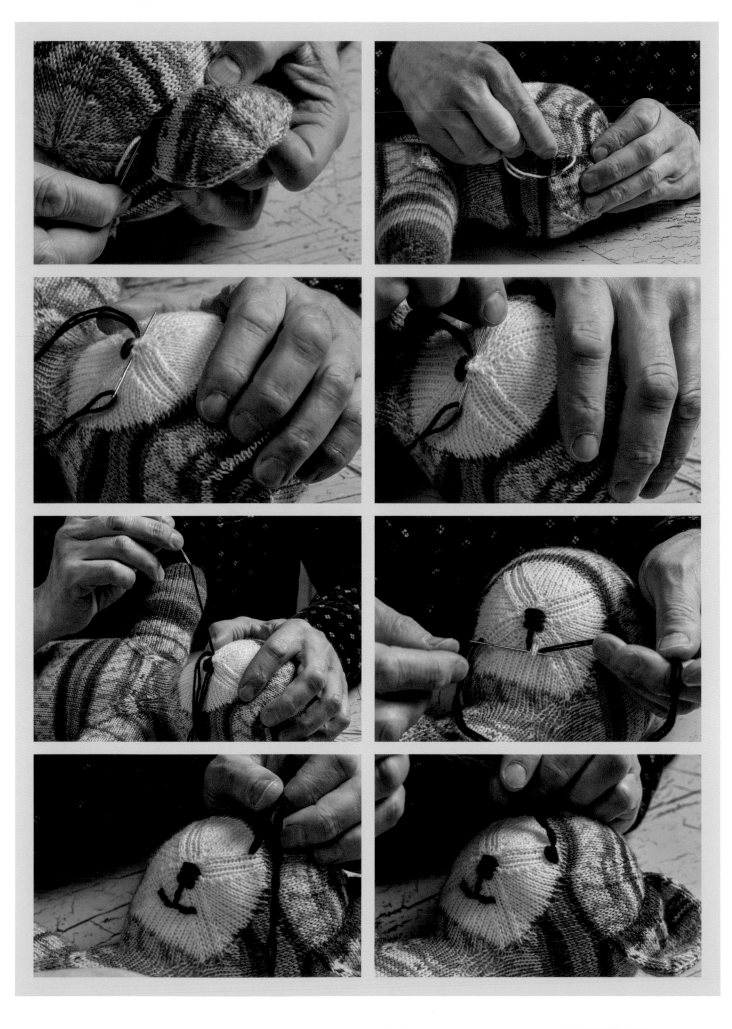

Horse Pillow

A few years ago, we found a rocking horse at an antiques shop. The seller mentioned he had two of them, one with a saddle and underside in blue and one with red. He'd bought them from a man who had given his son the blue one and his daughter the red one as gifts, sometime in the 1950s. The rocking horse was our inspiration for a printed T-shirt and the embroidered pillow.

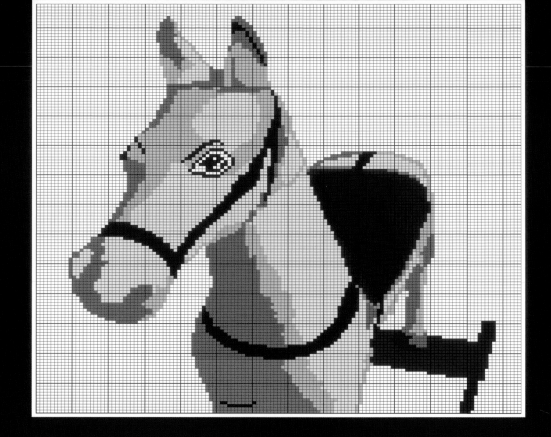

Count the holes in the canvas to calculate how many squares you'll need. Begin about ¾ in / 2 cm in and about ¾ in / 2 cm from a corner and cut the canvas to the necessary size. We recommending reinforcing the canvas with overlock all around the edges of the canvas to avoid tears. Use an embroidery frame and keep the canvas stretched as you work. Otherwise, the canvas can stretch on its own, unevenly, and make it increasingly difficult to stitch correctly, because the canvas softens as you embroider. Use a blunt needle. Embroider with half cross stitch.

After completing the embroidery, gently steam press the cover under a damp pressing cloth. Sew on the fabric backing. The backing can either be a heavy cotton or thin wool fabric. Cut out a longer and a shorter piece so they can overlap. Seam the pieces so the backing is the same size as the pillow front. With wrong sides out, sew the backing to the pillow front. Gently steam press the seams open and then turn the cover right side out through the back opening. Sew on snaps for closure or make buttonholes and sew on buttons.

LEVEL OF DIFFICULTY
Advanced

FINISHED MEASUREMENTS:
17¾ x 17¾ in / 45 x 45 cm.

MATERIALS
Yarn: Anchor Tapestry Wool from Coats (100% wool, 11 yd / 10 m skeins)
Yarn Amounts and Colors:
12 skeins White 8002
3 skeins Dark Gray 9792
2 skeins Medium Gray 9788
3 skeins Light Gray 9784
2 skeins Black 9646
1 skein Brown 9540
2 skeins Red 8216
1 skein Light Blue 8806
Other Materials: 4-thread canvas 2.6 (Permin product #703-26): 24 in / 60 cm; blunt tapestry needle for embroidery; embroidery frame; heavy cotton or thin wool fabric for backing (same size as canvas); pillow form slightly larger than cover

Knitted Dolls

For as long as we've worked creatively, we've worked with dolls in one way or another. And our knitted dolls aren't just for kids! The young at heart also love them. Even if you don't want to play with them, you can enjoy making clothes and accessories for them.

Materials for the Knitted Dolls

YARN

We swapped from the yarn originally suggested in *Knitted Dolls* to Schachenmayr, since some of the colors from the book are no longer available in the original yarn. You can use any other suitable yarn that you want, as long as it knits to the gauge on U.S. size 1.5 / 2.5 mm needles. We knitted a doll in pure new wool and put it in the washing machine set at 140°F / 60°C with some clothes. The doll came out half the size. Now it could wear the garments we had previously knit for a Barbie doll.

As far as yarn amounts, a ball of each color for the doll and its clothing will be plenty. The only exception is the long dress with the lace robe (see page 49). You'll need two balls of yarn for that outfit.

YARN COLORS

We've used several colors for doll skin, for the sake of diversity and variety—we are all unique! For the dolls we've knitted since our book was first published, we used **Schachenmayr Merino Extrafine 120** for the skin colors:

White 00101
Light Pink 00124
Camel 00105
Marone 00110
Chocolate 00111
Mocha 001112
Black 00199

There's no particular color we'd recommend over any other. Each doll has its own wonderful personality, which matters much more! Use whatever color you please for the hair and eyebrows. Feel free to choose for yourself!

In the section with the garment patterns, we list the color numbers and yarn types that we used for the various outfits. It's only natural when working with such small projects to search your stash for yarn instead of buying new balls! We list recommended needle sizes for all the garments, so you can use whatever yarn and colors you find as long as they work with those needles.

GAUGE

We knitted our dolls at a gauge of 3 sts = ⅜ in / 1 cm. We recommend that you knit a small gauge swatch to check the gauge before you start knitting a doll.

Knitting Tips

The yarns we suggest are machine-washable so the dolls won't shrink in the washer. One warning before machine-washing your doll—the doll should be firmly filled with wool.

We recommend using metal needles when knitting the dolls. The dolls need to be firmly knitted to stay durable, and it's usually not possible to knit as firmly with bamboo or wood needles. However, the garments can be worked on any needles you like.

We are all unique!

The Doll Body—Basic Instructions

We begin the dolls with the legs and work up. In addition to the eyes, there are only three seams to sew on the doll body: between the legs and under the arms. Fill the body with clean wool as you knit and make sure the filling is evenly distributed and not clumpy. The entire doll can be knitted in whatever skin color you prefer—but since the dolls are so thin, it's a little difficult to make undergarments for them. For that reason, we decided to knit the underclothes directly on the body. Milton is wearing a red "speedo" swimming suit; Kaja sports a patterned T-shirt while Sissel and Agnethe wear striped leggings.

RIGHT FOOT

With needles U.S. size 1.5 / 2.5 mm, CO 8 sts. Divide sts evenly over 4 dpn = 2 sts on each needle. Join, being careful not to twist cast-on sts.

Rnd 1: K8.
Rnd 2: *K1, inc 1, k1*; rep from * to * around.
Rnd 3: K12.
Rnd 4: *K1, inc 1, k1, inc 1, k1*; rep from * to * around.
Rnd 5: K20.
Rnd 6: *K1, inc 1, k3, inc 1, k1*; rep from * to * around = 28 sts.
Knit 8 rnds or ¾ in (2 cm).
Weave in yarn end at tip of toe neatly on WS, pulling end to close hole. Stuff foot with wool.

HEEL

Over a fourth of the stitches (=7 sts over Ndl 1), work 8 rows back and forth in St st (knit 1 row, turn and purl 1 row), beginning with a knit (RS) row.

Continue by working over all 4 needles as follows:
Ndl 1: K7.
Ndl 2: With an extra dpn, pick up and knit 5 sts from the side of the heel flap and then knit. Knit the 7 sts on Ndl 2 = 12 sts.
Ndl 3: K7.
Ndl 4: K7 and then pick up and knit 5 sts from the other side of the heel with Ndl 4 = 38 sts around. Pm for beginning of rnd between Ndls 1 and 4.

LEVEL OF DIFFICULTY
Intermediate

MATERIALS
Yarn for Body and Hair:
CYCA #3 (DK, light worsted), Schachenmayr Merino Extrafine 120 (100% Merino wool, 131 yd/120 m / 50 g)
Needles: U.S. size 1.5 / 2.5 mm: 2 sets of 5 dpn
Other Materials: 2.8 oz / 80 g wool for the filling
Gauge: The doll must be knitted firmly; go down a needle size if necessary. You don't want the wool stuffing to come out or show through the stitches.

LEGS AND THIGHS

Rnd 1: K7, k2tog, k27, k2tog.
Rnd 2: Knit around.
Rnd 3: K7, k2tog, k25, k2tog.
Rnd 4: Knit around.
Rnd 5: K7, k2tog, k23, k2tog.
Rnd 6: Knit around.
Rnd 7: K7, k2tog, k21, k2tog.
Rnd 8: Knit around.
Rnd 9: K7, k2tog, k19, k2tog.
Rnd 10: Knit around.
Rnd 11: (K1, k2tog, k1, k2tog, k1) around.
Rnd 12: K20.
Rnd 13: (K1, k2tog, k2) around.
Rnd 14: K16.
Rnd 15: (K1, k2tog, k1) around.
12 sts now remain.

RIGHT LEG

Begin with the right leg by dividing these 12 sts over 3 dpn = 4 sts per ndl; use the 4th ndl to knit with. Knit 70 rnds or 6¾ in / 17 cm. Use a thread marker to indicate the beginning of the round. Stuff the leg with wool as you work. Use a pencil or something similar to push the wool down. Don't fill the piece all the way to the top; that way the wool won't get caught in the knitting.

Finish the right leg as follows:
Rnd 1: K1, inc 1, k10, inc 1, k1.
Rnd 2: K14.
Rnd 3: K1, inc 1, k12, inc 1, k1.
Rnd 4: K16.
Rnd 5: K1, inc 1, k14, inc 1, k1.
Rnd 6: BO 2 sts, k14 (including the last st from the bind-off), BO the last 2 sts.
Divide the leg sts over 2 dpn = 7 sts on each needle.

LEFT FOOT AND LEG

CO 8 sts onto the other set of dpn and follow the instructions for the right leg.

Finish the left leg as follows:
Rnd 1: K5, inc 1, k2, inc 1, k5.
Rnd 2: K14.
Rnd 3: K6, inc 1, k2, inc 1, k6.
Rnd 4: K16.
Rnd 5: K7, inc 1, k2, inc 1, k7.
Rnd 6: K7, BO 4, k7 (including the last st from bind-off).

Divide the leg sts over 2 dpn = 7 sts on each needle.
Join the legs and knit over all sts.
Work 7 rnds or ¾ in / 2 cm.
Seam the groin and fill the legs with wool.

BODY AND ARMS WITH T-SHIRT
Change to the T-shirt color and knit 20 rnds or 1¾ in / 4.5 cm.

Rnd 21: BO 2 sts, k10 (including last st from bind-off), BO 4 sts, k10 (including last st from bind-off), BO the last 2 sts.
Place the 10 front sts on one needle and the 10 back sts on another needle.

BEGIN THE ARMS
CO 8 sts with arm color and U.S. size 1.5 / 2.5 mm needles; divide the sts evenly over 4 dpn = 2 sts per needle.
Rnd 1: K8.
Rnd 2: (K1, inc 1, k1) around.
Rnd 3: K12.
Rnd 4: (K1, inc 1, k1, inc 1, k1) around.
Rnd 5: K20.
Rnd 6: (K1, inc 1, k3, inc 1, k1) around.
Knit 9 rnds or ¾ in / 2 cm.
Weave in the yarn end from tip of hand neatly on WS, pulling it tight to close hole.

Rnd 16: (K1, k2tog, k1, k2tog, k1) around.
Rnd 17: K20.

Rnd 18: (K1, k2tog, k2) around.
Rnd 19: K16.
Rnd 20: (K1, k2tog, k1) around.
Divide remaining 12 sts over 3 dpn = 4 sts on each needle.

Continue by knitting 35 rnds or 3¼ in / 8 cm with skin color. Fill the arm with wool as you work.
Change to T-shirt color and knit 5 rnds.
Last rnd: BO 2 sts, k8 (including the last st from bind-off), BO the last 2 sts. Put the rem 8 sts onto 1 dpn.
Make the other arm the same way.

KNITTING THE BODY AND ARMS TOGETHER
Raglan Shaping:
Divide the sts over 4 dpn, with 8 sts for each arm and 10 sts for the front of the body and 10 sts for the back = 36 sts total.
With T-shirt color:
Rnd 1: K10 for back, k8 for one arm, k10 for front, and k8 for the other arm.
Rnd 2: Back: K1, k2tog, k4, k2tog, k1; arm: k8; front: k1, k2tog, k4, k2tog, k1; arm: k8.
Rnd 3: K32.
Rnd 4: (K1, k2tog, k2, k2tog, k1) around.
Rnd 5: K24.
Rnd 6: (K1, k2tog, k2tog, k1) around = 16 sts rem.
Seam the underarms and weave in all ends on WS.
Fill with wool.

We've made several designs for T-shirts and leggings which are knitted directly on the body—we have both single-color and patterned T-shirts as well as single-color leggings and striped leggings.

The Doll's Eyes, Nose, and Mouth

Now it's time to put life into the doll. Once the eyes are made, everything changes! The doll's something more than just a sweet little project you're working on, once it has eyes—after all, for many children, eyes attached to a sock are enough to turn it into a living creature. There's no turning back: the doll takes over and wants to have both a mouth and hair.

NECK AND HEAD

Rnd 1: K16.

Rnd 2: (K1, k2tog, k1) around.

Rnds 3-8: Knit.

Rnd 9: (K1, inc 1, k1, inc 1, k1) around.

Rnd 10: K20.

Rnd 11: (K1, inc 1, k3, inc 1, k1) around.

Rnd 12: K28.

Rnd 13: (K1, inc 1, k5, inc 1, k1) around.

Rnd 14: K36.

Rnd 15: (K1, inc 1, k7, inc 1, k1) around.

Rnd 16: K44.

Rnd 17: (K1, inc 1, k9, inc 1, k1) around.

Rnd 18: K52.

Rnd 19: (K1, inc 1, k11, inc 1, k1) around.

Rnd 20: K60.

Rnd 21: (K1, inc 1, k13, inc 1, k1) around.

Rnds 22-24: Knit.

NOSE

Rnd 25: Knit the nose as follows:

Ndl 1: K17.

Ndl 2: K17.

Ndl 3: K8, inc 5 by working (k1, p1, k1, p1, k1) into the 9th st.

Turn and purl the 5 sts.

Turn and k5.

Turn and p5.

Finish nose on RS by knitting the 5 sts on right ndl, and then passing the 2nd st over the 1st st; do the same with the 3rd, 4th, and then the 5th st. Pull the sts together and end with k8.

Ndl 4: K17.

Rnd 26: K68.

BEGIN THE HOLES FOR THE EYES

Rnd 27:

Ndl 1: K17.

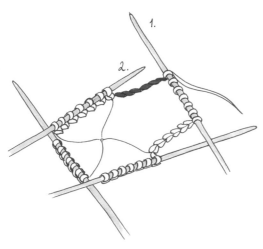

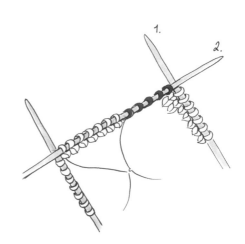

Ndl 2: K17.
Ndl 3: K2, BO 4, k5 (including the last st from bind-off), BO 4 sts, k2 (including last st from bind-off).
Ndl 4: K17.

Rnd 28:
Ndl 1: K17.
Ndl 2: K17.
Ndl 3: K2, CO 4, k5, CO 4, k2.
Ndl 4: K17.
Rnds 29-34: Knit.
Rnd 35: (K1, k2tog, k11, k2tog, k1) around.
Rnd 36: K60.
Rnd 37: (K1, k2tog, k9, k2tog, k1) around.
Rnd 38: K52.

Now prepare the eyes before you continue knitting:

KNITTED EYES
With desired eye color and dpn U.S. 1.5 / 2.5 mm, CO 8 sts.
Rnd 1: With White, k8 sts on 1 needle. Cut eye color and work with White only.
Rnd 2: Divide the 8 sts over 4 dpn and join = 2 sts on each ndl. Work (K1, inc 1, k1) on each of the 4 ndls.
Rnd 3: K12.
Rnd 4: (K1, inc 1, k1, inc 1, k1) around.
Rnd 5: K20.
BO. Make another eye the same way. Weave in ends on WS and carefully steam press the eyes (see page 39 for details).

Sometimes it's easier to sew on buttons for the eyes instead of knitting them! This is the only doll we knitted with pure new wool. She was washed in 140ºF / 60ºC water and came out half as large. She's wearing Barbie's sweater and trousers (the patterns for these garments are not in the book).

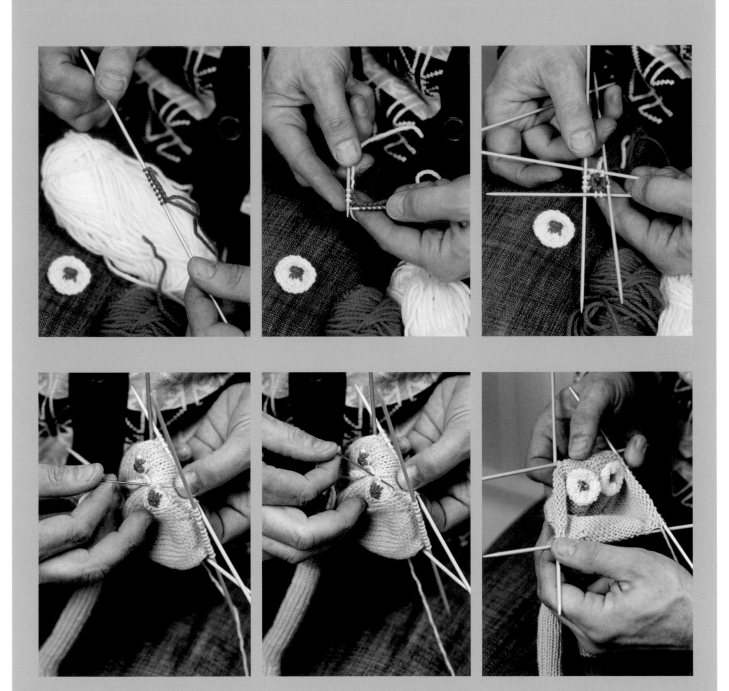

Position the eyes behind the holes, pressing them a little outwards so that the white pupils are somewhat rounded in the eye sockets. Decide which direction the doll will be looking. Sew in the eyes using yarn in the skin color you've chosen.

Caution: If you are making a doll for a young child, don't use buttons or other types of eyes that can be pulled off. Knitted or embroidered eyes are the safest if there are young children in the house.

FINISH HEAD

Rnd 39: (K1, k2tog, k7, k2tog, k1) around.

Rnd 40: K44.

Rnd 41: (K1, k2tog, k5, k2tog, k1) around.

Rnd 42: K36.

Check to make sure the neck is filled properly. If it's not fully stuffed, fill it up well so that the head won't hang down when the doll is finished.

Rnd 43: (K1, k2tog, k3, k2tog, k1) around.

Rnd 44: K28.

Rnd 45: (K1, k2tog, k1, k2tog, k1) around.

Rnd 46: K20.

Rnd 47: (K1, k2tog, k2) around.

Rnd 48: K16.

Rnd 49: (K1, k2tog, k1) around.

Cut yarn and pull end through remaining 12 sts.

Fill the head with wool and sew the hole at the top together. Embroider on the eyelashes with back stitch and embroider on straight stitches for longer eyelashes if you like. We are all different!

MOUTH

Embroider the mouth on with back stitches.

Agnethe has neat black
embroidered eyelashes
while Kaja has lovely
long red lashes.

The Doll's Hair

Use special colors for the hair so each of the dolls will have its own personality. If you're going to machine-wash the doll, it's important that you knot the hair in well so that it doesn't felt—unless you want a doll with dreadlocks, like Ulla! If you want that effect, use a pure wool yarn so the hair will felt and clump after a few cycles in the washing machine. Ulla's hair is made with wool embroidery yarn that we had lying around. Arne and Milton's curly hair came from yarn that we unraveled from an old sweater.

We begin by marking the hairline around the head. Cut the yarn to desired length. We usually wrap the yarn around a notebook (ours are 11½ x 8¼ in / A4) for long hair. Fold the yarn lengths at the center and use a crochet hook to draw the yarn through a stitch. Pull the ends through the yarn loop and tighten. We used one or two strands in each hair length for thinner or thicker hair.

When you've added hair all around the head along the marked hairline, you can choose to section off the area between the decreases at the front. Take all the hair, pull it up and make a ponytail attached to the highest point. If you want, you can add in short yarn lengths for bangs.

Alternately, you can continue to attach hair at various points around the whole head. This means a lot of hair, but you'll have more options for making fun hairstyles and cutting hair to different lengths than if you only make the version with the ponytail.

Siv only has hair around the hairline. We pulled the hair up into a ponytail. The doll with green hair has thicker hair because we attached lengths of yarn at various points around the head.

Milton

MILTON'S BATHING SUIT

We added Milton's bathing suit directly
to the body as we finished the legs. We
changed from the body color to the
swimsuit color, Merino Extrafine 120
Red 00131, and knitted 7 rounds before
we changed back to the body color. We
then seamed the groin with red to finish
the swimsuit.

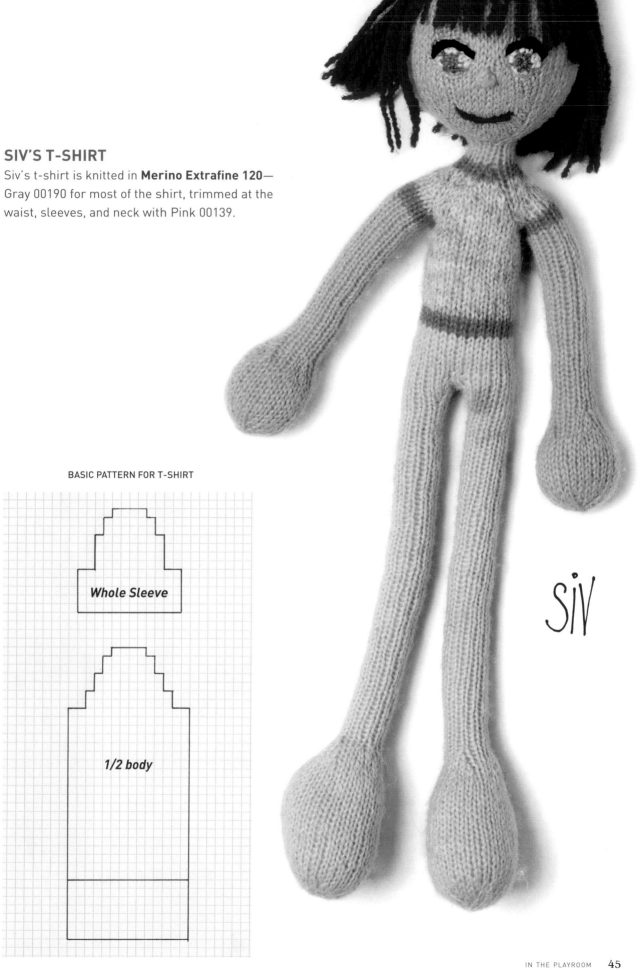

SIV'S T-SHIRT

Siv's t-shirt is knitted in **Merino Extrafine 120**—
Gray 00190 for most of the shirt, trimmed at the
waist, sleeves, and neck with Pink 00139.

BASIC PATTERN FOR T-SHIRT

Whole Sleeve

1/2 body

SiV

The mouth, nose, and eyes are worked in duplicate stitch. To make the face look like a skull, we sewed a black thread from the center of the eyes and out through the back of the head, pulled the yarn until it drew in the eyes, and tied it well. We did the same thing with the nose. The head has deep crevices at the back, but when the hair was attached, it covered them! Even if the crevices show a little, it doesn't matter—this is a spooky doll, after all!

This doll has long, scary fingers. The thumb is knitted with 6 rounds, the index finger with 9 rounds, the middle finger has 11 rounds, the ring finger 10 rounds, and the little finger 6 rounds.

See pattern instructions on page 50.

CHART FOR HEAD

LEVEL OF DIFFICULTY
Intermediate

MATERIALS
Yarn:
CYCA #3 (DK, light worsted),
Schachenmayr Merino Extrafine
120 (100% Merino wool, 131 yd/
120 m / 50 g)
Yarn Colors and Amounts:
Black 00199, 50 g
White 00101, 50 g
Red 00131, 50 g
Needles: U.S. sizes 1.5 and 2.5 /
2.5 and 3 mm: sets of 5 dpn and
short circulars
Gauge: 30 sts on smaller needles
= 4 in / 10 cm.
Although the yarn ball band
recommends U.S. sizes 2.5-6 /
3-4 mm needles and a gauge of
22 sts in 4 in / 10 cm, we think
that is too loose for a doll, so we
went down to U.S. 1.5 / 2.5 mm
needles for a gauge of 30 sts in
4 in / 10 cm.

All Hallows Eve

DRESS

With larger short circular and Black, CO 100 sts. Join, being careful not to twist cast-on row. Pm for beginning of rnd.

Rnd 1: Purl.
Rnd 2: Work (K1tbl, yo, k3, sl 1, k2tog, psso, k3, yo) around.
Rnd 3: Knit.
Rnd 4: (K2, yo, k2, sl 1, k2tog, psso, k2, yo, k1) around.
Rnd 5: Knit.
Rnd 6: K1 and place a long thread marker between this and the next st, (yo, k2, yo, k1, sl 1, k2tog, psso, k1, yo, k1, k2tog) around.
Rnd 7: Knit.
Rnd 8: (K2, k2tog, yo, sl 1, k2tog, psso, yo, ssk, k1) around.
Rnd 9: Knit.
Rnd 10: (K1, k2tog, yo, k1tbl, yo, k1tbl, yo, k1tbl, yo, ssk) around. Slip the marker to the front after the last yarnover.
Rnd 11: Knit.
Rnd 12: (Sl 1, k2tog, psso, yo, k7, yo) around.
Rnd 13: Knit.
Rep Rnds 2-13 6 times.
Rep Rnds 2-9 once more.
Rnd 94: (K1, k2tog, k3, ssk) around.
Rnd 95: Knit.
Divide the sts onto 4 dpn = 15 sts per needle.
Rnds 96-100: Knit.
Rnd 101: (K1, k2tog, k9, k1) around.
Rnds 102-106: Knit.
Rnd 107: (K1, k2tog, k7, k2tog, k1) around.
Rnds 108-112: Knit.
Rnd 113: (K1, k2tog, k5, k2tog, k1) around.
Rnds 114-118: Knit.
Rnd 119: (K1, k2tog, k3, k2tog, k1) around.
Rnd 120: BO 2, k10 (including last st from bind-off), BO 4, k10 (including last st from bind-off), BO 2. Place 10 sts on one needle for front and the rem 10 sts on another needle for the back.

SLEEVES

With smaller dpn and Black, CO 24 sts. Divide sts evenly onto 4 dpn and join, being careful not to twist cast-on row. Pm for beginning of rnd.

Rnd 1: Purl.
Rnd 2: Knit.
Rnd 3: Purl.
Rnds 4-33: Change to larger dpn and knit (30 rnds).
Rnd 34: BO 2 sts, k20 (including last st from bind-off), BO last 2 sts.
Place st on a holder and make the second sleeve the same way.

Join Sleeves and Body:

Rnd 121: K10 for the back, pm, k20 for left sleeve, pm, k10 for front, pm, k20 for right sleeve, pm = 60 sts.
Rnd 122: (Knit to marker, sl m, k1, k2tog, k14, k2tog, k1, sl m) 2 times. The decreases are at the beginning and end of each sleeve.
Rnd 123: K56.
Rnd 124: (Knit to marker, sl m, k1, k2tog, k12, k2tog, k1, sl m) 2 times.
Rnd 125: K52.
Rnd 126: (Knit to marker, sl m, k1, k2tog, k10, k2tog, k1, sl m) 2 times.
Rnd 127: K48.
Rnd 128: (Knit to marker, sl m, k1, k2tog, k8, k2tog, k1, sl m) 2 times.
Rnd 129: K44.
Rnd 130: (Knit to marker, sl m, k1, k2tog, k6, k2tog, k1, sl m) 2 times = 40 sts rem.

Change to smaller dpn and work 15 rnds of k2, p2 ribbing. BO in ribbing.
Seam the underarms. Weave in all ends neatly on WS. Gently steam press the dress, except for the ribbing for the neckband, under a damp pressing cloth.

Hands with Fingers

In our *Easter Knits* book, we knitted an Easter hen with claws. We knitted the claws over two needles but later learned to knit I-cords, and then we realized that the dolls could have hands with fingers! We didn't completely agree about using fingers on the knitted dolls; fingers are fun to knit, but they also seemed a bit too realistic. For our All Hallows Eve doll, we knitted longer fingers than described in this pattern so they would look a little scarier. Use needles the same size as for the rest of the doll.

Begin with the I-cord fingers with 2 dpn:

I-cord: Knit across sts on dpn. *Do not turn. Slide sts to front tip of needle, pull yarn on WS and knit across*. Rep from * to * for specified number of rows.

Thumb: CO 4 sts and knit 4 I-cord rows.
Cut yarn. Use beginning end to close cast-on sts and bring end up through thumb. Place thumb on a holder.

Little Finger: CO 4 sts and knit 4 I-cord rows.
Cut yarn. Use beginning end to close cast-on sts and bring end up through finger. Place little finger on holder.

Ring Finger: CO 4 sts and knit 6 I-cord rows.
Cut yarn. Use beginning end to close cast-on sts and bring end up through finger. Place ring finger on holder.

Middle Finger: CO 4 sts and knit 8 I-cord rows.
Cut yarn. Use beginning end to close cast-on sts and bring end up through finger. Place middle finger on holder.

Index Finger: CO 4 sts and knit 5 I-cord rows.
Do *not* cut yarn. Use beginning end to close cast-on sts and bring end up through finger. Place index finger on holder.
Do not cut yarn after working index finger.

Divide the fingers over 4 dpn in this sequence:

Ndl 1: 4 sts of index finger.
Ndl 2: 2 sts from middle finger + 2 sts of ring finger.
Ndl 3: 4 sts from little finger.
Ndl 4: 2 sts from ring finger + 2 sts of middle finger.

Now continue, working in the round, knitting with the yarn from index finger, beginning 1st rnd with the first st of middle finger.

Rnd 1:
Ndl 1: K2 of middle finger and k2 from ring finger.
Ndl 2: K4 of little finger.
Ndl 3: K2 from ring finger and k2 from middle finger.
Ndl 4: K4 from index finger.
Rnds 2–3: K16, drawing in the working yarn at the end of each needle.
Rnd 4: Increase at the index finger: K13, M1, k2, M1, k1.
Rnd 5: K18. Add the thumb to the hand on the next rnd, dividing sts as follows:
Rnd 6:
Ndl 1: Place the 2 last sts of Ndl 4 onto the needle you are knitting with and k3 from Ndl 2 together with the 2 sts, move last st to Ndl 2.
Ndl 2: K5 + k1 from Ndl 3.
Ndl 3: K3 from Ndl 3 and k2 from Ndl 4.
Ndl 4: K1 from Ndl 4 + k4 from thumb + k1 from Ndl 4.
Rnd 7: K22.
Rnd 8: K7, k2tog, k9, k2tog, k2.
Rnd 9: K20.
Sew up any holes between the fingers, leaving the yarn ends to use as filling for the hand.
Rnd 10: (K1, k2tog, k2) around.
Rnd 11: K16.
Rnd 12: (K1, k2tog, k1) around.
Divide rem 12 sts over 3 dpn = 4 sts per needle.
With skin color, knit 35 rnds (3¼ in / 8 cm).
Fill hand and arm with wool as you knit.
Change to T-shirt color and knit 5 rnds.
Last rnd: BO 2 sts, k8 (including last st from bind-off), BO last 2 sts. Place the rem 8 sts on a

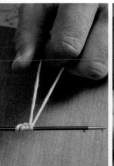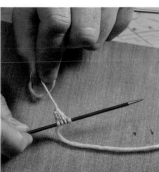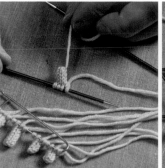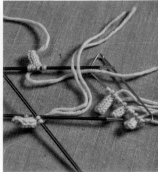

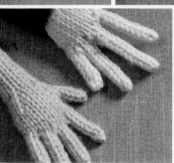

dpn. On this rnd, you can also shift the binding off of the 4 sts so that the hand faces the direction you want. The thumb, as a general rule, points in towards the body; if it points straight ahead, the index finger is over it and almost looks as if the arm is set wrong. We like the thumb to point in the same direction on both hands when the arms are joined to the body. Make the second hand/arm the same way.

Ears

Our knitted dolls don't usually have any ears because they don't work well with the hairdos on the original dolls in our book. But many people have asked how they could make ears, so we recommend this simple method.

We crochet both ears the same way, but if you don't want one to look as if the wrong side is out when the right side is facing out on the other ear, you can crochet one of the ears backwards. Personally, we don't care very much if there is a wrong-side and a right-side ear. We usually draw them in a bit so they look good in any case! Even if they aren't completely the same, that just makes them better. No one has two identical feet, two arms the same length, or hands or ears that are precisely the same...

EAR CONSTRUCTION

Ch 7, work 1 tr / UK dtr into the 2nd ch from hook, and then work 1 tr / UK dtr, 2 dc / UK tr, and end with 1 sl st in last ch. Cut yarn and draw end through the sl st.

MATERIALS

Yarn for the body and hair:
CYCA #3 (DK, light worsted), Schachenmayr Merino Extrafine 120 (100% Merino wool, 131 yd/120 m / 50 g)
Needles: U.S. size 1.5 / 2.5 mm: 2 sets of 5 dpn
Other Materials: 2.8 oz / 80 g wool for the filling
Gauge: The doll must be knitted firmly; go down a needle size if necessary. You don't want the wool stuffing to come out or show through the stitches.

EARS

CYCA #3 (DK/ight worsted), Schachenmayr Merino Extrafine 120 (100% Merino wool, 131 yd/120 m / 50 g)
Crochet Hook: U.S. size C-2 / 2.5 mm

- = ch
- = dc/UK tr
- = tr/UK dtr

EAR CHART

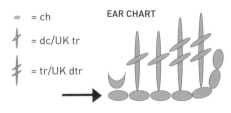

Well, another freezing winter has passed. We tried to dress for the cold and went outside as little as possible. Now sunshine makes a regular appearance and water is once again running in the streams and waterfalls. We dream about spring, about summer and long, warm days. By the time Easter comes, we actually dig out our winter coats again, grab our backpacks, and go up into the mountains in search of snow. The mountains call, and we forget that we scraped ice off the cars and cursed winter and the darkness for many months. We freeze and enjoy ourselves, recognize that we are alive, that we are nearer the sun up on the mountains and closer to the sky. We Norwegians are remarkable people.

Easter at Our House

Easter Eggs—The Basic Pattern

LEVEL OF DIFFICULTY
Intermediate

The charted stitches are repeated over four double-pointed needles. Once you've sewn the hole at the base to close it, you can use the yarn end as a marker.

When there are long stretches between pattern colors, to avoid holes, catch the yarns by twisting the pattern and background colors on the WS.

If a color is used for only a small number of stitches, it will be easier to work it in with duplicate st after the egg is finished, to avoid too many twisted yarns and long floats.

After sewing the hole at the top of the egg closed, crochet a 30-st chain for the hanging loop. The ends can then be sewn through the ball or egg and fastened off at the base.

Cast on 12 sts over dpn U.S. 2.5 / 3 mm. Divide these 12 sts over 4 dpn = 3 sts per ndl. These stitches are the bottom row of the chart.
Rnd 1: K12.
Rnd 2: (K2, inc 1, k1) around. (See page 259 for increase method.)
Rnd 3: K16.
Rnd 4: (K1, inc 1, k2, inc 1, k1) around.
Rnd 5: K24.

Rnd 6: (K1, inc 1, k4, inc 1, k1) around.
Rnd 7: K32.
Rnd 8: (K1, inc 1, k6, inc 1, k1) around.
Rnd 9: K40.
Rnd 10: (K1, inc 1, k8, inc 1, k1) around.
Rnds 11-19: K48.
Rnd 20: (K1, k2tog, k6, k2tog, k1) around.
Rnds 21-23: K40.
Rnd 24: (K1, k2tog, k4, k2tog, k1) around.
Rnds 25-27: K32.
Rnd 28: (K1, k2tog, k2, k2tog, k1) around.
Rnds 29-31: K24.
Rnd 32: (K1, k2tog, k2tog, k1) around.
Rnds 33-35: K16.
Rnd 36: (K2tog, k2tog) around.
Cut yarn and pull end through remaining 8 sts.

Sew the hole at the bottom of the egg together and then steam the egg before filling it with wool, stuffed in from the top. If you are knitting an egg with several colors, weave in the ends as you work so the egg will be smoother.
Run the yarn tail through the stitches at the top of the egg once more and then crochet a hanging loop with 40 chain stitches (see page 260 for details).
Thread the ends from the hanging loop through the egg from the top down to the base and then secure the ends at the bottom of the egg.

Chick in the Egg

The red and blue stitches are worked in
duplicate stitch.

Egg with Outhouse

You can sit in here and think quietly, at least
until someone bangs on the door.

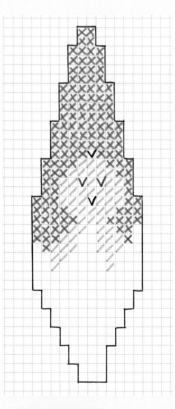

MATERIALS
Yarn:
CYCA #1 (fingering),
Schachenmayr
Merino Extrafine 170
(100% Merino wool,
185 yd/169 m / 50 g)
**Yarn Colors and
Amounts:**
White 0001, 50 g
Yellow 00020, 50 g
Green 00074, 50 g
Blue 00051, 50 g
Red 00031, 50 g

MATERIALS
Yarn:
CYCA #3 (DK, light
worsted), Schachenmayr
Merino Extrafine 120
(100% Merino wool,
131 yd/120 m / 50 g)
**Yarn Colors and
Amounts:**
White 00101, 50 g
Light Blue 00152, 50 g
Dark Blue 00153, 50 g
Red 00131, 50 g

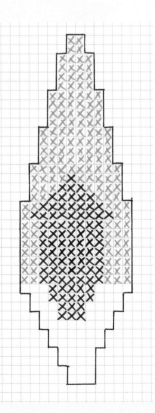

Five Colors of Small Crosses

Hearts

Five colors of small crosses against a single color background—simple yet decorative.

Hearts are a favorite motif for many children and don't get any better than red on pink.

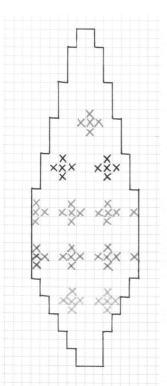

MATERIALS
Yarn:
CYCA #3 (DK, light worsted), Schachenmayr Merino Extrafine 120 (100% Merino wool, 131 yd/120 m / 50 g)
Yarn Colors and Amounts:
Dark Blue 00153, 50 g
Yellow 00122, 50 g
Pink 00136, 50 g
Light Blue 00165, 50 g
Purple 00147, 50 g

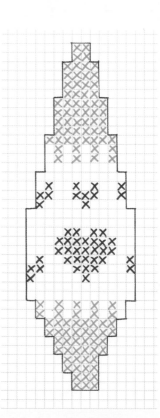

MATERIALS
Yarn:
CYCA #3 (DK, light worsted), Schachenmayr Merino Extrafine 120 (100% Merino wool, 131 yd/120 m / 50 g)
Yarn Colors and Amounts:
Light Blue 00165, 50 g
Pink 00136, 50 g
Red 00140, 50 g

⋆ *Egg with a Little Tulip* ⋆

⋆ *Egg with a Flower Motif* ⋆

Tulips can be knitted in any color from around the world. These eggs will invite spring into your home.

You can vary this motif endlessly.

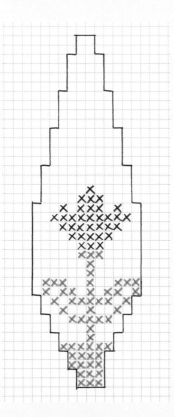

MATERIALS
Yarn:
CYCA #3 (DK, light worsted), Schachenmayr Merino Extrafine 120 (100% Merino wool, 131 yd/120 m / 50 g)
Yarn Colors and Amounts:
White 00101, 50 g
Green 00173, 50 g
The flowers can be in any color you like. We recommend:
Blue 00153
Purple 00148
Yellow 00121
Red 00131
Orange 00125

MATERIALS
Yarn:
CYCA #3 (DK, light worsted), Schachenmayr Merino Extrafine 120 (100% Merino wool, 131 yd/120 m / 50 g)
Yarn Colors and Amounts:
Light Blue 00152, 50 g
Orange 00125, 50 g
Red 00131, 50 g

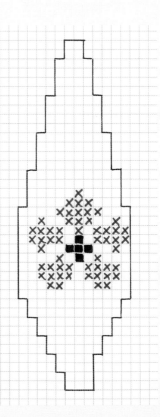

✦ *The Only Rooster in the Basket* ✦

✦ *Spotted Egg* ✦

A rooster motif inspired by an
embroidery design.

Knit the eggs with designs painted
by children.

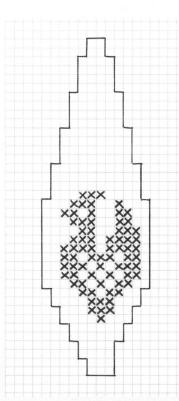

MATERIALS
Yarn:
CYCA #3 (DK, light
worsted),
Schachenmayr
Merino Extrafine
120 (100% Merino
wool, 131 yd/120 m
/ 50 g)
**Yarn Colors and
Amounts:**
Red 00131, 50 g
Pink 00135, 50 g

MATERIALS
Yarn:
CYCA #3 (DK, light
worsted), Schachen-
mayr Merino Extrafine
120 (100% Merino
wool, 131 yd/120 m /
50 g)
**Yarn Colors and
Amounts:**
Flax 00103, 50 g
Orange 00125, 50 g
Red 00130, 50 g
Yellow 00121, 50 g
Green 00170, 50 g
Blue 00153, 50 g

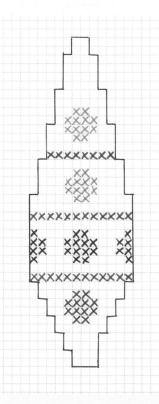

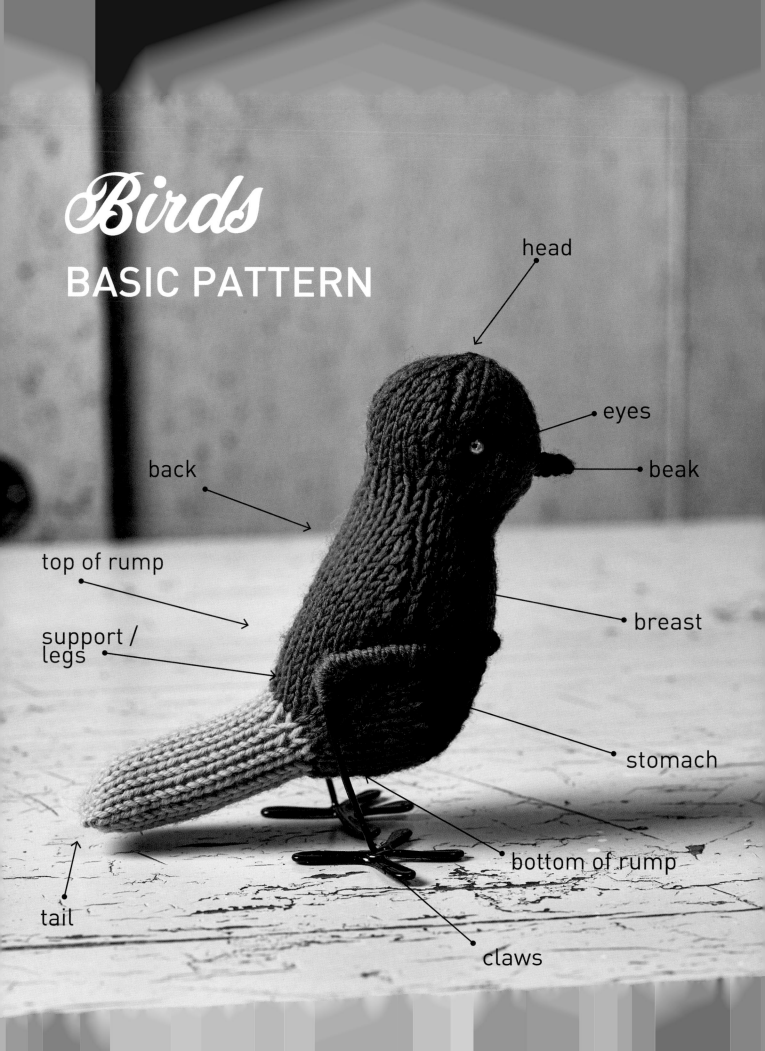

Birds
BASIC PATTERN

head

eyes

beak

back

breast

top of rump

support / legs

stomach

bottom of rump

tail

claws

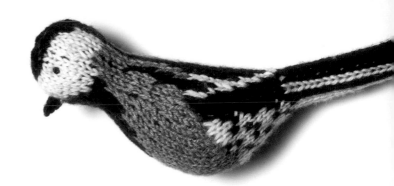

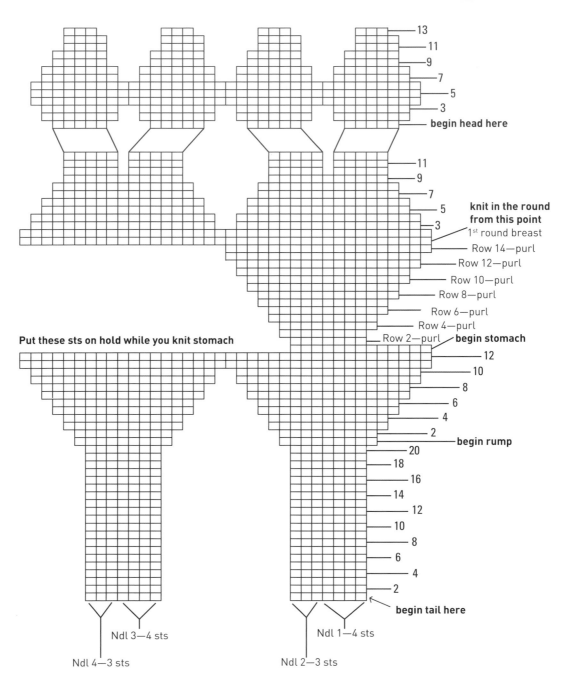

13
11
9
7
5
3
begin head here

11
9
7
5
knit in the round from this point
3
1st round breast
Row 14—purl
Row 12—purl
Row 10—purl
Row 8—purl
Row 6—purl
Row 4—purl
Row 2—purl **begin stomach**

Put these sts on hold while you knit stomach

12
10
8
6
4
2 **begin rump**

20
18
16
14
12
10
8
6
4
2 **begin tail here**

Ndl 3—4 sts
Ndl 4—3 sts
Ndl 1—4 sts
Ndl 2—3 sts

Birds—Basic Pattern

Needles: U.S. size 0-2.5 / 2-3 mm: set of 5 dpn

TAIL:
CO 14 sts and divide sts over 4 dpn: 4 + 3 + 4 + 3 sts. Knit 20 rnds.

NOTE: Make sure the floats on the WS do not pull in when knitting birds with a pattern on the tail. As you knit, periodically use your index finger to stretch out the "tube" for the tail. Also make sure that the stitches lie smoothly next to each other. If you pull too tightly when knitting the pattern, the contrast color stitches can become quite small or disappear altogether between the main color stitches. After completing the tail, insert a pen or pencil into the tail and use it to press the stitches into a smooth conformation. Work increases with RLI (see page 259 for increase method).

RUMP:
Shape the rump by increasing at the sides. Work stitches within parentheses 2 times per round.
Rnd 1: (K1, inc 1, k5, inc 1, k1) around.
Rnd 2: K18.
Rnd 3: (K1, inc 1, k7, inc 1, k1) around.
Rnd 4: K22.
Rnd 5: (K1, inc 1, k9, inc 1, k1) around.
Rnd 6: K26.
Rnd 7: (K1, inc 1, k11, inc 1, k1) around.
Rnd 8: K30.
Rnd 9: (K1, inc 1, k13, inc 1, k1) around.
Rnd 10: K34.
Rnd 11: (K1, inc 1, k15, inc 1, k1) around.
Rnd 12: K38.

STOMACH:
Work back and forth in short rows (as for turning the heel of a sock), with knit over knit and purl over purl as stitches face you.
Always slip the first stitch purlwise with yarn in back on RS and yarn in front on WS.
Row 1: K13; turn.
Row 2: Sl 1, p6; turn.
Row 3: Sl 1, k7; turn.
Row 4: Sl 1, p8; turn.

Row 5: Sl 1, k9; turn.
Row 6: Sl 1, p10; turn.
Row 7: Sl 1, k11; turn.
Row 8: Sl 1, p12; turn.
Row 9: Sl 1, k13; turn.
Row 10: Sl 1, p14; turn.
Row 11: Sl 1, k15; turn.
Row 12: Sl 1, p16; turn.
Row 13: Sl 1, k17; turn.
Row 14: Sl 1, p18; turn.
Now return to knitting in the round.

BREAST:
The breast is shaped by decreasing at the sides. Stitches within parentheses are worked 2 times per round.
Rnd 1: Sl 1, k37.
Rnd 2: K38.
Rnd 3: (K1, k2tog, k13, k2tog, k1) around.
Rnd 4: K34.
Rnd 5: (K1, k2tog, k11, k2tog, k1) around.
Rnd 6: K30.
Rnd 7: (K1, k2tog, k9, k2tog, k1) around.
Rnd 8: K26.
Rnd 9: (K1, k2tog, k7, k2tog, k1) around = 22 sts remain.
Rnd 10: (K4, k2tog, k5) around.
Rnd 11: K20.
Rnd 12: K20.

HEAD:
Stitches within parentheses are worked 4 times per round.
Rnd 1: K20.
Rnd 2: (K1, inc 1, k3, inc 1, k1) around.
Rnd 3: K28.
Rnd 4: (K1, inc 1, k5, inc 1, k1) around.
Rnd 5: K36.
Rnd 6: K36.
Rnd 7: (K1, k2tog, k3, k2tog, k1) around.
Rnd 8: K28.
Rnd 9: (K1, k2tog, k1, k2tog, k1) around.
Rnd 10: K20.
Rnd 11: (K1, k2tog, k2) around.
Rnd 12: K16.
Rnd 13: (K1, k2tog, k1) around.

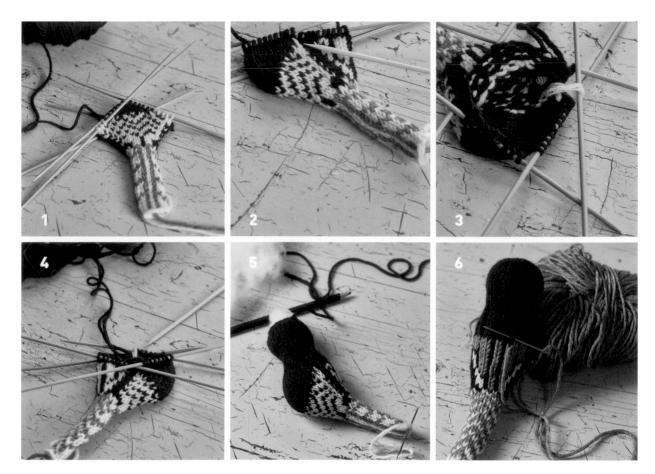

Cut yarn and draw end through remaining 12 sts. Sew the tail together flat at the cast-on row, making sure that the top and bottom sides lie correctly.

Fill with wool, fiberfill, or yarn ends from other birds or other projects.

Tighten the yarn holding final stitches of the head. Weave in any ends to inside of bird.

Crochet the beak: a 3-dc / British 3-tr cluster (see details on page 65).

1 After the tail has been completely knitted, insert a pencil into the tail and press it around to smooth out the stitches. The stomach is worked back and forth with knit and purl short rows, as for the heel turn on a sock.

2 Check to make sure the stitches on the stomach are not too loose. The stitches from turning and working back on knit and purl rows can sometimes be a little loose.

3 We tighten up any loose stitches and then trim any long strands so we can then knot them to-gether, or, for any very long strands, we let them hang until we can pick them up onto the needle on the next round to knit together with a stitch.

4 If there are any long strands after we've tight-ened the knitting, we knit them together with a stitch. We always start the round by knitting the long strand together with the first stitch. If you lift the strand onto the needle and knit it together with the last stitch on the round, it will be visible on the right side.

5 Fill the bird with wool or fiberfill. You can also use yarn ends from the birds or other projects: card the yarn, and then use the batting as filling for the knitted birds.

6 Now you can decorate the bird with duplicate stitch if necessary.

Eyes

Sew on two beads, one on each side of the head. You will need a size 9 or 10 beading needle, rather than a regular sewing needle, to fit through most small beads. First attach one bead with a stitch and then bring the needle through the head over to the opposite side where you will place the second eye. Sew back and forth through the beads and then down on the outside of each bead until they sit smoothly on the head.

Glasses

You'll need steel wire, super glue, and yarn in the same color as the frame.

Shape the frames with fine steel wire (the type used for floral decorations). Begin with the first arm of the glasses, bend the wire toward the lenses and form them into the shape you want. At the end piece (at the bend between the arm and the top bar), bend the wire down to and across the bottom of the lens, up to the nose and back to the top bar. Wrap the wire for the top bar above the lens and then over to the second lens. Start with the top bar, shaping the top, side, and then the

bottom of the lens, and then up to the nose before you twist the wire for the top bar of the lens. End with the second arm. Smooth out the glasses one last time. Reinforce with super glue on the end piece of the first arm, and then at all the places where the frame made a turn. With the color you want, wrap wool yarn around the frame. You'll need glue that can be used on metal – protect your fingers because this glue is strong.

Beak

CROCHET 3 DC TOGETHER (3-DC CLUSTER) / UK 3 TR TOGETHER (3-TR CLUSTER) AS FOLLOWS:
Begin with ch 2 around a stitch at the center of the face.

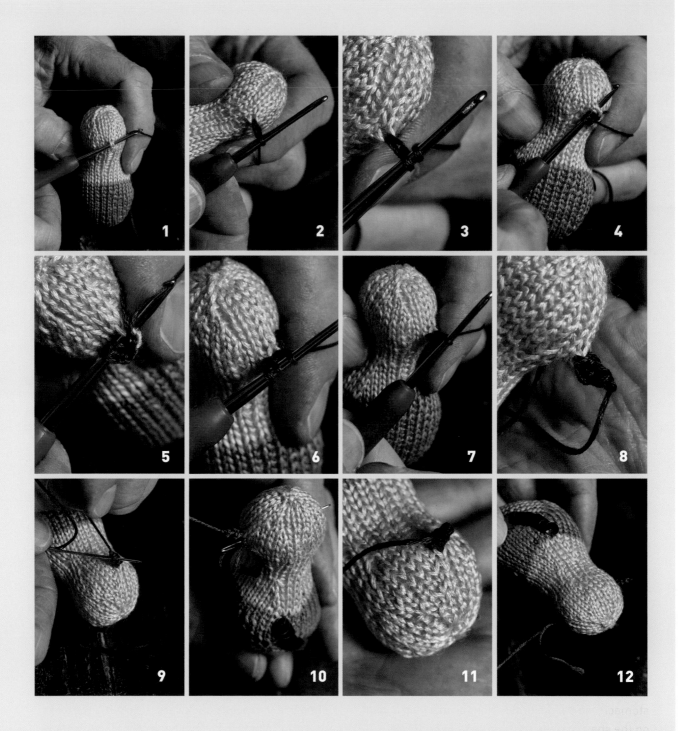

For the first dc / UK tr: Yarn around hook, insert hook into the 1st st up from the one side of the 1st ch and through the nearest strand of the st above. Yarn around hook and through 2 loops.

Second dc / UK tr: Yarn around hook, insert hook into st above ch, yarn around hook and through first 2 loops on hook.

Third dc / UK tr: Yarn around hook, insert hook into st on opposite side of ch, yarn around hook and

through first 2 loops on hook.

Yarn around hook and bring through remaining loops on hook all at once.

End the beak by cutting yarn and drawing the end through the last st of the 3-dc / UK 3-tr cluster. Use the two yarn ends to sew back and forth through the beak to make it stronger. Thread the ends through the head and fasten off.

Birds—Basic Pattern

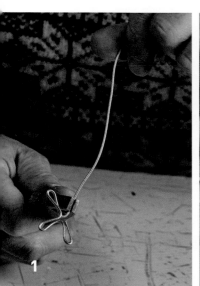 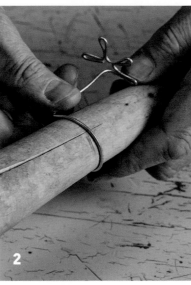 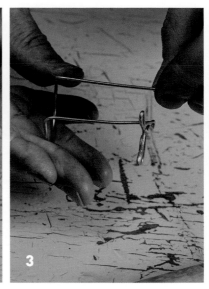 

Supports for the birds

1 Begin at the end of the steel wire with the left foot. Place the pliers ⅝ in / 1.5 cm up from the bottom of the steel wire, bend the wire and clamp the piece together carefully. You've made the back claw. Make the three front claws by bending and clamping the wire. Shape the claws so they all smoothly point in the correct direction, one at the back and three front claws fanning out on the other side.

2 Bend the steel wire so it is perpendicular to the front claws and is centered behind the three claws that point forward. To form the bowed brace for the stomach, we used a broom handle, marking a point on the shaft that fits the stomachs of our birds. Place the steel wire on the point you have marked, about 1¼ in / 3 cm from the bend over the leg, and

shape the wire around the broom shaft or a round dowel. If you've used a round dowel, you don't need to mark it.

3 Eyeball the measurement and bend the steel wire down again so the bow shape you made around the dowel looks even on both sides of the legs. Check to make sure the legs are the same length. Ours are about 2 in / 5 cm long.

4 Bend the wire into four claws for the right foot as for the left foot. When you've formed the fourth claw (the one that points backwards), cut off any excess wire and clamp it in. Shape the four claws so they lie flat, three pointing forwards and one backwards. Bend the claws so they stand level on a tabletop.

MATERIALS
Galvanized steel wire, 1.5 mm
Universal varnish/enamel paint
Pliers
Dowel
Super glue for metal
Each leg has four claws

2 in / 5 cm

Painting the Support

If you want to paint the support, it's best to just dip the legs individually into a can of varnish/enamel paint. Let the varnish/enamel paint drip off and turn the support so the varnish/enamel paint doesn't clump up. Have some paper at the ready in case you need to remove a few drops. Leave the support upside down to dry.

When the support has dried, you can work single crochet/UK double crochet starting with about ⅜ in / 1 cm on top of the left leg, across the bowed stomach brace, and then down about ⅜ in / 1 cm on the right leg. Use one or two of the colors in the bird where the bow comes over the rump and stomach. Or you can attach thread with super glue around the steel wire from the top of one leg, across the bow, to the top of the other leg. You can also attach the support to the bird with the same yarn colors the steel wire lies over, or just leave the metal plain.

Birds—Basic Pattern on page 62

LEVEL OF DIFFICULTY
Intermediate

MATERIALS
Yarn:
CYCA #3 (DK, light worsted), Schachenmayr
Merino Extrafine 120 (100% Merino wool,
131 yd/120 m / 50 g)
Yarn Colors and Amounts:
Color Version 1:
Green 00170, 50 g
Red 00131, 50 g
Yellow 00121, 50 g
Pink 00137, 50 g
Color Version 2:
Red 00131, 50 g
Purple 00146, 50 g
Blue 00165, 50 g
Yellow 00121, 50 g
Needles: U.S. size 2.5 / 3 mm: 1 set of 5 dpn
Crochet Hook: U.S. size D-3 / 3 mm

Pedro and Juanita

PERUVIAN HAT
CO 12 sts and divide evenly onto 4 dpn = 3 sts per
needle.
Rnd 1: K12.
Rnd 2: (K1, inc 1, k2) around.
Rnd 3: K16.
Rnd 4: (K1, inc 1, k2, inc 1, k1) around.
Rnd 5: K24.
Rnd 6: (K1, inc 1, k4, inc 1, k1) around.
Rnds 7–16: K32 following the chart.
Rnd 17: K3, BO 10 sts, k7, including last st after
bind-off, BO 8, k4, including last st after bind-off.
Divide sts 7-7 onto two dpn and work the first earflap.
Row 1: Sl 1, p6,
Row 2: Sl 1, k6.
Row 3: Sl 1, p6.
Row 4: Sl 1, k2tog, k1, k2tog, k1.
Row 5: Sl 1, p4.
Row 6: Sl 1, k2tog, k2.
Row 7: Sl 1, p3.
BO rem sts and cut yarn.
BO 4 sts at back of hat and then make the other
earflap the same way.

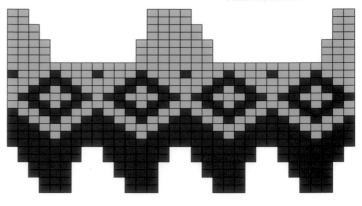

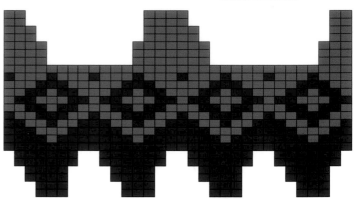

Weave in all ends neatly on WS. Sew the hole at top
of hat and then, with yellow or blue, work single /
British double crochet all around the edge, including
earflaps.
For each earflap, ch 7 with same color as sc / dc
edging. Make 3 small pompoms and sew one to the
top of the hat and one onto end of each cord. The
pompoms shown here are pink and yellow, ⅝ in /
16 mm and ½ in / 12 mm in diameter.

SHORT CARDIGAN

LEVEL OF DIFFICULTY

Advanced

MATERIALS

Yarn:

CYCA #3 (DK, light worsted),
Schachenmayr Merino Extrafine 120
(100% Merino wool, 131 yd/
120 m / 50 g)

Yarn Colors and Amounts:

Light Blue 00165, 50 g

Dark Turquoise 00168, 50 g

Other Materials: 4 small mother-
of-pearl buttons

Needles: U.S. sizes 1.5 and 2.5 /
2.5 and 3 mm: sets of 5 dpn

DRESS WITH BIRD DESIGN

LEVEL OF DIFFICULTY

Advanced

MATERIALS

Yarn:

CYCA #3 (DK, light worsted),
Schachenmayr Merino Extrafine 120
(100% Merino wool, 131 yd/
120 m / 50 g)

Yarn Colors and Amounts:

Light Gray 00190, 50 g

Yellow 00121, 50 g

Light Blue 00165, 50 g

Red 00120, 50 g

Yellow 00122, 50 g

Capri 00168, 50 g

White 00101, 50 g

Black 00199, 50 g

Needles: U.S. sizes 1.5 and 2.5 /
2.5 and 3 mm: sets of 5 dpn

For basic dress pattern,
see page 171.

1/4 dress

SHORT CARDIGAN

Wind two small balls of Dark Turquoise, and work the garter st edge with one ball. Knit each of the button bands with a separate ball of yarn, twisting the light and dark yarns around each other each time they intersect. The neckband is knitted with Dark Turquoise.

GARTER STITCH LOWER BAND WITH BUTTONHOLE

Body: With smaller needles and Dark Turquoise, CO 52 sts.

Rows 1-3: Knit 52 sts back and forth.

Row 4: K49, yo, k2tog, k1.

Rows 5-7: Knit 52 sts back and forth.

Row 8 (WS): Change to larger needles and begin working bands in Dark Turquoise and body in Light Blue: K5, p42, k5.

Row 9: K52.

Row 10: K5, p42, k5.

Row 11: K52.

Row 12: K5, p42, k2, yo, k2tog, k1.

Row 13: K52.

Row 14: K5, p42, k5.

Row 15: K52.

Row 16: K5, p42, k5.

Row 17: K12, BO 4 sts, k20 (including last st of bind-off), BO 4 sts, k12 (including last st of bind-off).

Set 44 rem body sts aside while you knit the sleeves.

SLEEVES

With smaller dpn and Dark Turquoise, CO 24 sts. Divide sts evenly onto 4 dpn and join = 6 sts per needle.

Work the garter stitch edging as follows:

Rnd 1: Purl.

Rnd 2: Knit.

Rnd 3: Purl.

Rnd 4: Knit.

Rnd 5: Purl.

Change to larger dpn and Light Blue: Knit 24 rnds (= 1½ in / 4 cm).

BO 2 sts, k20 (including last st of bind-off), BO 2 sts.

Now join the body and sleeves:

Row 18: Place the sts of sleeves and body onto larger needles as follows. Pm at each intersection of body and sleeve. Continue front bands and front in stitches/colors as set; slip markers as you come to them.
With WS facing, K5, p7 for front, p20 for sleeve, p20 for back, p20 for sleeve, p7 and k5 for front = 84 sts total.

Row 19: K12 for front, (k1, k2tog, k14, k2tog, k1) for sleeve, (k1, k2tog, k14, k2tog, k1) for back, (k1, k2tog, k14, k2tog, k1) for sleeve, k12 for front = 78 sts rem.

Row 20: K5, Purl until 5 sts rem and end with k2, yo, k2tog, k1 (buttonhole).

Row 21: K9, k2tog, k2, k2tog, k12, k2tog, k2, k2tog, k12, k2tog, k2, k2tog, k12, k2tog, k2, k2tog, k9 = 70 sts rem.

Row 22: K5, purl until 5 sts rem and end k5.

Row 23: K8, (k2tog, k2, k2tog, k10) 3 times, and end with k2tog, k2, k2tog, k8 = 62 sts rem.

Row 24: K5, purl until 5 sts rem and end k5.

Row 25: K7, (k2tog, k2, k2tog, k8) 3 times, and end with k2tog, k2, k2tog, k7 = 54 sts rem.

Row 26: K5, purl until 5 sts rem and end k5.

Row 27: K6, (k2tog, k2, k2tog, k6) 4 times = 46 sts rem.

Row 28: K5, purl until 5 sts rem and end with k2, yo, k2tog, k1 (buttonhole).

Row 29: Cut Light Turquoise and continue with Dark Turquoise only for neckband: K5, (k2tog, k2, k2tog, k4) 3 times and end with k2tog, k2, k2tog, k5 = 38 sts rem.

Row 30: Knit.

Row 31: K4, (k2tog, k2, k2tog, k2) 3 times, and end with k2tog, k2, k2tog, k4 = 30 sts rem.

Row 32: Knit.

Row 33: K6, (k2tog, k2tog, k2) 2 times, and end with k2tog, k2, k2tog, k6 = 24 sts rem.

Row 34: Knit.

BO rem sts. Seam underarms. Weave in all ends neatly on WS. Gently steam press sweater under damp pressing cloth. Sew on buttons.

See page 195 for tips on joining the body and sleeves.

This short sweater is a bit easier to knit than the long sweater in the same style—there are fewer steps to worry about. The easy-to-knit red skirt features the same same red as the sweater.

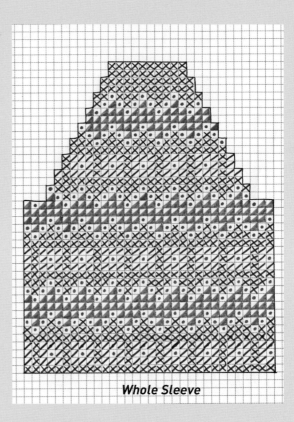

Whole Sleeve

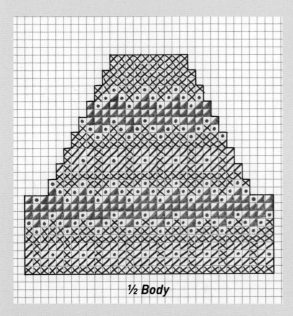

½ Body

SHORT "HEN KNITTING" SWEATER

LEVEL OF DIFFICULTY
Advanced

MATERIALS
Yarn:
CYCA #3 (DK, light worsted), Schachenmayr Merino Extrafine 120 (100% Merino wool, 131 yd/120 m / 50 g)
Yarn Colors and Amounts:
Red 00031, 50 g
Burgundy 00033, 50 g (we couldn't find the same brown we used for the version in the picture, but this substitute color goes well with the red, pink, and yellow)
Pink 00035, 50 g
Lurex: Concorde from Rauma
Needles: U.S. sizes 1.5 and 2.5 / 2.5 and 3 mm: sets of 5 dpn
Crochet Hook: U.S. size D-3 / 3 mm for crocheted cord on Version 2

BODY
With Burgundy and smaller dpn, CO 48 sts and divide evenly onto 4 dpn; join and pm for beginning of rnd = 12 sts per needle
Rnds 1-5: (K2, p2) around.
Rnd 6: Change to larger dpn. (K3, inc 1) around = 64 sts (see page 259 for increase method).
Begin working charted pattern.
Rnds 7-15: Knit 9 rnds for the short model or **Rnds 7-27**, 21 rnds for longer version.
Rnd 16 (28): BO 3 sts, k26 (including last st of bind-off), BO 6 sts, k26 (including last st of bind-off), BO 3 sts.
Place the sts of front and back each on a separate needle = 26 sts per needle.

SLEEVES
With Burgundy and smaller dpn, CO 24 sts and divide evenly onto 4 dpn; join and pm for beginning of rnd = 6 sts per needle.
Rnds 1-5: (K2, p2) around.

Rnd 6: Change to larger dpn. (K3, inc 1) around = 32 sts. Begin working charted pattern with 21 rnds for the long sleeves or 9 rnds for short sleeves.

Rnd 16 (28): BO 3 sts, k26 (including last st of bind-off), BO 3 sts.

Join the body and sleeves:

Rnd 29: K26 for the back, k26 for a sleeve, k26 for the front, k26 for second sleeve.

Rnd 30: (K1, k2tog, k20, k2tog, k2, k1) around.

Rnd 31: K96.

Rnd 32: (K1, k2tog, k18, k2tog, k2, k1) around.

Rnd 33: K88.

Rnd 34: (K1, k2tog, k16, k2tog, k2, k1) around.

Rnd 35: K80.

Rnd 36: (K1, k2tog, k14, k2tog, k2, k1) around.

Rnd 37: K72.

Rnd 38: (K1, k2tog, k12, k2tog, k2, k1) around.

Rnd 39: K64.

Rnd 40: (K1, k2tog, k10, k2tog, k2, k1) around.

Rnd 41: K56.

Rnd 42: (K1, k2tog, k8, k2tog, k2, k1) around.

Rnd 43: K48.

Rnd 44: (K1, k2tog, k6, k2tog, k2, k1) around.

Rnd 45: K40.

Version 1: Change to smaller dpn *at the same time* as you continue

Rnd 46: (K2, p2) around for ribbed collar.
BO in ribbing.

Version 2: Work (k2tog, yo, p2) around.
Work 8 rnds in k2, p2 ribbing. BO in ribbing.
Crochet a chain and draw it through the eyelets in neckband. Make 2 small pompoms and sew them securely to the ends of the chain cord.

Version 3: Work 10 rnds in k2, p2 ribbing. BO in ribbing. (This is the version shown in the photo.)

FINISHING

Seam the underarms. Weave in all ends neatly on WS. Gently steam press sweater under a damp pressing cloth. Do not press any of the ribbing.

RED SKIRT
For Basic Pattern, see page 77.

LEVEL OF DIFFICULTY
Easy

MATERIALS

Yarn:
CYCA #3 (DK, light worsted), Schachenmayr Merino Extrafine 120 (100% Merino wool, 131 yd/120 m / 50 g)

Yarn Colors and Amounts:
Red 00031, 50 g

Burgundy 00033, 50 g (we couldn't find the same brown we used for the version in the picture, but this color goes well with the red)

Needles: U.S. sizes 1.5 and 2.5 / 2.5 and 3 mm: sets of 5 dpn

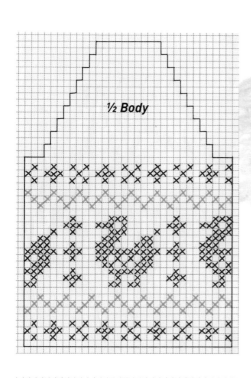

½ Body

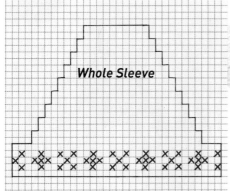

Whole Sleeve

Ulla

PULLOVER WITH BIRD MOTIFS

For Basic Pattern, see page 72.

We designed this pattern with leftovers from a bazaar prize—a blanket produced by Th. Lunde of Lillehammer. The pattern on the blanket was from an old spot weaving in Gudbrandsdalen.

LEVEL OF DIFFICULTY
Advanced

MATERIALS
Yarn:
CYCA #3 (DK, light worsted), Schachenmayr Merino Extrafine 120 (100% Merino wool, 131 yd/120 m / 50 g)
Yarn Colors and Amounts:
Yellow 00120, 50 g
Red 00031, 50 g
Turquoise 00167, 50 g
Purple 00147, 50 g
Needles: U.S. sizes 1.5 and 2.5 / 2.5 and 3 mm: sets of 5 dpn

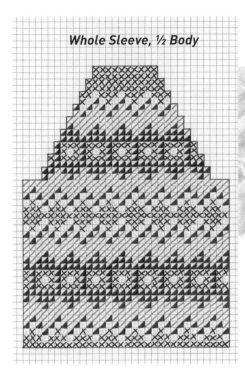

Whole Sleeve, ½ Body

LONG "HEN KNITTING" PULLOVER

For Basic Pattern, see page 72.

LEVEL OF DIFFICULTY
Advanced

MATERIALS
Yarn:
CYCA #3 (DK, light worsted),
Schachenmayr Merino Extrafine 170
(100% Merino wool, 131 yd/120 m /
50 g)
Yarn Colors and Amounts:
Red 00031, 50 g
Burgundy 00033, 50 g (we couldn't
find the same brown we used for
the version in the picture, but
this substitute color goes well
with the red, pink, and yellow)
Pink 00035, 50 g
Lurex: Concorde from Rauma
Needles: U.S. sizes 1.5 and 2.5 / 2.5
and 3 mm: sets of 5 dpn
Crochet Hook: U.S. size D-3 / 3 mm
for crocheted cord on Version 2

This sweater features pattern motifs and colors inspired by hand-painted Mexican birds.
There are a lot of ends to weave in so we just trimmed the ends and tied them in pairs.

HEAVY SWEATER
LEVEL OF DIFFICULTY
Intermediate

MATERIALS
Yarn:
CYCA #4 (worsted/afghan/aran), Schachenmayr Merino Extrafine 85 (100% Merino wool, 93 yd/85 m / 50 g)
Yarn Color and Amount:
Purple 00249, 50 g
Needles: U.S. sizes 7 and 8 / 4.5 and 5 mm: sets of 5 dpn

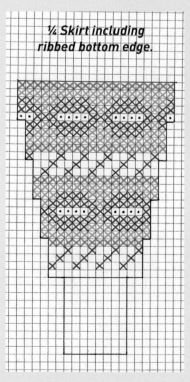

¼ Skirt including ribbed bottom edge.

BODY
With smaller needles, CO 32 sts. Divide sts evenly onto 4 dpn and join; pm for beginning of rnd = 8 sts per dpn.
Work 5 rnds of k2, p2 ribbing.
Change to larger dpn and work around in St st for 2½ in / 6 cm or desired length.

Armhole Shaping: BO 1 st, k14 (including last st from bind-off), BO 2 sts, k14 (including last st from bind-off), BO 1 st. Divide body sts onto 2 dpn with 14 sts on each needle.

SLEEVES
With smaller dpn, CO 16 sts. Divide sts evenly onto 4 dpn and join; pm for beginning of rnd = 4 sts per dpn.
Work 5 rnds k2, p2 ribbing. Change to larger dpn and work around in St st for 2½ in / 6 cm or desired length.
Underarm Shaping: BO 1 st, k14 (including last st of bind-off) BO 1 st. Place sts on 1 dpn and work the second sleeve the same way.

Join body and sleeves:
Arrange sleeves and front/back on 4 larger dpn (= 56 sts) and work around as follows:
Rnd 1: Knit.
Rnd 2: (K1, k2tog, k8, k2tog, k1) around = 48 sts rem.
Rnd 3: Knit.
Rnd 4: (K1, k2tog, k6, k2tog, k1) around = 40 sts rem.
Rnd 5: Knit.
Rnd 6: (K1, k2tog, k4, k2tog, k1) around = 32 sts rem.
Rnd 7: Knit.
Rnd 8: (K1, k2tog, k2, k2tog, k1) around = 24 sts rem.
Rnd 9: Knit.

Change to smaller dpn and work in k2, p2 ribbing for 5 rnds or to desired length for neckband. Seam underarms. Weave in all ends neatly on WS. Gently steam press sweater, except for ribbing, under a damp pressing cloth.

"HEN KNITTING" SKIRT
LEVEL OF DIFFICULTY
Advanced

MATERIALS
Yarn:
CYCA #1 (fingering), Schachenmayr Merino Extrafine 170 (100% Merino wool, 185 yd/169 m / 50 g)

Yarn Colors and Amounts:
Gray 00090, 50 g
Navy Blue 00050, 50 g
Green 00075, 50 g
Light Blue 00068, 50 g
Orange 00023, 50 g
Lurex: Concorde from Rauma
Needles: U.S. sizes 1.5 and 2.5 / 2.5 and 3 mm: set of 5 dpn

Ulla has toned down her outfit with a simple purple sweater worn with her colorful skirt. The skirt panels were inspired by our collection of Mexican wooden birds.

The skirt is worked from the top down by following chart from bottom up.

With Gray and smaller dpn, CO 32 sts and divide evenly onto 4 dpn = 8 sts per needle. Join and pm for beginning of rnd.
Work 10 rnds in k2, p2 ribbing.
Change to larger dpn and work (K2, inc 1) around = 48 sts (see page 259 for increase method).

Work following the color pattern on the chart, increasing on every 5th rnd. Begin each increase rnd with k1, inc 1, and end with inc 1, k1.

Continue increasing as shown on the chart until there are 20 sts on each needle (= 80 sts total). Work 4 more rnds after the last increase rnd. Finish with 4 purl rnds using Gray. BO. Cut yarn and weave in all ends neatly on WS.

"HEN KNITTING" ONESIE
LEVEL OF DIFFICULTY
Advanced

MATERIALS
Yarn:
CYCA #3 (DK, light worsted), Schachenmayr
Merino Extrafine 120 (100% Merino wool,
131 yd/120 m / 50 g)
Yarn Colors and Amounts:
Gray 00192, 50 g
Red 00031, 50 g
Blue 00168, 50 g
Orange 00125, 50 g
Yellow 00120, 50 g
Black 00199, 50 g
White 00101, 50 g
Other Materials: 5 small buttons
Needles: U.S. sizes 1.5 and 2.5 / 2.5 and 3 mm:
sets of 5 dpn
Crochet Hook: U.S. size C-2 or D-3 / 3.5 or 3 mm
for front and edgings

LEGS

With Red and smaller dpn, CO 36 sts. Divide sts evenly onto 4 dpn = 9 sts per needle. Join and pm for beginning of rnd.

Work 5 rnds in k2, p2 ribbing.

Change to larger dpn and work the pattern repeat (see marked section on chart below) two times. After completing charted rep, BO the first and last 3 sts of the rnd.

Divide the leg sts onto 2 dpn = 15 sts per needle. Set aside.

Make the second leg the same way.

Now join the legs, beginning with the doll's right leg.

Continuing in charted pattern, knit across front, pm. Work in pattern for 1¼ in / 3 cm. Move the marker to the center front. From this point, begin all rows with k3 for the button bands as you continue in pattern, working back and forth in St st, for 1½ in / 4 cm.

Shape underarms on RS sts follows:

K12, BO 6 sts, k24 (including last st of bind-off), BO 6 sts, k12 (including last st of bind-off). Set body aside.

SLEEVES

With Red and smaller dpn, CO 36 sts. Divide sts evenly onto 4 dpn = 9 sts per needle. Join and pm for beginning of rnd.

Work 5 rnds in k2, p2 ribbing.

Change to larger dpn and begin charted pattern where indicated, with 2 rnds Gray. Continue following chart through Rnd 20.

Rnd 21: BO 3 sts, k30 (including last st of bind-off), BO 3 sts. Set sleeve aside.

Make the second sleeve the same way.

Join the body and sleeves as follows:

Arrange the body and sleeve sts onto 4 dpn, matching underarms. Pm at each intersection of sleeve and body.

Work yoke with Gray, beginning with 1 purl row on WS.

On every RS row, work raglan shaping: (Knit until 2 sts before marker, ssk, sl m, k2tog) around, knitting to end of row after last decrease. When front panels each have 5 sts rem, continue decreasing only on sleeves and back. When 30 sts rem, decrease only on the sleeves for the final decrease row.

Change to smaller dpn and work 5 rows in k2, p2 ribbing with Red. BO in ribbing.

Front Bands: With Red and RS facing, work a row of single crochet along left front band. Fasten off. Work row of crochet/UK double crochet along right front band the same way and then make a row of 5 button loops with single crochet and chain sts evenly spaced down band. Make sure the buttons fit into the loops. Fasten off.

FINISHING

Weave in all ends neatly on WS. Seam underarms and crotch. Gently steam press onesie under a damp pressing cloth. Sew on buttons.

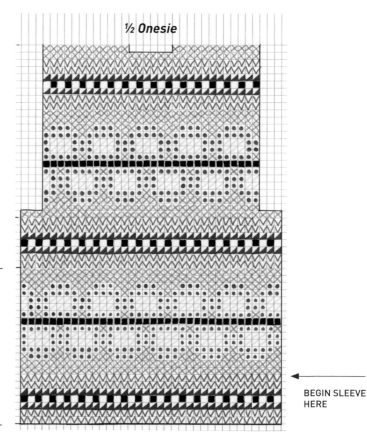

½ Onesie

1 REPEAT

BEGIN SLEEVE HERE

Three-Color Clog Slippers

These are slippers for Dad, knitted in black and gray. The design could be considered quite traditional, but the pattern came more or less of its own accord. The red stripe defines the slippers' form quite well. The slippers show how effective the cast-on with one strand can be—the edge rolls nicely after felting.

NOTE: Alternate two strands of yarn on every stitch throughout (as for two-end or Fair Isle knitting).

With one strand of Red and circular, CO 56 (60, 64) sts; join, being careful not to twist cast-on row. Join second strand of Red and knit 1 rnd, alternating the 2 strands of yarn on each stitch. Cut Red and change to Black. Knit 2 rnds, alternating two strands of yarn on every stitch.

Now work the heel in charted pattern and as follows:

HEEL

Row 1: K14 (15, 16), knitting last st with both strands; turn.
Row 2: Sl 1, p27 (29, 31), purling last st with both strands; turn.

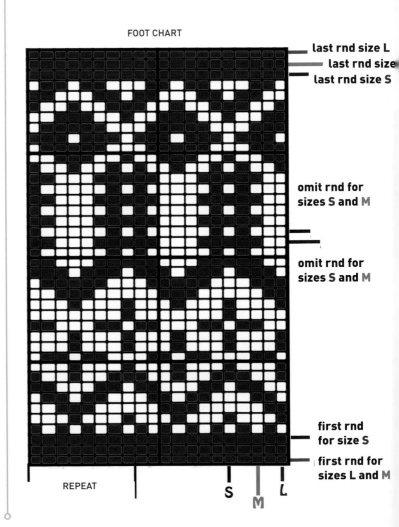

FOOT CHART

last rnd size L
last rnd size
last rnd size S

omit rnd for sizes S and M

omit rnd for sizes S and M

first rnd for size S

first rnd for sizes L and M

REPEAT

S M L

HEEL CHART

L S
M

Back—begin here

Work another 11 rows back and forth in St st over the 28 (30, 32) heel sts, always slipping the first st.

HEEL TURN

Row 14: P13 (15, 17), p2tog, p1 with both strands; turn.
Row 15: K3 (5, 7), k2tog, k1 with both strands; turn.
Rows 16-23: Continue St st and shaping, with 1 more st before the decrease on each row (the decrease joins the sts before/after the gap).
Row 24: P12 (14, 16), p2tog, p1 with both strands; turn.
Row 25: K13 (15, 17), k2tog with both strands; turn. (This row ends with k2tog and not k1 as previously.)
Row 26: P13 (15, 17), p2tog, p1 with both strands; turn.

FOOT

Set-up Rnd: Ssk, k6 (7, 8). Pm at center of sole, k7 (8, 9), pick up and knit 7 sts evenly spaced across one side of the heel flap, k28 (30, 32) across instep, pick up and knit 7 sts evenly spaced across other side of heel flap and k7 (8, 9) on sole. The beginning of the rnd is at center of sole.

Foot: Following the chart, beginning at the stitch and rnd for your size, knit 34 (37, 40) rnds on the 56 (60, 64) sts of foot.

Toe Shaping

Divide the sts onto 4 dpn with 14 (15, 16) sts on each needle. With Black only, shape toe as follows, with 8 sts decreased on each decrease rnd.
Rnd 1 (decrease rnd): At beginning of each needle: K1, k2tog. At end of each needle: K2tog, k1.
Rnd 2: Knit.
Repeat Rnds 1-2 until 16 (20, 16) sts rem. Cut yarn and draw end through remaining sts. Pull tight and weave in all ends neatly on WS. Steam press and then felt slippers.

Felting: Felt slippers on Easy Care program, at 104-140°F / 40-60°C. Wash with a mild wool-safe liquid soap, using 6 tablespoons / 100 ml soap for about 2.2 lb / 1 kg knitted fabric. The water temperature can vary from machine to machine, so start with the lower temperature and check the felting occasionally.

LEVEL OF DIFFICULTY
Advanced

MATERIALS
Yarn:
CYCA #4 (worsted/afghan/aran) Rauma Vamsegarn (100% wool), 91 yd/83 m / 50 g)

Yarn Colors and Amounts:
Black V10, 50 g
Gray V13, 50 g
Red V23, 50 g
Needles: U.S. size 8-10 / 5-6 mm: circular and set of 5 dpn
Recommended Gauge: 14-16 sts = 4 in / 10 cm

Everyone knows that a pair of rabbits means there will soon be more. Before long, you'll have a whole armful.

LEVEL OF DIFFICULTY
Intermediate

MATERIALS
Yarn:
CYCA #3 (DK, light worsted), Schachenmayr Merino Extrafine 120 (100% Merino wool, 131 yd/120 m / 50 g)
Yarn Colors and Amounts:
Body
White 00102, 50 g
Pink 00136, 50 g
Nose and Mouth
Black 00199, 50 g
Eyes
Red 00031, 50 g
Black 00199, 50 g
Other Materials: wool batting or fiberfill, 50 g
Needles: U.S. size 1.5 / 2.5 mm: set of 5 dpn
Crochet Hook: U.S. size C-2 / 2.5 mm for joining ears

The Easter Bunny

It's not Easter without the Easter bunny! We've knitted a whole bunch of them in a variety of colors.

LEFT LEG

With dpn, CO 8 sts and divide onto 4 dpn = 2 sts per needle. Join, being careful not to twist cast-on row; pm for beginning of rnd. (See page 259 for increase method.)

Rnd 1: K8.
Rnd 2: (K1, inc 1, k1) around.
Rnd 3: K12.
Rnd 4: (K1, inc 1, k1, inc 1, k1) around.
Rnd 5: K20.
Rnd 6: (K1, inc 1, k3, inc 1, k1) around.
Rnds 7-12: K28.
Rnd 13: (K1, k2tog, k1, k2tog, k1) around.
Rnds 14-19: K20.
Rnd 20: (K1, k2tog, k2) around.
Rnds 21-26: K16.

Begin the heel by working 6 rows St st (knit on RS and purl on WS) back and forth over the sts on the first needle.

Now you have a little strip on the first needle. With Ndl 4, pick up and knit 4 sts along the side of the strip and place a locking ring marker (or move up beginning yarn tail) between Ndls 1 and 4. With Ndl 2, pick up and knit 4 sts on the other side of the strip on Ndl 1.

Rnd 27: Ndl 1: K4; Ndl 2: k8; Ndl 3: k4; Ndl 4: k8.
Rnd 28: Ndl 1: K4; Ndl 2: k2tog, k6; Ndl 3: k4; Ndl 4: k6, k2tog.
Rnd 29: Ndl 1: K4; Ndl 2: k7; Ndl 3: k4; Ndl 4: k7.
Rnd 30: Ndl 1: K4; Ndl 2: k2tog, k5; Ndl 3: k4; Ndl 4: k5, k2tog.
Rnd 31: Ndl 1: K4; Ndl 2: k6; Ndl 3: k4; Ndl 4: k6.
Rnd 32: Ndl 1: K4; Ndl 2: k2tog, k4; Ndl 3: k4; Ndl 4: k4, k2tog.
Rnd 33: Ndl 1: K4; Ndl 2: k5; Ndl 3: k4; Ndl 4: k5.
Rnd 34: Ndl 1: K4; Ndl 2: k2tog, k3: Ndl 3: k4; Ndl 4: k3, k2tog.
Rnd 35: K16.
Rnd 36: (K1, k2tog, k1) around.

Fill the foot with wool or fiberfill.

Rnds 37-67: K12 (= 30 rounds).
Rnd 68: K1, inc 1, k10, inc 1, k1.
Rnd 69: K14.
Rnd 70: K1, inc 1, k12, inc 1, k1.
Rnd 71: K16.
Rnd 72: BO 2, k12 (including last st from bind-off), BO 2.
Divide leg sts onto 2 dpn (6 sts per needle).

RIGHT LEG

Work as for left leg, Rnds 1-67.
Rnd 68: K5, inc 1, k2, inc 1, k5.
Rnd 69: K14.
Rnd 70: K6, inc 1, k2, inc 1, k6.
Rnd 71: K16.
Rnd 72: K6, BO 4, k6 (including last st from bind-off).
Divide leg sts onto 2 dpn (6 sts per needle).
Fill legs with wool.

JOIN THE LEGS AND KNIT THE BODY

Rnd 1: Continue knitting with the strand of yarn from the right leg: Ndl 1: K6 from right leg; Ndls 2 and 3: K6 from left leg; Ndl 4: K6 from right leg. Move the marker up to the side here. The 4 sts bound-off on each leg should face each other between the legs.

Rnds 2-23: K24 (= 22 rounds).

Rnd 24: BO 2 sts, k8 (including the last st of bind-off), BO 4, k8 (including last st of bind-off), BO 2.

Place the 8 sts each sts of front and back onto separate needles.

KNIT THE ARMS

With dpn, CO 6 sts and divide sts onto 3 dpn. Join, being careful not to twist cast-on row.

Rnd 1: K6.

Rnd 2: (K1, inc 1, k1) around.

Rnd 3: K9.

Rnd 4: (K1, inc 1, k1, inc 1, k1) around.

Rnd 5: K15.

Rnd 6: (K1, inc 1, k3, inc 1, k1) around.

Rnds 7-13: K21.

Rnd 14: (K1, k2tog, k1, k2tog, k1) around.

Rnd 15: K15.

Rnd 16: (K1, k2tog, k2) around.

Rnd 17: K12.

Rnd 18: (K1, k2tog, k1) around.

Rnds 19-40: K9 (= 22 rnds).

Rnd 41: BO 2, k5 (including last st after bind-off), BO 2.

Put the arm sts on a holder and make the other arm the same way.

KNIT THE BODY AND ARMS TOGETHER ON 4 DPN

Rnd 1: Back: K8; left arm: k5; front: k8; right arm: k5.

Rnd 2: Back: K1, k2tog, k2, k2tog, k1; arm: k5; front: k1, k2tog, k2, k2tog, k1; arm: k5.

Rnd 3: K22.

Rnd 4: Back: K2, k2tog, k2; arm: k5; front: k2, k2tog, k2; arm: k5.

Rnd 5: K20.

Rnd 6: (K1, k2tog, k2) around.

Rnd 7: K16.

Rnd 8: (K1, k2tog, k1) around = 12 sts remain.

Seam the underarms and stuff the arms and body with wool.

Rnds 9-12: Knit.

BEGIN HEAD

Rnd 13: (K1, inc 1, k1, inc 1, k1) around.

Rnd 14: K20.

Rnd 15: (K1, inc 1, k3, inc 1, k1) around.

Rnd 16: K28.

Rnd 17: (K1, inc 1, k5, inc 1, k1) around.

Rnd 18: K36.

Rnd 19: Ndl 1: K9; Ndl 2: k11 onto the needle; Ndl 3: k5; Ndl 4: place the 2 last sts on Ndl 3 onto Ndl 4 and k11.

Rnd 20: K20; on Ndl 3, shape head with short rows: k5; turn and p5; turn, k5; turn and p5; turn, k5; turn and p5; turn, k5; turn and p5. Now, with Ndl 2, pick up and knit 5 sts on the side of the strip on Ndl 3. On the other side of the strip, with Ndl 4, pick up and knit 5 sts. K21 to finish round.

Rnd 21: K46.

Rnd 22: K17, k2tog, k17, k2tog, k8.

Rnd 23: K44.

Rnd 24: K17, k2tog, k15, k2tog, k8.

Rnd 25: K42.

Rnd 26: K17, k2tog, k13, k2tog, k8.

Rnd 27: K40.

Move 2 sts from Ndl 2 onto Ndl 3 and move 2 sts from Ndl 4 to Ndl 3.

Rnd 28: K17, k2tog, k11, k2tog, k8.

Rnd 29: K38.

Rnd 30: K17, k2tog, k9, k2tog, k8.

Rnd 31: K36.

Rnd 32: (K1, k2tog, k3, k2tog, k1) around.

Rnd 33: K28.

Rnd 34: (K1, k2tog, k1, k2tog, k1) around.

Rnd 35: K20.

Rnd 36: (K1, k2tog, k2) around.

Rnd 37: K16.
Rnd 38: (K1, k2tog, k1) around.

Cut yarn and pull end through remaining 12 sts.
Fill with wool.
Pull tail through remaining sts once more and
weave in ends to WS.

EMBROIDERING ON THE MOUTH AND NOSE
Sew 4 stitches for the tip of the nose, then make a
straight line of back stitches down to the mouth
(where you can see the shift in the knitting from the
strip that was knit back and forth); at that line,
embroider the mouth with back stitches.

EARS FOR THE RABBIT
Each ear is made with 2 layers, one in Pink and the
other in the same color as for the rabbit body (for
example, White). The ears are worked in St st: knit
on the RS and purl on the WS.
With dpn, CO 5 sts.
Row 1 (WS): P5.
Row 2: K5.
Row 3: P5.
Row 4: K5.
Row 5: P5.
Row 6: K1, inc 1, k3, inc 1, k1.
Rows 7-13: Continue in St st with knit on RS and
purl on WS.
Row 14: K1, inc 1, k5, inc 1, k1.
Rows 15-27: Continue in St st with knit on RS and
purl on WS.
Row 28: K1, k2tog, k3, k2tog, k1.
Row 29: P7.
Row 30: K1, k2tog, k1, k2tog, k1.
Row 31: P5.
Row 32: K1, k2tog, k2.
Row 33: P4.
Row 34: K1, k2tog, k1.
Row 35: P3.
Row 36: BO knitwise.

Gently steam press the two parts of the ear and lay
them together with WS facing WS. Crochet the two
pieces together with single crochet/UK double

crochet into the outermost stitches around.
Crochet with the skin color side facing you.
Make the other ear the same way.
Sew the ears to the head, approx. ⅜ in / 1 cm from
each other on each side of the finishing at the top
of the head.

EYES
Embroider the eyes with your choice of color and
cross stitch where the decreases were made over
the nose.
With Black, embroider a small seed stitch at the
center of the cross stitch.

Make a pompom tail to sew on the back (see page 262).

SWEATER FOR THE EASTER BUNNY
LEVEL OF DIFFICULTY
Intermediate

MATERIALS
Yarn:
CYCA #4 (worsted/afghan/aran),
Schachenmayr Merino Extrafine 85
(100% Merino wool, 93 yd/85 m / 50 g)
Needles: U.S. sizes 7 and 8 / 4.5 and 5
mm: sets of 5 dpn

Sweater for the Easter Bunny

We decided to make just one garment for the Easter bunny, a sweater knitted with a heavy yarn. The sizes of the stitches on the sweater are in proportion to the rabbit's size. The sweater was designed so that the legs must be up in the sweater first and then the sweater can be pulled on. With the pompom tail, we decided against making trousers; but if you want, you can knit the legs and half of the body in a different color from the bunny's "fur" color, and then switch back to the "fur" color for the pompom tail, to create the appearance of trousers.

BODY

With smaller needles, CO 24 sts and divide evenly over 4 dpn = 6 sts per dpn. Join and pm for beginning of rnd.

Work 4 rnds k2, p2 ribbing.

Change to larger dpn.

Rnds 1-3: Knit.

Rnd 4: BO 2 sts, k8 (including last st from bind-off), BO 4, k8 (including last st from bind-off), BO 2. Place 8 sts for front on one needle and 8 sts for back on another needle.

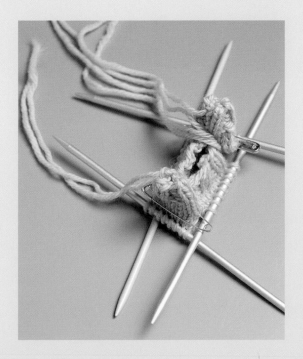

SLEEVES

With smaller dpn, CO 12 sts and divide onto 3 dpn (= 4 sts per needle); join.

Work 4 rnds k2, p2 ribbing.

Change to larger dpn.

Rnds 1-7: Knit.

Rnd 8: BO 2, k8 (including last st from bind-off), BO 2.

Place sleeve sts on a holder and then make another sleeve the same way.

Divide the body and sleeve sts onto larger dpn: 8 sts for back on Ndl 1, 8 sts of left sleeve on Ndl 2, 8 sts for front on Ndl 3, 8 sts of right sleeve on Ndl 4.

Rnd 1: K32.

Rnd 2: (K1, k2tog, k2, k2tog, k1) around.

Rnd 3: K24.

Rnd 4-7: Change to smaller needles and work (k2, p2) ribbing around.

BO and cut yarn. Seam underarms. Weave in ends neatly on WS. Gently steam press sweater except for ribbing.

Mother's Knitting Tips:
Attach the sleeves to the body with safety pins so it'll be easier to knit the body and sleeves together.

LEVEL OF DIFFICULTY
Advanced

MATERIALS
Yarn:
CYCA #4 (worsted/afghan/aran) Rauma
Vamsegarn (100% wool), 91 yd/83 m / 50 g),
Orange V43, 150-200 g
DMC Embroidery Thread
4 hanks White (Blanc)
1 hank Red 666
3 hanks Green 505
Aida 354 waste canvas
Sewing needle
Needles: U.S. size 8-10 / 5-6 mm: circular and
set of 5 dpn
Recommended Gauge: 14-16 sts = 4 in / 10 cm

Rabbit and Carrot Slippers

These slippers feature an embroidered rabbit sitting behind a carrot, so obviously the slippers must be knitted with orange yarn. The embroidery requires some patience, because the amount of space for it gets a bit tight at the tip of the slipper.

NOTE: Alternate two strands of yarn on every stitch throughout (as for two-end or Fair Isle knitting).

With one strand of Orange and circular, CO 56 (60, 64) sts and then add second strand of Orange. Knit 10 rows back and forth in garter st, alternating the two strands on every stitch.
Join the "collar": work 28 (30, 32) sts to center back, pm for beginning of rnd, and knit 13 rnds. Divide the work in half and continue over 28 (30, 32) sts for the heel.

HEEL
Row 1: K14 (15, 16), knitting last st with both strands; turn.
Row 2: Sl 1, p27 (29, 31), purling last st with both strands; turn.
Work another 11 rows back and forth in St st over the 28 (30, 32) heel sts, always slipping the first st.

Heel Turn
Row 14: P13 (15, 17), p2tog, p1 with both strands; turn.
Row 15: K3 (5, 7), k2tog, k1 with both strands; turn.
Rows 16-23: Continue the same way, working back and forth in St st and shaping, with 1 more st before the decrease on each row (the decrease joins the sts before/after the gap).
Row 24: P12 (14, 16), p2tog, p1 with both strands; turn.
Row 25: K13 (15, 17), k2tog with both strands; turn. (This row ends with k2tog and not k1 as previously.)

Row 26: P13 (15, 17), p2tog, p1 with both strands; turn.

FOOT
Set-up Rnd: Ssk, k6 (7, 8). Pm at center of sole, k7 (8, 9), pick up and knit 7 sts evenly spaced across one side of the heel flap, k28 (30, 32) across instep, pick up and knit 7 sts evenly spaced across other side of heel flap and k7 (8, 9) on sole. The beginning of the rnd is at center of sole.
Foot: Knit 33 (36, 39) rnds on the 56 (60, 64) sts of foot.

Toe Shaping
Divide the sts onto 4 dpn with 14 (15, 16) sts on each needle. Shape toe as follows, with 8 sts decreased on each decrease rnd.
Rnd 1 (decrease rnd): At beginning of each needle: K1, k2tog. At end of each needle: K2tog, k1.
Rnd 2: Knit.
Repeat Rnds 1-2 until 16 (20, 16) sts rem. Cut yarn and draw end through remaining sts. Pull tight and weave in all ends neatly on WS.

FINISHING
Steam press slippers and then felt slippers (see page 81).
Place the waste canvas centered on the slipper, with the edge directly below the split in the collar. Do not divide the plies of the embroidery thread. Begin the embroidery with the white ear at the center of the motif, with the top of the first cross

stitch in the 12th hole from the top of the canvas. Continue working from the chart. When the embroidery is complete, remove the threads from the canvas. Be careful when removing the threads from the outer edge of the embroidery; it's easy to pull a little too hard and distort the stitches.

CROSS STITCH

Photo 1: Sew the first stitch on the diagonal from one hole to the second hole on the next row.

Photo 2: When working several crosses in the same color one after the other, sew the first step of each cross at the same time.

Photo 3: Sew the second and last step of the cross on the diagonal on the way back so the threads will cross the same way throughout.

Photo 4: Carefully remove the waste canvas after you've completed all the embroidery.

EMBROIDERY FOR THE FIRST SLIPPER

EMBROIDERY FOR THE SECOND SLIPPER

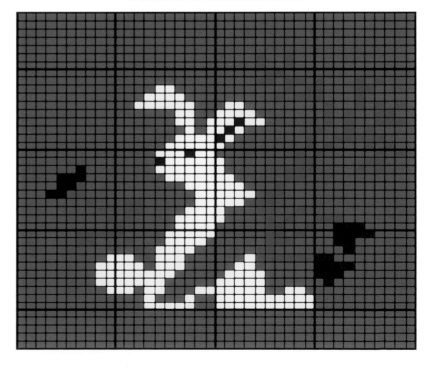

LEVEL OF DIFFICULTY
Advanced

FINISHED MEASUREMENTS
17¾ x 17¾ in / 45 x 45 cm

MATERIALS
Yarn:
CYCA #4 (worsted/afghan/aran)
Rauma Vamsegarn (100% wool),
91 yd/83 m / 50 g
Yarn Colors and Amounts:
Color 1: Beige V05, 200 g
Color 2: Red V24, 50 g
Color 3: Blue V82, 50 g
Color 4: Orange V43, 50 g
Color 5: Purple V71, 50 g
Color 6: Green V80, 50 g
NOTE: Hold 2 strands of yarn
together throughout.
Needles: U.S. size 10½ / 6.5 mm:
32 in / 80 cm circular
Other Materials: Pillow form,
24 x 24 in / 60 x 60 cm.
Gauge: 10 sts and 14 rnds =
4 x 4 in / 10 x 10 cm.
Adjust needle size to obtain
correct gauge if necessary.

Pillow with Åkle Tapestry Motifs

We knitted this pillow a few years ago so we can't guarantee that the colors we used are still available. We've made some suggestions for substitutions in the Materials list.

The finished pillow measures approx. 17¾ x 17¾ in / 45 x 45 cm, but we used a pillow form slightly larger than that, since a form the exact same size as the pillow cover flattens out with use. The larger form helps the pillow keep its shape and plumpness longer.

PILLOW

With 2 strands of Color 1 held together, CO 100 sts. Join, being careful not to twist cast-on row. Pm for beginning of round. Work (P1, k49) 2 times. The cast-on row + the first row worked correspond to the first 2 rows of the chart. Continue, following the chart and working knit over knit and purl over purl, until 1 row remains on chart. BO with Color 1.

FINISHING

Weave in ends neatly on WS and then steam press pillow cover under a damp pressing cloth. With Color 1, seam one end of the pillow, making sure the purl stitches are at the sides. Insert pillow form. Use Color 1 to seam the other end of the pillow and weave in remaining ends.

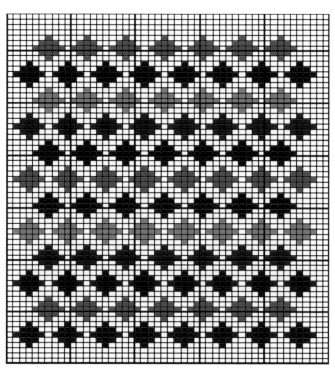

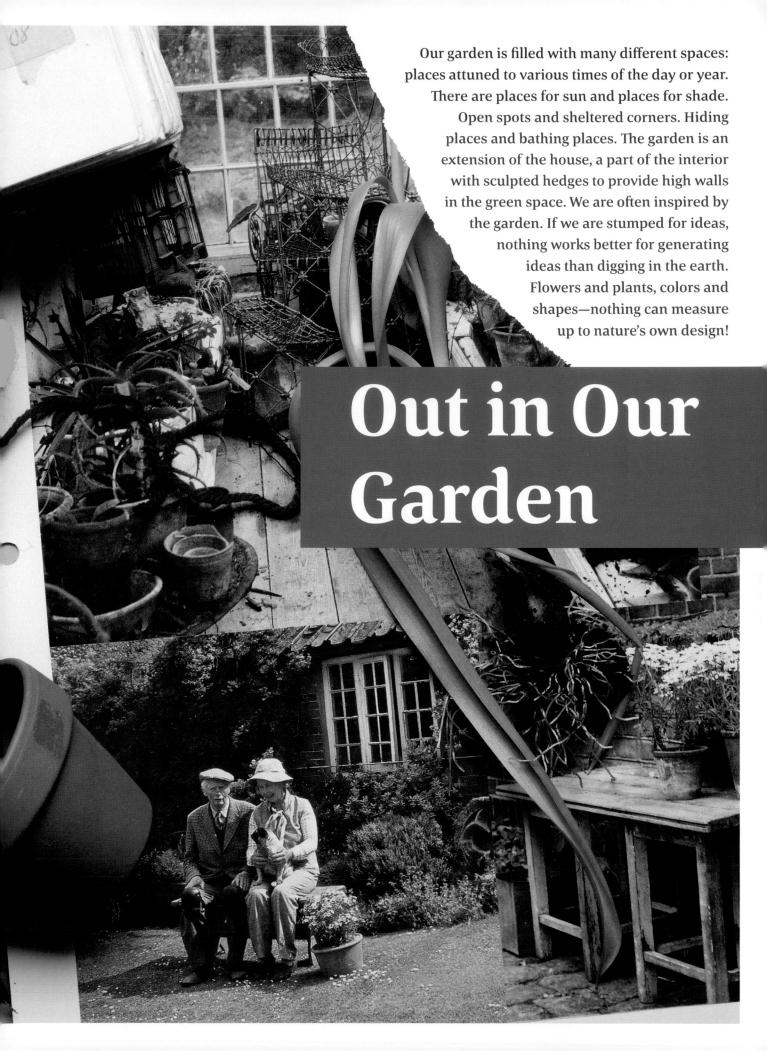

Our garden is filled with many different spaces: places attuned to various times of the day or year. There are places for sun and places for shade. Open spots and sheltered corners. Hiding places and bathing places. The garden is an extension of the house, a part of the interior with sculpted hedges to provide high walls in the green space. We are often inspired by the garden. If we are stumped for ideas, nothing works better for generating ideas than digging in the earth. Flowers and plants, colors and shapes—nothing can measure up to nature's own design!

Out in Our Garden

LEVEL OF DIFFICULTY
Advanced

FINISHED MEASUREMENTS
17¾ x 17¾ in / 45 x 45 cm

MATERIALS
Yarn:
CYCA #3 (DK, light worsted), Schachenmayr Merino
Extrafine 120 (100% Merino wool, 131 yd/120 m / 50 g)
Yarn Colors and Amounts:
Color 1: White 00102, 100 g
Color 2: Blue 00151, 50 g
Color 3: Pink 00137, 50 g
Color 4: Orange 00125, 50 g
Color 5: Green 00173, 50 g
Color 6: Yellow 00120, 50 g
Needles: U.S. size 2.5 / 3mm: 24 in / 60 cm circular
Other Materials: Pillow form, 24 x 24 in / 60 x 60 cm

Flower Pillow

We knitted this pillow for the first time for an article in a Japanese magazine covering our work and our garden.

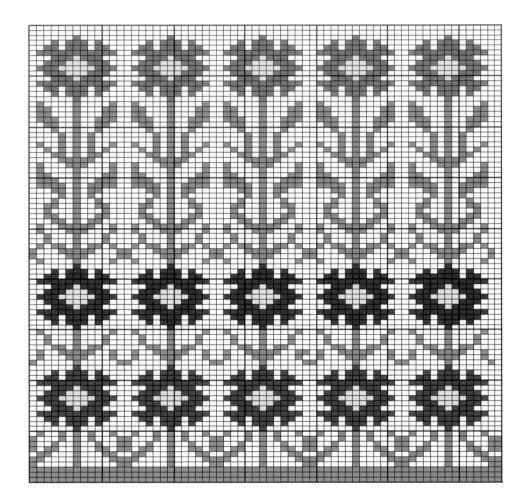

With Color 5, CO 132 sts. Join, being careful not to twist cast-on row. Pm for beginning of round. Work (P1, k65) 2 times. Work following the chart, with knit over knit and purl over purl, until 1 row remains on chart. BO with Color 1.

FINISHING
Weave in ends neatly on WS and then steam press pillow cover under a damp pressing cloth. With Color 1, seam top end of the pillow, making sure the purl stitches are at the sides. Insert pillow form. Use Color 5 to seam bottom end of the pillow and weave in remaining ends.

In the summer of 2015, a new guest popped up in our
garden. Its appearance and behavior matched the
description of a European robin, although its breast
was less red than in pictures we'd seen. So we made
two versions—one with an orange breast and one
with red, just to be sure. The bird wasn't especially
shy. It came out of the bushes and perennials and
stared at us when we sat in the garden. We hope it
has come to stay, because it's a really nice guest to
have in the garden! But if that doesn't happen, we
can put out one we've knitted ourselves.

LEVEL OF DIFFICULTY
Advanced

MATERIALS
Yarn:
CYCA #3 (DK weight) Schachenmayr Merino
Extrafine 120 DK, 100% wool (131 yd/120 m / 50 g)
Yarn Colors and Amounts:
White 00101, 50 g
Black 00199, 50 g
Orange 00125, 50 g
Gray 00191, 50 g
Needles: U.S. size 0-2.5 / 2-3 mm:
set of 5 dpn
Gauge: 30 sts and 40 rnds in 4 x 4 in /
10 x 10 cm. Adjust needle size to
obtain correct gauge if necessary.

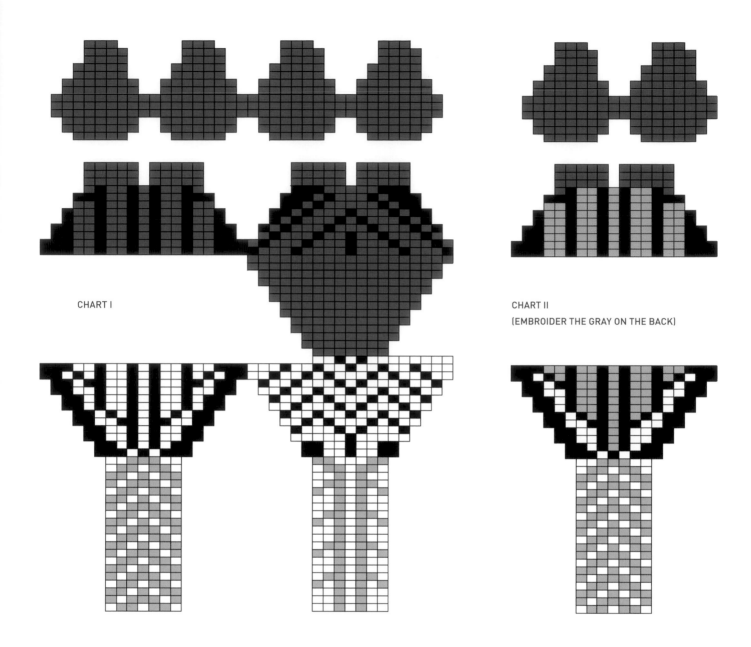

CHART I

CHART II
(EMBROIDER THE GRAY ON THE BACK)

European Robin

Erithacus Rubecula

With White, CO 14 sts and divide onto 4 dpn: 4 + 3 + 4 + 3. Join to work in the round.

TAIL

Work following the Basic Pattern on page 62 and Chart I on this page.

Cut yarn and draw end through rem 12 sts.

Flatten the tail and sew the end at the cast-on row, making sure the top and bottom sides are correctly oriented. Stretch the body well and tighten any stitches that are too loose.

Block by gently steam pressing under a damp pressing cloth. Fill the bird and sew the hole at top of head to close.

Crochet the beak and sew on the eyes. This bird has a black beak and black eyes.

With Gray, following Chart II, embroider in duplicate stitch between the two black stitches on the back and up to the last black row at the neck.

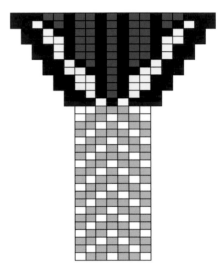

Tea Cozy with a European Robin

LEVEL OF DIFFICULTY
Advanced

MATERIALS
Yarn:
CYCA #3 (DK weight) Schachenmayr Merino Extrafine 120 DK, 100% wool (131 yd/120 m / 50 g)
Yarn Colors and Amounts:
Blue 00153, 50 g
Orange 00125, 50 g
White 00102, 50 g
Black 00199, 50 g
Needles: U.S. sizes 2.5 and 4 / 3 and 3.5 mm: set of 5 dpn and 16 in / 40 cm circulars
Gauge: 22 sts and 30 rnds on larger needles = 4 x 4 in / 10 x 10 cm.

We knitted this tea cozy with the same colors as for the robin, but added a little blue to brighten up the cozy. To match, the robin on top has blue over its back, as well as a blue beak and blue eyes.

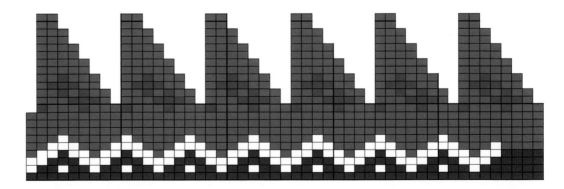

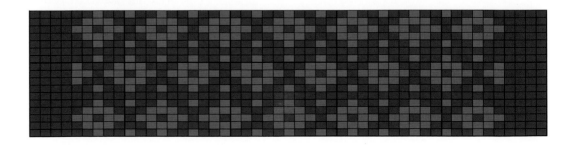

Tea Cozy with a Robin

With Black and short circular U.S. size 2.5 / 3 mm, CO 96 sts. Join, being careful not to twist cast-on row; pm for beginning of rnd.

Work 15 rnds in k2, p2 ribbing.

Change to larger circular and knit 1 rnd, increasing 2 sts evenly spaced around = 98 sts.

Now work each side of the cozy separately. Rows for one side are worked back and forth on the circular, with the other half of the stitches (= 49 sts) resting on the same circular or on a holder.

Work 49 sts following the bottom chart on page 100; begin each row of the chart with sl 1, k3, and end with k4 (= garter stitch vertical panel).

When beginning a row with a slip st, it is important to make sure that the yarn at the beginning of the row doesn't tighten the slipped stitch. The edge stitches should lie smoothly, one above the other, along the edge.

All of the edge stitches should be "open." One method for making an open chain edge is to begin each row with sl 1 knitwise with yarn in back and end each row with p1.

Chart: Work back and forth in knit and purl St st rows. After completing the 17 rows of lower chart for one side, work the other side of the cozy the same way.

Now join the two pieces on Row 18 (1st row of top chart):

Sl 1, k3, p44, purl the last st of piece 1 together with the first st of piece 2. The opening for the spout is complete; continue with p44, k4.

Work back and forth over 97 sts following the chart:

Begin the row with sl 1, k96.

Work 7 more rows in stockinette following the chart.

Begin each row of the chart with sl 1, k3, and end with k4.

Rnd 8: Now work in the round again—begin with k1 and then sl the last st of row 7 over the knit st = 96 sts rem. The opening for the handle is complete.

Continue following the chart:

Rnd 9: (K2tog, k6) around.

Rnd 10: K84.

Move sts to dpn on the next rnd, dividing them evenly onto 4 larger dpn.

Rnd 11: (K2tog, k5) around.

Rnd 12: K72.

Rnd 13: (K2tog, k4) around.

Rnd 14: K60.

Rnd 15: (K2tog, k3) around.

Rnd 16: K48.

Rnd 17: (K2tog, k2) around.

Rnd 18: K36.

Rnd 19: (K2tog, k1) around.

Rnd 20: K24.

Change to smaller dpn and finish the cozy with 15 rnds k2 p2 ribbing.

BO knitwise.

Weave in all ends neatly on WS and tighten any loose strands, especially in the section worked back and forth.

Gently steam press the cozy (except for ribbing) under a damp pressing cloth.

Knit a bird.

For this cozy, we sewed a robin on top. So that the bird won't roll off, insert a ring of cardboard under the top ribbing and then fold the ribbing over it.

Baste the bird to the top.

If you want a smaller bird on the tea cozy, make one with a smaller needle size.

Garter Stitch

Many years ago, we knitted a garter-stitch band to make an easy pin cushion with five rolled rings. Our pin cushion has now been transformed into a flower made of seven circles.

INSTRUCTIONS

All of the bands are worked on two needles, back and forth over 10 sts. The length is determined by the number of ridges. 1 ridge = 2 knit rows, worked back and forth. Leave a long tail when you finish knitting and you can use it for joining the bands. The ends of the bands are sewn together into a ring before the long sides are folded down. This way, different bands can lie inside each other to form shapes.

Bands have 8, 18, 28, 38, 50, or 70 ridges. When counting ridges, hold the piece towards you with the cast-on tail on the right side. When you bind off, the tail should end up on the left side of the piece.

JOINING THE BANDS

Lay the bands inside each other, shaping as shown, and, using the yarn tails, sew them together through the edge stitches on the wrong/under side of the piece. End on the right side, sewing and shaping the piece using thread the same color as for the outermost band. Check the right side and then weave in the ends on the underside so the pieces don't shift and lose their shape.

LEVEL OF DIFFICULTY
Easy

MATERIALS
Wool yarn suitable for knitting on needles U.S. size 2.5 / 3 mm (sport weight recommended)
Needles: straight U.S. size 2.5 / 3 mm
Other Materials: Blunt tapestry needle

LEVEL OF DIFFICULTY
Easy

MATERIALS
Yarn: CYCA #3 (DK weight) Schachenmayr
Merino Extrafine 120 DK, 100% wool
(131 yd/120 m / 50 g)
Yarn Colors and Amounts:
Dark Purple 00148, 50 g
Light Purple 00147, 50 g
Yellow 00122, 50 g
Needles: U.S. size 2.5 / 3 mm

INSTRUCTIONS
See opposite page for general instructions and joining.

Knit 6 Light Purple bands with 8 ridges each.
Knit 6 Dark Purple bands with 18 ridges each.
Knit 1 Yellow band with 8 ridges.
Knit 1 Yellow band with 18 ridges.

Seat Cushion
Inspired by Blue Poppies

Warm up your cold garden chair with one of these thick and lovely seat cushions. If you want to bring in a little taste of summer for the rest of the year, set the cushion on a kitchen stool.

The flowers are composed of bands with 8 and 18 ridges. The flower's center is a yellow ring surrounded by six blue rings for flower petals. Each ring has a 70-ridge band around it. Between the flowers are rings with 8, 18, and 28 ridges. Sew the flowers together securely with brown yarn.

INSTRUCTIONS
See page 104 for general instructions and joining.

Knit:
9 Yellow bands with 8 ridges each.
9 Yellow bands with 18 ridges each.
12 Deep Blue bands with 8 ridges each.
12 Deep Blue bands with 18 ridges each.
18 Pool Blue bands with 8 ridges each.
18 Pool Blue bands with 18 ridges each.
18 Royal Blue bands with 8 ridges each.
18 Royal Blue bands with 18 ridges each.
6 Enzian Blue bands with 8 ridges each.
6 Enzian Blue bands with 18 ridges each.
4 Brown bands with 8 ridges each.
4 Brown bands with 18 ridges each.
4 Brown bands with 28 ridges each.
9 Brown bands with 70 ridges each.

LEVEL OF DIFFICULTY
Easy

MATERIALS
Yarn: CYCA #3 (DK weight) Schachenmayr Merino Extrafine 120 DK, 100% wool (131 yd/120 m / 50 g)

Yarn Colors and Amounts:
Enzian Blue 00153, 50 g
Royal Blue 00151, 50 g
Pool Blue 00165, 50 g
Deep Blue 00158, 50 g
Yellow 00122, 50 g
Brown 00110, 250 g
Needles: U.S. size 2.5 / 3 mm

Butterfly
Lysandra bellargus

A table mat shaped like a butterfly. Play around with various color combinations to make your own butterfly! You can even arrange the rings in other ways to create your own butterfly species.

LEVEL OF DIFFICULTY
Easy

MATERIALS
Yarn: CYCA #3 (DK weight)
Schachenmayr Merino Extrafine
120 DK, 100% wool (131 yd/120
m / 50 g)
Yarn Colors and Amounts:
Pool Blue 00165, 150 g
Dark Blue 00150, 50 g
White 00101, 50 g
Needles: U.S. size 2.5 / 3 mm

INSTRUCTIONS
See page 104 for general instructions
and joining.

Knit:
14 Dark Blue bands with 8 ridges each.
1 Dark Blue band with 70 ridges.
2 Pool Blue bands with 8 ridges each.
4 Pool Blue bands with 18 ridges each.
4 Pool Blue bands with 28 ridges each.
4 Pool Blue bands with 50 ridges each.
2 Pool Blue bands with 70 ridges each.
6 White bands with 8 ridges each.

LEVEL OF DIFFICULTY
Advanced

MATERIALS
Yarn: CYCA #3 (DK weight) Schachenmayr Merino Extrafine 120 DK, 100% wool (131 yd/120 m / 50 g)
Yarn Colors and Amounts: Choose your own selection of colors
Crochet Hook: U.S. size E-4 / 3.5 mm

Butterfly Throw

Butterfly Throw

When we reorganize our yarn supply after a long winter, we usually end up crocheting a new throw with the leftover yarns. We often work with butterflies as a theme, and this version of a granny square blanket features butterfly shaping.

SPECIAL STITCHES

1st dc / UK tr = ch 3.

dc cluster (dc cl) / UK tr cluster (UK tr cl) = 2 (3) dc / UK tr joined as follows:

2 (3) dc cluster / UK tr cluster = *work 1 dc / UK tr, but do not bring yarn through last 2 loops on hook. Repeat from * 1 (2) more times until there are 3 (4) loops on hook; yarn around hook and through all remaining loops.

dc group (dc gr) / UK tr group (UK tr gr) = 3 dc / UK tr into 1 stitch

NOTE: U.S. stitch names will be followed by British stitch names throughout.

BUTTERFLY BODY

Ch 8 and join into a ring with 1 sl st into 1st ch.

Row 1: Ch 3, 1 dc / UK tr, ch 1, 2 dc / UK tr around ring = 1st body segment.

Row 2: Work back: Ch 3, (1 dc / UK tr, ch 1, 1 dc / UK tr) around ch between the 2 center dc / UK tr of previous round and 1 dc / UK tr in top of ch 3 at beginning of row.

Repeat Row 2 10 times—12 body segments.
End with ch 3, (1 dc / UK tr, ch 1, 1 dc / UK tr) around ch between the 2 center dc / UK tr of previous row, 1 dc / UK tr in top of ch 3 at beginning of row.
The last 2 dc / UK tr are crocheted together.

ANTENNAE

Ch 10, 1 sc / UK dc in 6th ch from hook, and then work 1 sc / UK dc in each of the next 3 ch, 1 sl st between the 2 dc / UK tr in the center of the previous segment of the body, ch 10, 1 sc / UK dc in 6th ch from hook; 1 sc / UK dc in each of next 3 ch, 1

sl st between the 2 dc / UK tr in center of the last segment on body; cut yarn and fasten off.

BACK WINGS

Make both wings alike on Rounds 1-2.

First Color

Ch 8 and join into a ring with 1 sl st into 1st ch.

Rnd 1: Ch 4 (= 1 dc / UK tr + ch 1), (1 dc / UK tr, ch 1) around ring 9 times and end with 1 sl st into 3rd ch at beginning of rnd.
Cut yarn and fasten off = 10 dc / UK tr around circle.

Second Color

Rnd 2: Work around the ch st between each dc / UK tr of Rnd 1. Begin with (ch 3 and 2-dc cl / UK 2-tr cl) around ch loop, ch 4, (3-dc cl / UK 3-tr cl around next ch loop, ch 4) around; end with ch 4 and 1 sl st into top of 1st dc cl / UK tr cl.

Third Color

Rnd 3: Join the right back wing to the body.
Work (2 sc / UK dc, ch 3 = picot, 2 sc / UK dc) in 1st ch loop between dc clusters / UK tr clusters on Rnd 2, ch 2.
The wing is joined to the body in two places as follows:
2 sc / UK dc around the next ch loop between dc clusters / UK tr clusters on Rnd 2. 1 tr / UK dtr around dc / UK tr on side of body in 5th segment from bottom, on right side from back, 2 sc / UK dc around ch loop of wing, ch 2, 2 sc / UK dc in next ch loop between dc cl / UK tr cl on Rnd 2, 1 dc / UK tr around dc / UK tr on right side of body in 3rd segment as counted from bottom up on back, 2 sc /

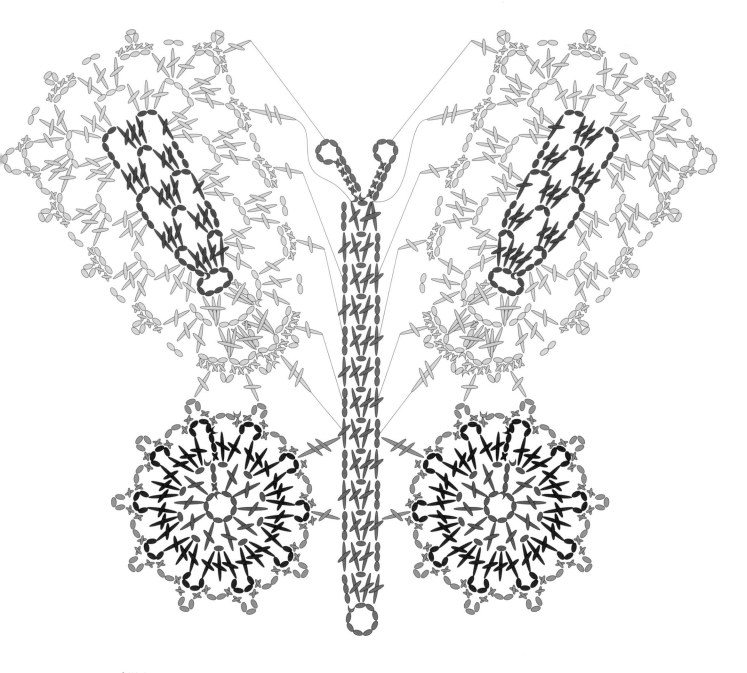

✖ = sc/UK dc

● = ch

☽ = sl st

⊦ = dc/UK tr

⧧ = tr/UK dtr

⧣ = dtr/Uk trtr

⧥ = trtr/UK quadtr

⋔ = 3-dc cl/UK 3-tr cl

BUTTERFLY CHART

UK dc back around ch loop on wing, ch 2. *(2 sc / UK dc, ch 3, 2 sc / UK dc, ch 2) in next ch loop between dc cl / UK tr cl on Rnd 2*; rep from * to * in all ch loops. End with 1 sl st in 1st sc / UK dc.

Join left back wing to body

Work (2 sc / UK dc, ch 3, 2 sc / UK dc) in 1st ch loop between dc clusters / UK tr clusters on Rnd 2, ch 2. The wing is joined to the body in two places as follows:

Work 2 sc / UK dc in next ch loop between dc cl / UK tr cl on Rnd 2, 1 dc / UK tr around left side of body in 3rd segment as counted from the bottom of back, 2 sc / UK dc back around ch loop of wing, ch 2. 2 sc / UK dc around next ch loop between dc clusters / UK tr clusters on Rnd 2. 1 tr / UK dtr around dc / UK tr on left side of body at 5th segment from bottom of body, 2 sc / UK dc back around ch loop on wing, ch 2, *(2 sc / UK dc, ch 3, 2 sc / UK dc, ch 2) in next ch loop between dc cl / UK tr cl on Rnd 2*; repeat from * to * in every ch loop.

End with 1 sl st into 1st ch.

Cut yarn and fasten off.

FRONT WINGS

Make both wings alike up to round joining wing to body.

First Color

Ch 8 and join into a ring with 1 sl st into 1st ch.

Row 1: Ch 5, 3 dc / UK tr, ch 2, 1 dc / UK tr around ring.

Row 2: Turn and ch 3, 2 dc / UK tr around ch loop, ch 2, 3 dc / UK tr around last ch loop; turn.

Row 3: Ch 5, 3 dc / UK tr around ch loop, ch 2, 1 dc / UK tr in last dc / UK tr of previous row.

Row 4: Turn with ch 3, 2 dc / UK tr around 1st ch loop, ch 2, 3 dc / UK tr around last ch loop; turn.

Row 5: Ch 5, 3 dc / UK tr around ch loop, ch 2, 1 dc / UK tr in last dc / UK tr of previous row. Cut yarn and fasten off.

Second Color

Attach yarn around ring beginning First Color section above. Ch 3 and work 2-dc cl / UK 2-tr cl around bottom of ring.

Ch 4, 3-dc cl / UK 3-tr cl around ring, ch 3 and then (3 dc / UK tr, ch 3) in each of the next 2 ch loops along side of wing.

Corner: *(3 dc / UK tr, ch 4, 3 dc / UK tr) around ch loop in corner, ch 3* and, in next corner, work * to * once more, work (3 dc / UK tr, ch 3) in each of next 2 ch loops along other side of wing.

End with 1 sl st into top of 1st dc cl / UK tr cl.

Third Color

Begin at lower edge of wing between 2 dc clusters / UK tr clusters; work around the 4-ch loop.

Work (ch 3, 2-dc cl / UK 2-tr cl, ch 3, 3-dc cl / UK 3-tr cl) in same ch loop, ch 3, *3 dc / UK tr, ch 3*; rep from * to * around the next 3 ch loops. In the corner work (3 dc / UK tr, ch 4, 3 dc / UK tr, ch 3), 3 dc / UK tr in center ch loop, ch 3, and, in next corner, work (3 dc / UK tr, ch 4, 3 dc / UK tr, ch 3), *3 dc / UK tr, ch 3*; rep from * to * in the next 3 ch loops. End with 3-dc cl / UK 3-tr cl in 1st ch loop (where you have already worked a 2-dc cl / UK 2-tr cl), ch 3, and 1 sl st into top of 1st dc cl / UK tr cl.

Join body and back wings in the same color as follows:

RIGHT WING

Begin with 2 sc / UK dc in 1st ch loop, 1 dc / UK tr in 1st picot from body on back wing, 2 sc / UK dc back in ch loop on wing, ch 2.

In the 2nd ch loop (between 2 dc groups / UK tr groups), work 2 sc / UK dc, 1 dc / UK tr in 2nd picot from body on back wing, 2 sc / UK dc back around ch loop on wing, ch 2.

Work *(2 sc / UK dc, ch 3, 2 sc / UK dc, ch 2) around next ch loop*; rep from * to * around the 3rd, 4th, and 5th ch loops. Around ch loop in corner work: (2 sc / UK dc, ch 4, 2 sc / UK dc, ch 2) and then continue *(2 sc / UK dc, ch 3, 2 sc / UK dc, ch 2) around next ch loop*; rep from * to * around the 7th and 8th ch loops.

Work 2 sc / UK dc in ch loop in corner, ch 3, 1 sc / UK dc, 1 dc / UK tr in ch circle at end of 1st antenna, 2 sc / UK dc back in same ch loop on wing, ch 2.

10th ch loop: 2 sc / UK dc, 1 tr / UK dtr in top of segment where antenna is crocheted from, 2 sc / UK dc back in same ch loop on wing, ch 2.
11th ch loop: 2 sc / UK dc, 1 dc / UK tr around dc / UK tr at side of 3rd segment from top, 2 sc / UK dc back, ch 2.
12th ch loop: 2 sc / UK dc, 1 dc / UK tr around dc / UK tr at side of 5th segment from top, 2 sc / UK dc back, ch 2.
13th ch loop: 2 sc / UK dc, 1 dc / UK tr around dc / UK tr at side of 7th segment from top, 2 sc / UK dc back, ch 2.
14th ch loop: 2 sc / UK dc, 1 tr / UK dtr around same dc / UK tr at side where tr / UK dtr from back wing is worked, 2 sc / UK dc back, ch 2.

End with 1 sl st into 1st sc / UK dc; cut yarn and fasten off.

LEFT WING

1st ch loop: 2 sc / UK dc, 1 tr / UK dtr around same dc / UK tr on left side where tr / UK dtr from back wing was worked, 2 sc / UK dc back in same ch loop on wing, ch 2.
2nd ch loop: (between 2-dc cl / UK 2-tr cl) 2 sc / UK dc, 1 dc / UK tr around dc / UK tr at side of 7th segment from top, 2 sc / UK dc back, ch 2.
3rd ch loop: 2 sc / UK dc, 1 dc / UK tr around dc / UK tr at side of 5th segment from top, 2 sc / UK dc back, ch 2.
4th ch loop: 2 sc / UK dc, 1 dc / UK tr around dc / UK tr at side of 7th segment from top, 2 sc / UK dc back, ch 2.

5th ch loop: 2 sc / UK dc, 1 tr / UK dtr in top of segment where antenna is crocheted from, 2 sc / UK dc back, ch 2.

2 sc / UK dc around ch loop in corner, 1 dc / UK tr in ch-ring at end of second antenna, 1 sc / UK dc back in same ch loop on wing, ch 2.

6th ch loop: (2 sc / UK dc, ch 3, 2 sc / UK dc, ch 2) in corner, *2 sc / UK dc, ch 3, 2 sc / UK dc, ch 2*; rep * to * around 7th and 8th ch loops.

Around the ch loop in corner, work: (2 sc / UK dc, ch 3, 2 sc / UK dc, ch 2), work *2 sc / UK dc, ch 3, 2 sc / UK dc, ch 2* around 10th, 11th, and 12th ch loops.

13th ch loop: Work 2 sc / UK dc, 1 dc / UK tr in 2nd picot of body, on back wing, 2 sc / UK dc back in ch loop, ch 2.
14th ch loop: Work 2 sc / UK dc, 1 dc / UK tr in 1st picot of body, on back wing, 2 sc / UK dc back in ch loop, ch 2.

End with 1 sl st in 1st sc / UK dc; cut yarn and fasten off.

Weave in all ends neatly on WS.

Background Color for Joining Butterflies
We decided to crochet with Black all around the butterflies. Begin by working around each butterfly as follows.

WORK BETWEEN THE WINGS AND BODY BACK:
Ch 6 and join into a ring with 1 sl st into 1st ch.
Rnd 1: Ch 3, 1 sc / UK dc in 2nd picot from body on right wing, ch 3, 1 sc / UK dc back around ring.
Ch 3, 1 sc / UK dc in 1st picot from body on right wing.
Ch 3, 1 sc / UK dc back around ring.
Ch 3, 1 sc / UK dc in ring at end of body, ch 3, 1 sc / UK dc back around ring.
Ch 3, 1 sc / UK dc in 1st picot from body on left wing.

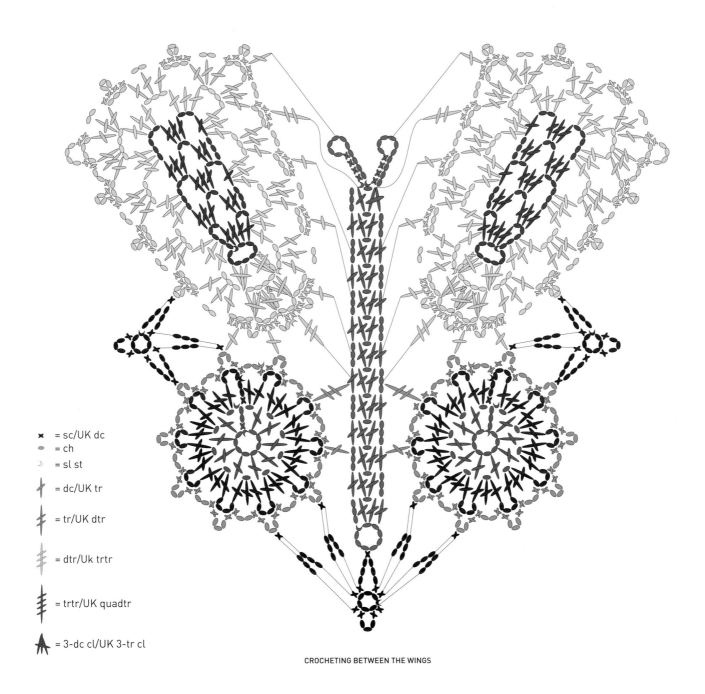

= sc/UK dc

= ch

= sl st

= dc/UK tr

= tr/UK dtr

= dtr/Uk trtr

= trtr/UK quadtr

= 3-dc cl/UK 3-tr cl

CROCHETING BETWEEN THE WINGS

Ch 3, 1 sc / UK dc back around ring.

Ch 3, 1 sc / UK dc in 2nd picot from body on left wing.

Ch 3, 1 sc / UK dc back around ring.

End with 1 sc / UK dc around ring, ch 3, and 1 sc / UK dc around ring.

Cut yarn and fasten off.

WORK BETWEEN THE FRONT AND BACK WINGS:

Ch 6 and join into a ring with 1 sl st into 1st ch.

Ch 3, 1 sc / UK dc in 1st picot on front wing from join between front and back wings.

Ch 3, 1 sc / UK dc back around ring.

Ch 3, 1 sc / UK dc around join between front and back wings, ch 3, 1 sc / UK dc back around ring.

Ch 3, 1 sc / UK dc in 1st picot on back wing from join between front and back wings.

Ch 3, 1 sc / UK dc back around ring.

End with 1 sc / UK dc around ring, ch 3, 1 sc / UK dc around ring.

Cut yarn and fasten off.

Work the same way on the other side of the butterfly's body, but begin with the back wing.

Butterfly Throw

Crochet around the butterfly with the same color, beginning in the left corner at top of front wing and then continue towards the left in all picots.

Rnd 1:
1st picot: Ch 3, 2 dc / UK tr, ch 2.
2nd picot: 4 dc / UK tr, ch 2.
3rd picot: 4 tr / UK dtr, ch 2.
4th picot: 4 dtr / UK tr tr (= 3 yarnovers over hook to begin stitch), ch 2.
5th picot: Work around the 3 ch from join between wings, 4 dc / UK tr, ch 2.
6th picot: 4 tr tr / UK quadtr (= 4 yarnovers over hook to begin stitch), ch 2.
7th picot: Corner, 3 tr tr / UK quadtr, ch 4, 3 tr tr / UK quadtr, ch 2.
8th picot: 4 dc / UK tr, ch 2.
9th picot: 4 sc / UK dc, ch 2.
10th picot: 4 tr / UK dtr, ch 2.
11th picot: Around the ch 3 of join between wings, work 4 sc / UK dc, ch 2.
12th picot: 4 tr / UK dtr, ch 2.
13th picot: 4 sc / UK dc, ch 2.
14th picot: 4 dc / UK tr, ch 2.
15th picot: Corner, 3 tr tr / UK quadtr, ch 4, 3 tr tr / UK quadtr, ch 2.
16th picot: 4 tr tr / UK quadtr, ch 2.
17th picot: Around the ch 3 of join between wings, work 4 dc / UK tr, ch 1.
18th picot: 4 dtr / UK tr tr, ch 2.
19th picot: 4 tr / UK dtr, ch 2.
20th picot: 4 dc / UK tr, ch 2.
21st picot: Corner, 3 dc / UK tr, ch 4, 3 dc / UK tr, ch 2.
22nd picot: 4 sc / UK dc, ch 2.
23rd picot: 4 sc / UK dc, ch 2.
24th picot: 4 dc / UK tr, ch 2.
In the ring on the antennae, work 2 tr / UK dtr in 1st antenna and 2 tr / UK dtr in the other one, ch 2.
25th picot: 4 dc / UK tr, ch 2.

26th picot: 4 sc / UK dc, ch 2.
27th picot: 4 sc / UK dc, ch 2.
End with 3 dc / UK tr in 1st corner, ch 4, and 1 sl st into top of 1st dc / UK tr.
Turn work and crochet back:

Rnd 2:
Ch 4, 3 tr / UK dtr around ch loop, ch 4, 4 tr / UK dtr around same ch loop, ch 2.

On the long side, work 4 tr / UK dtr around ch loop, and ch 2 between dc groups / UK tr groups. In each corner, work (4 tr / UK dtr, ch 4, 4 tr / UK dtr, ch 2). End with 1 sl st into 4th ch at beginning of rnd. Cut yarn and fasten off. Weave in all ends neatly on WS.

JOINING ALL THE BUTTERFLY BLOCKS
Begin with the 1st butterfly block and work from corner to corner on one side.
Begin in the 1st corner with (1 sc / UK dc, ch 3, and 1 sc / UK dc) around the same ch loop.
Continue with 1 sc / UK dc between the 1st and 2nd tr / UK dtr, (1 sc / UK dc, ch 3, 1 sc / UK dc) between the 2nd and 3rd tr / UK dtr, 1 sc / UK dc between the 3rd and 4th tr / UK dtr, (1 sc / UK dc, ch 3, 1 sc / UK dc) around ch loop; end with (1 sc / UK dc, ch 1, 1 dc / UK tr) in corner in second end of side you are working on.
Continue with ch 1 and 1 sc / UK dc in corner on block you are joining the 1st one to.
From the corner on the next block, work 1 dc / UK tr in corner of 1st block. Work along the side of the 2nd block the same way as for the 1st, but the ch 3 is now ch 1, 1 sc / UK dc around ch loop on 1st block, and ch 1.
Join all the blocks for the first strip (tier) the same way. Work each strip separately and then join the strips.

JOINING TWO BLOCKS

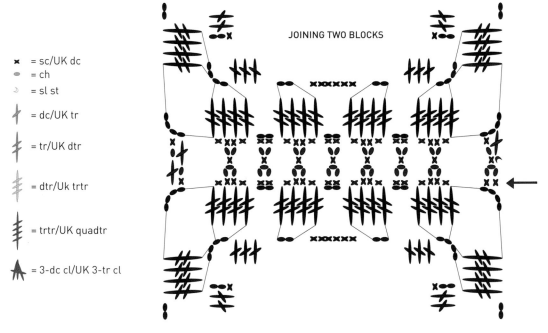

✖ = sc/UK dc

● = ch

☽ = sl st

⊬ = dc/UK tr

⨰ = tr/UK dtr

⨰ = dtr/Uk trtr

⨰ = trtr/UK quadtr

⋏ = 3-dc cl/UK 3-tr cl

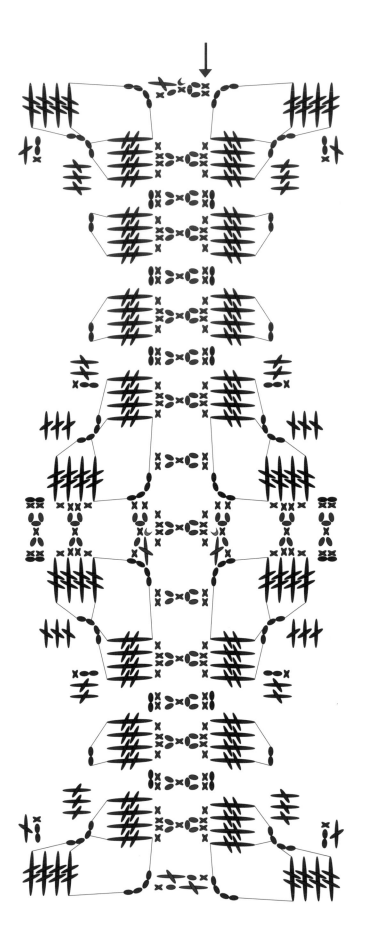

Slippers

with Art Deco Flowers

These slippers were inspired by a Grindley china service from 1930 with the pieces encircled by relief pansies. At first we only had one bowl from Arne's great-grandmother but we've added to our collection by shopping at auctions over the past few years.

With one strand of Brown and circular, CO 56 (60, 64) sts and knit 15 rows back and forth in garter st, alternating the two strands on every stitch.
Join the "collar": work 28 (30, 32) sts to center back, pm for beginning of rnd, and knit 13 rnds.

HEEL
Row 1: K14 (15, 16), knitting last st with both strands; turn.
Row 2: Sl 1, p27 (29, 31), purling last st with both strands; turn.
Work another 11 rows back and forth in St st over the 28 (30, 32) heel sts, always slipping the first st.

Heel Turn
Row 14: P13 (15, 17), p2tog, p1 with both strands; turn.
Row 15: K3 (5, 7), k2tog, k1 with both strands; turn.
Rows 16-23: Continue the same way, working back and forth in St st and shaping, with 1 more st before the decrease on each row (the decrease joins the sts before/after the gap).
Row 24: P12 (14, 16), p2tog, p1 with both strands; turn.
Row 25: K13 (15, 17), k2tog with both strands; turn. (This row ends with k2tog and not k1 as previously.)
Row 26: P13 (15, 17), p2tog, p1 with both strands; turn.

FOOT
Set-up Rnd: Ssk, k6 (7, 8). Pm at center of sole, k7 (8, 9), pick up and knit 7 sts evenly spaced across one side of the heel flap, k28 (30, 32) across instep,

LEVEL OF DIFFICULTY
Intermediate

MATERIALS
SLIPPERS
Yarn:
CYCA #4 (worsted/afghan/aran), Rauma Vamsegarn (100% wool, 91 yd/83 m / 50 g), Dark Brown Heather V64, 150-200 g
Needles: U.S. size 8-10 / 5-6 mm: circular and set of 5 dpn
Recommended Gauge: 14-16 sts = 4 in / 10 cm

FLOWERS AND LEAVES
Yarn:
CYCA #3 (DK/light worsted), Rauma Mitu (50% superfine alpaca and 50% wool, 109 yd/100 m / 50 g) Our flowers and leaves were crocheted with scrap yarns. The colors we used correspond to the suggested colors of Mitu below.
Yarn Colors and Amounts:
Orange 0784, 50 g
Yellow 6240, 50 g
Pink 8141, 50 g
Green 2196 (darker than shown here), 50 g
Purple 5090 (darker than shown here), 50 g
If you have a good yarn stash, you can find the yarn quality and colors from your leftovers.
Crochet Hook: U.S. size D-3 / 3 mm

NOTE: Alternate two strands of yarn on every stitch throughout (as for two-end or Fair Isle knitting).

pick up and knit 7 sts evenly spaced across other side of heel flap and k7 (, 9) on sole. The beginning of the rnd is at center of sole.
Foot: Knit 33 (, 39) rnds on the 56 (, 64) sts of foot.

Toe Shaping
Divide the sts onto 4 dpn with 14 (, 16) sts on each needle. Shape toe as follows, with 8 sts decreased on each decrease rnd.
Rnd 1 (decrease rnd): At beginning of each needle: K1, k2tog. At end of each needle: K2tog, k1.
Rnd 2: Knit.
Repeat Rnds 1-2 until 16 (, 16) sts rem. Cut yarn and draw end through remaining sts. Pull tight and weave in all ends neatly on WS.

FINISHING
Steam press and then felt slippers.

Felt slippers
Use a wool-safe liquid soap. For 2.2 lb / 1 kg knitted fabric, you should use about 6 tablespoons / 100 ml soap. Set the water temperature for the machine at 104-140°F / 40-60°C (the temperature options vary from machine to machine). Start at the lower temperature and check the degree of felting occasionally.

FLOWERS
Wrap the Yellow yarn around your finger 2-3 times and crochet around the ring at the same time as catching and covering the yarn tail:
Rnd 1: 1 sc / UK dc, (ch 3, 1 sc / UK dc) 6 times (= 6 ch loops).

Cut yarn and bring tail through last st; tighten.
Crochet the petals with Orange, Purple, or Pink as follows:
Rnd 2: Around each ch loop, work (1 sc / UK dc, ch 3, 2 tr / UK dtr, ch 3, 1 sl st around loop). End rnd with 1 sl st around last loop.
Cut yarn and fasten off all ends. Steam press flowers gently.

LEAVES
With Green, ch 8.
Work back along the chain, as follows:
2 dc / UK tr in 3rd ch from hook.
2 tr / UK dtr in 4th ch from hook.
1 dc / UK tr in 5th ch from hook,
1 dc / UK tr in 6th ch from hook.
1 sl st in 1st ch (7th ch from hook), ch 3 and 1 sl st into same st as previous sl st.
Now work along opposite side of foundation chain:
1 dc / UK in 6th ch.
1 dc / UK in 5th ch.
2 tr / UK dtr in 4th ch.
1 dc / UK tr, ch 2 and 1 sl st in 3rd ch.
Cut yarn and pull end through last st; tighten.
Weave in all ends neatly on WS. Gently steam press the leaves.
Fold down collar and arrange the flowers and leaves around each slipper collar. The pair shown is size M.
One slipper has 1 pink, 2 purple, 2 orange flowers, and 8 leaves. Sew flowers on using matching sewing thread.

LEVEL OF DIFFICULTY
Advanced

MATERIALS
Yarn:
CYCA #4 (worsted/afghan/aran), Rauma Vamsegarn
(100% wool, 91 yd/83 m / 50 g)
Yarn Colors and Amounts:
Brown V55, 150–200 g
Light Yellow V20, 50 g
Red V18, 50 g
Spring Green V45, 50 g
Small amounts of Orange V43, Clover Pink V65, Light Lilac
V71, and Deep Rose Pink V44.
Needles: U.S. size 8-10 / 5-6 mm: circular and set of 5 dpn
Recommended Gauge: 14–16 sts = 4 in / 10 cm

Slippers
Bordered with Tulips

The motif for these slippers was inspired by a tulip vase that Arne bought for his mother many years ago. The flowers on the slippers are knitted in while the green leaves are embroidered afterwards with duplicate stitch.

NOTE: Alternate two strands of yarn on every stitch throughout (as for two-end or Fair Isle knitting).

With one strand of Yellow and circular, CO 56 (60, 64) sts; join, being careful not to twist cast-on row. Join second strand of Yellow and knit around following the chart, beginning at marker for your size; the first row of the chart = cast-on row. After completing charted rows, continue with Brown only.

HEEL
Row 1: K14 (15, 16), knitting last st with both strands; turn.
Row 2: Sl 1, p27 (29, 31), purling last st with both strands; turn.
Work another 11 rows back and forth in St st over the 28 (30, 32) heel sts, always slipping the first st.

HEEL TURN
Row 14: P13 (15, 17), p2tog, p1 with both strands; turn.
Row 15: K3 (5, 7), k2tog, k1 with both strands; turn.
Rows 16-23: Continue the same way, working back and forth in St st and shaping, with 1 more st before the decrease on each row (the decrease joins the sts before/after the gap).
Row 24: P12 (14, 16), p2tog, p1 with both strands; turn.
Row 25: K13 (15, 17), k2tog with both strands; turn. (This row ends with k2tog and not k1 as previously.)

Row 26: P13 (15, 17), p2tog, p1 with both strands; turn.

FOOT
Set-up Rnd: Ssk, k6 (7, 8). Pm at center of sole, k7 (8, 9), pick up and knit 7 sts evenly spaced across one side of the heel flap, k28 (30, 32) across instep, pick up and knit 7 sts evenly spaced across other side of heel flap and k7 (8, 9) on sole. The beginning of the rnd is at center of sole.
Foot: Knit 33 (36, 39) rnds on the 56 (60, 64) sts of foot.

Toe Shaping
Divide the sts onto 4 dpn with 14 (15, 16) sts on each needle. Shape toe as follows, with 8 sts decreased on each decrease rnd.
Rnd 1 (decrease rnd): At beginning of each needle: K1, k2tog. At end of each needle: K2tog, k1.
Rnd 2: Knit.
Repeat Rnds 1-2 until 16 (20, 16) sts rem. Cut yarn and draw end through remaining sts. Pull tight and weave in all ends neatly on WS.

FINISHING
Steam press slippers.
Embroider the green leaves and flower details onto the slippers with duplicate stitch embroidery (see charts on next page).
Steam press embroidery and then felt slippers.

Begin here

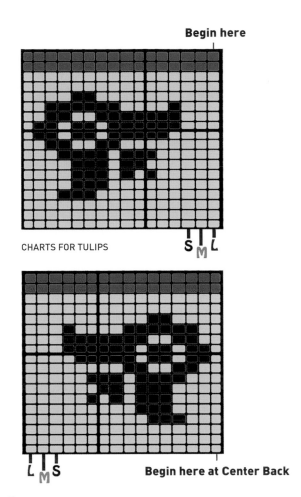

CHARTS FOR TULIPS

L M S

Begin here at Center Back

Slippers Bordered with Tulips

TULIP EMBROIDERY

Felt slippers

Use a wool-safe liquid soap. For 2.2 lb / 1 kg knitted fabric, you should use about 6 tablespoons / 100 ml soap. Set the water temperature for the machine at 104-140°F / 40-60°C (the temperature options vary from machine to machine). Start at the lower temperature and check the degree of felting occasionally.

Embroidered Table Mats

MATERIALS

Yarn:
CYCA #1 (fingering),
Schachenmayr Merino
Extrafine 170 (100% Merino
wool, 185 yd/169 m / 50 g)

Yarn Colors and Amounts:
Small amounts each of:
Light Blue 00052
Purple 00046
Red 00031
Pink 00035
Black 00099
Yellow 00020
White 00001

Canvas: Aida 4.4 from Permin

Coasters

for Glasses and Mugs

INSTRUCTIONS

Rnd 1: Ch 8 and join into a ring with 1 sl st into 1st ch.

Rnd 2: Ch 6 (= 1 tr / UK dtr + ch 2), (1 tr / UK dtr around ring, ch 2) a total of 12 times. End with 1 sl st into 4th ch at beg of rnd.

Rnd 3: Ch 3 (= 1 dc / UK tr), 2 dc / UK tr in 1st ch loop, ch 1, (3 dc / UK tr in next ch loop, ch 1) around and end with 1 sl st into top of ch 3.

Rnd 4: Turn and work 1 sc / UK dc in 1st ch loop, *ch 14, 1 sc / UK dc in the same loop, ch 2, 1 sc / UK dc in the next ch loop. Turn and ch 3, 15 tr / UK dtr around the 14-ch loop. Ch 3 and work 1 sc / UK dc in the top of the 1st tr / UK dtr where the petal is attached*. Rep * to * a total of 12 times, ending with 1 sc / UK dc in the ch loop where the 1st petal was worked.

Weave in ends on WS and gently steam press. Shape the petals so they are slightly angled. Pull the trebles / UK double trebles into place so they sit evenly on the chain loops.

LEVEL OF DIFFICULTY

Intermediate

MATERIALS

Yarn: CYCA #3 (DK weight) Schachenmayr Merino Extrafine 120 DK, 100% wool (131 yd/120 m / 50 g)

Yarn Colors and Amounts:

100 g total is enough for 5 flowers

Red 00140

Orange 00125

Pink 00136

Yellow 00122

Crochet hook: U.S. size E-4 / 3.5 mm

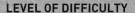

Chair Cushion

With this cushion, you'll feel as if you are sitting in a meadow full of daisies.

FLOWER

Rnd 1: Ch 8 and join into a ring with 1 sl st into 1st ch.

Rnd 2: Ch 6 (= 1 tr / UK dtr + ch 2), (1 tr / UK dtr around ring, ch 2) a total of 12 times. End with 1 sl st into 4th ch at beg of rnd.

Rnd 3: Ch 3 (= 1 dc / UK tr), 2 dc / UK tr in 1st ch loop, ch 1, (3 dc / UK tr in next ch loop, ch 1) around and end with 1 sl st in top of beg ch.

Rnd 4: Turn and work 1 sc / UK dc in 1st ch loop, *ch 14, 1 sc / UK dc in the same loop, ch 2, 1 sc / UK dc in the next ch loop. Turn and ch 3, 15 tr / UK dtr around the 14-ch loop. Ch 2 and work 1 sc / UK dc in the 14-ch loop, ch 3 and 1 sc / UK dc in the top of the 1st tr / UK dtr where the petal is attached*. Rep * to * a total of 12 times, ending with 1 sc / UK dc in the ch loop where the 1st petal was worked.

BACKGROUND

The background begins at the dc groups / UK tr groups around the chain loops behind the flower petals.

Rnd 1: Ch 4 (= 1 tr / UK dtr), 2 tr / UK dtr in ch loop, ch 3 and 3 tr / UK dtr in the same ch loop, *(ch 2, 3 tr / UK dtr in the next ch loop) 2 times, ch 2, 3 tr / UK dtr in the next ch loop, ch 3, 3 tr / UK dtr in the same ch loop*; rep * to * a total of 3 times. Work (ch 2, 3 tr / UK dtr in the next ch loop) 2 times, ch 2 and end with 1 sl st into top of ch at beg.

Rnd 2: Turn and crochet back. Begin the 1st tr group / UK dtr group with ch 4. Continue as for Rnd 1, with one more 3-tr group / UK 3-dtr group along each side between corners.

Rnd 3: Turn and work back. Begin the 1st tr group / UK dtr group with ch 4. Continue as for Rnd 1, with one more 3-tr group / UK 3-dtr group along each side between corners.

JOINING THE SQUARES

Join the squares one by one, beginning with an edge on the first square or strip, until the cushion is desired width.

Attach yarn to one corner and work 1 sc / UK dc in the ch loop, ch 3, 1 sc / UK dc in the same loop, *1 sc / UK dc between the 1st and 2nd tr / UK dtr of the tr group / UK dtr group, ch 3, 1 sc / UK dc between the 2nd and 3rd tr / UK dtr of the tr group / UK dtr group, 1 sc / UK dc in the ch loop, ch 3, 1 sc / UK dc in the same loop*; rep * to * to the corner, 1 sc / UK dc in ch loop, ch 1. Now crochet the first square together with the second square or strip without cutting the yarn.

Beginning at the corner of the second square, work 1 dc / UK tr in the ch loop, ch 1 and 1 sc / UK dc in the same loop. Work 1 dc / UK tr in the sc / UK dc at the corner of the first square and then 1 sc / UK dc in the ch loop you just worked into on the second square. *1 sc / UK dc between the 1st and 2nd tr / UK

dtr of the tr group / UK dtr group of the second square, ch 1, 1 sc / UK dc in the next ch loop of the first square, ch 1, 1 sc / UK dc between the 2nd and 3rd tr / UK dtr of the tr group / UK dtr group on the second square, 1 sc / UK dc in the ch loop of the second square, ch 1, 1 sc / UK dc in the next ch loop of the first square, ch 1, 1 sc / UK dc in the same loop of the second square*; rep * to * to the corner.

Cut yarn and pull end through last st to fasten off.

Join the strips one by one as for joining the squares until the piece is desired length, but in the space between the squares, work 1 sc / UK dc in the tr / UK dtr of one strip, ch 3, and 1 sc / UK dc in the tr / UK dtr of the second strip.

Crochet Tip: **Catch yarn ends as you work so you won't have to weave them in later on.**

LEVEL OF DIFFICULTY
Intermediate

MATERIALS
Yarn:
CYCA #4 (worsted, afghan, Aran), Schachenmayr Merino Extrafine 85 (100% Merino wool, 93 yd/85 m / 50 g)
Yarn Colors and Amounts:
Yellow 00221, 50 g for centers of daisies
White 00201, 100 g for petals
Green 00277, 100 g
Black 00299, 50 g
Crochet Hook: U.S. size E-4 / 3.5 mm. We used a smaller hook than usual for this yarn so the cushion would be firmer than if worked with a larger hook.

Place Mat

The flowers are crocheted together and then joined to the knitting as the stitches are cast on for the place mat. The mat is worked back and forth.

CHART FOR FLOWERS

✖ = sc/UK dc

● = ch

∿ = sl st

↟ = dc/UK tr

‡ = tr/UK dtr

‡ = dtr/Uk trtr

‡ = trtr/UK quadtr

⋔ = 3-dc cl/UK 3-tr cl

LEVEL OF DIFFICULTY
Intermediate

MATERIALS
Yarn: CYCA #2 (sport/ baby), Schachenmayr Catania (100% cotton, 137 yd/125 m / 50 g)
Yarn Colors and Amounts:
Light Blue 00173, 50 g
Pink 00246, 50 g
White 00106, 50 g
Crochet Hook: U.S. size D-3 / 3 mm
Needles: U.S. size 2.5 / 3 mm: 12 in / 33 cm long straights or short circular

FLOWERS
Rnd 1: With White, ch 8 and join into a ring with 1 sl st into 1st ch.
Rnd 2: Ch 3 (= 1 dc / UK tr), 15 dc / UK tr around ring (= 16 dc / UK tr total). End with 1 sl st into top of ch 3.
Rnd 3: Change to Pink and work 1 sc / UK dc between 2 dc / UK tr, ch 5, (1 sc / UK dc between the 2nd and 3rd dc / UK tr from hook, ch 5) around (= 8 ch loops). End with 1 sl st into 1st sc.
Rnd 4: (1 sc / UK dc in ch loop, ch 3, 2 tr / UK dtr in same ch loop, ch 3, 1 sc / UK dc in top of the last tr / UK dtr, 2 tr / UK dtr in same ch loop, ch 3, 1 sc / UK dc in same loop) in each ch loop around. End with 1 sl st into 1st sc / UK dc. Make 5 flowers for the width of the place mat.

See next page for the instructions for the knitted part of the mat.

JOINING FLOWERS

Place Mat

JOINING

Crochet the flowers together in 2 of the petals at each side as follows:

With Pink, ch 1, 1 sc / UK dc in the picot of the 1st flower, ch 1, 1 sc / UK dc in the picot of the 2nd flower. Repeat for the next petal.

Crochet the 5 flowers together.

PLACE MAT

With Blue, cast on sts for the place mat *at the same time* as you attach the flower border to the cast-on row. Cast on through the picots of the 2 petals on each flower along the long side of the flower border as follows:

CO 1 st through the 1st picot, CO 7 sts between two petals, 1 st in the next picot, 7 sts to the next flower; rep * to * and end with 1 st through the last picot. Work the mat in garter st, knitting all rows until place mat is desired length.

Our place mat has 5 flowers across and is 17¼ in / 44 cm long, including the flowers. If you want a wider mat, make more flowers and work in garter st with one color of yarn for a longer length. The size will vary depending on your gauge; both of us knit and crochet rather tightly.

Primroses edging place mats and kitchen towels

For our outdoor summer table, we crocheted the edges of the place mats and matching kitchen towels with primroses. You can also use the kitchen towels as napkins.

Kitchen Towel

A flower border on a cotton kitchen towel—maybe that seems like too much work for something to be used only for drying, but, of course, you can also make these towels for show, or knit several and use them as napkins!

Follow the instructions for the Place Mat (page 131) but use Yellow for the first 2 rnds of the flowers and White for the rest of the flower and knitted towel.

LEVEL OF DIFFICULTY
Intermediate

MATERIALS
Yarn: CYCA #2 (sport/baby), Schachenmayr Catania (100% cotton, 137 yd/ 125 m / 50 g)
Yarn Colors and Amounts:
Yellow 00280, 50 g
White 00106, 50 g
Crochet Hook: U.S. size D-3 / 3 mm
Needles: U.S. size 2.5 / 3 mm: 12 in / 33 cm long straights or short circular

This towel has 7 flowers across the width on one side and is 34 in / 86 cm long, including the flower border.

Primrose Throw

We crocheted masses of little flowers and then crocheted them together for a large throw. The only "rule" was that the same two colors never meet. This is a project for anyone with plenty of time and patience.

WHOLE FLOWER

Rnd 1: Ch 6 and join into a ring with 1 sl st into 1st ch.

Rnd 2: Ch 5 (= 1 tr / UK dtr + 1 ch), (1 tr / UK dtr around ring, ch 1) around until there are a total of 12 tr / UK dtr and 12 ch. End with 1 sl st into 1st tr / UK dtr (= 4th ch at beg).

Rnd 3: Change color and ch 4 (= 1 tr / UK dtr), 1 tr / UK dtr around ch loop, (ch 2, 2 tr / UK dtr in next ch loop) around and end with 1 sl st into top of beg ch.

Rnd 4: Change color. Turn work, (2 sc / UK dc around ch loop, ch 3, 2 sc / UK dc around same ch loop) in each ch loop around. End with 1 sl st into 1st sc / UK dc; cut yarn and bring end through rem st.

For rest of the flowers, crochet one flower to another on the 4th rnd.

See following two pages for charts.

LEVEL OF DIFFICULTY
Intermediate

MATERIALS
Yarn: Leftover yarns suitable for crochet hook size
Crochet Hook: U.S. size E-4 / 3.5 mm and leftover yarn suitable for hook size

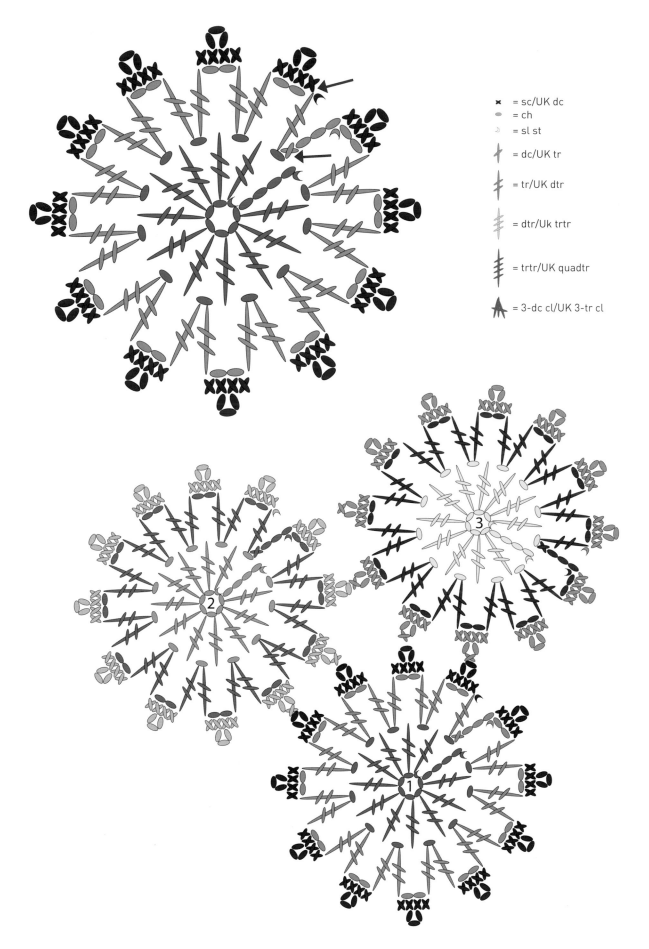

= sc/UK dc
= ch
= sl st
= dc/UK tr
= tr/UK dtr
= dtr/Uk trtr
= trtr/UK quadtr
= 3-dc cl/UK 3-tr cl

Primrose Throw

JOINING

Crochet with the yarn for 2nd flower. Work *2 sc / UK dc around a ch loop of 2nd flower, ch 1 and 2 sc / UK dc around a ch loop of 1st flower. Ch 1, 2 sc / UK dc around the same ch loop on 2nd flower*; rep * to * 2 times to join the flowers.

Two flowers meet only in two ch loops and are crocheted together with 2 picots.

HALF FLOWERS FOR THE EDGING

Rnd 1: Ch 6 and join into a ring with 1 sl st into 1st ch.

Rnd 2: Ch 5 (= 1 tr / UK dtr + 1 ch), (1 tr / UK dtr around ring, ch 1) around 6 times and end with 1 tr / UK dtr.

Rnd 3: Turn and change color. Ch 4 (= 1 tr / UK dtr), 1 tr / UK dtr around ch loop, ch 2 (2 tr / UK dtr in next ch loop, ch 2) around and end with 2 tr / UK dtr into last ch loop.

Rnd 4: Crochet as for the whole flower when the flower is joined with another.

This throw has 21 whole and 2 half flowers across the width and is 25 whole and 2 half flowers in length. We also used a total of 11 half flowers as an edging on the short side and 26 half flowers on the long side.

We edged the throw with 4 tr / UK dtr in the center of every half flower and 4 tr / UK dtr around the outermost tr / UK dtr of the half flowers. We rounded the corners with 10 tr / UK dtr.

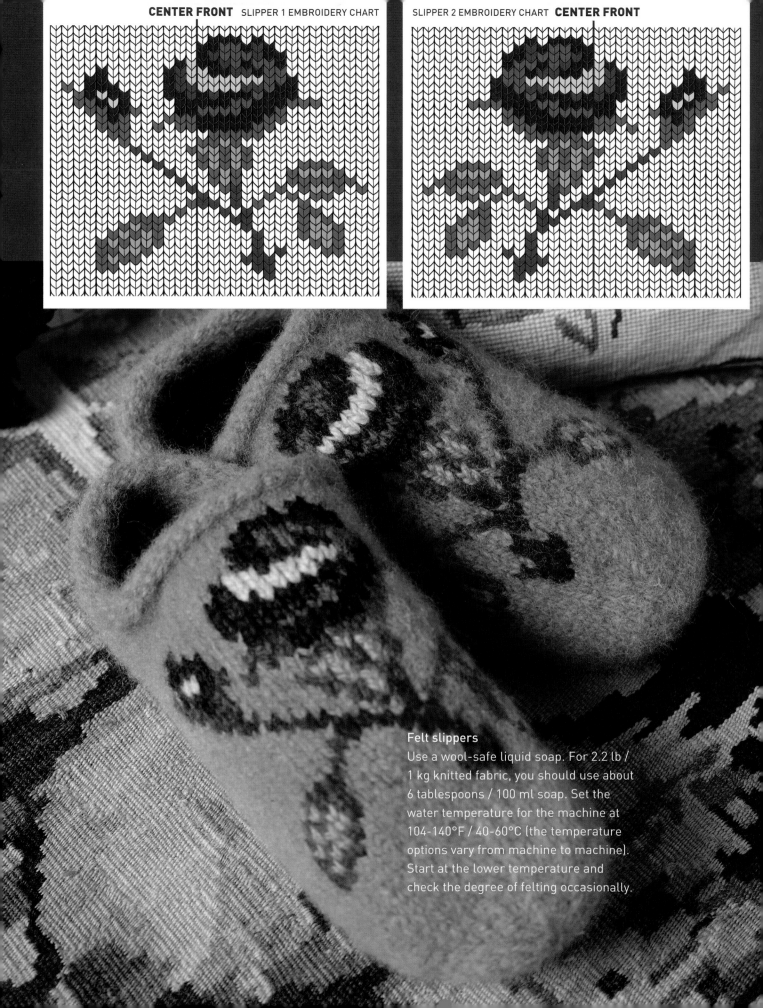

Felt slippers

Use a wool-safe liquid soap. For 2.2 lb / 1 kg knitted fabric, you should use about 6 tablespoons / 100 ml soap. Set the water temperature for the machine at 104–140°F / 40–60°C (the temperature options vary from machine to machine). Start at the lower temperature and check the degree of felting occasionally.

Rose Slippers

Our rose motifs were inspired by an old cross-stitch embroidered pillow

NOTE: Alternate two strands of yarn on every stitch throughout (as for two-end or Fair Isle knitting).

With one strand of Purple and circular, CO 56 (60, 64) sts; join, being careful not to twist cast-on row. Join second strand of Purple and knit 3 rnds, alternating strands on every stitch.

HEEL
Row 1: K14 (15, 16), knitting last st with both strands; turn.
Row 2: Sl 1, p27 (29, 31), purling last st with both strands; turn.
Work another 11 rows back and forth in St st over the 28 (30, 32) heel sts, always slipping the first st.

Heel Turn
Row 14: P13 (15, 17), p2tog, p1 with both strands; turn.
Row 15: K3 (5, 7), k2tog, k1 with both strands; turn.
Rows 16-23: Continue the same way, working back and forth in stockinette and shaping, with 1 more st before the decrease on each row (the decrease joins the sts before/after the gap).
Row 24: P12 (14, 16), p2tog, p1 with both strands; turn.
Row 25: K13 (15, 17), k2tog with both strands; turn. (This row ends with k2tog and not k1 as previously).
Row 26: P13 (15, 17), p2tog, p1 with both strands; turn.

FOOT
Set-up Rnd: Ssk, k6 (7, 8). Pm at center of sole, k7 (8, 9), pick up and knit 7 sts evenly spaced across one side of the heel flap, k28 (30, 32) across instep, pick up and knit 7 sts evenly spaced across other side of heel flap and k7 (8, 9) on sole. The beginning of the rnd is at center of sole.
Foot: Knit 33 (36, 39) rnds on the 56 (60, 64) sts of foot.

Toe Shaping
Divide the sts onto 4 dpn with 14 (15, 16) sts on each needle. Shape toe as follows, with 8 sts decreased on each decrease rnd.
Rnd 1 (decrease rnd): At beginning of each needle: K1, k2tog. At end of each needle: K2tog, k1.
Rnd 2: Knit.
Repeat Rnds 1-2 until 16 (20, 16) sts rem. Cut yarn and draw end through remaining sts. Pull tight and weave in all ends neatly on WS.

FINISHING
Steam press slippers.
Embroider the rose motif onto the slippers with duplicate stitch embroidery. The motif is worked over 28 stitches.
Center the motif on each slipper instep or as you like so that it is smooth and balanced.
Steam press the embroidery and then felt slippers (see felting tips on opposite page).

LEVEL OF DIFFICULTY
Intermediate

MATERIALS
Yarn:
CYCA #4 (worsted/ afghan/aran), Rauma Vamsegarn (100% wool, 91 yd/83 m / 50 g)
Yarn Color and Amount:
Purple V71, 150-200 g

Yarn for Embroidery:
Old Rose V65, 50 g
Red V18, 50 g
Brown V64, 50 g
Dark Green V87, 50 g
Signal Green V45, 50 g
Pale Rose Pink V66, 50 g
Needles: U.S. size 8-10 / 5-6 mm: circular and set of 5 dpn
Recommended Gauge:
14-16 sts = 4 in / 10 cm

*I saw a ship sailing
on the sea's watery way,
and the ship was filled
with good things for you.*

From *Rhymes and Rules for Every Child*,
retold in Norwegian by Alf Prøysen.

Whole Sleeve, ½ Body

*Blue and white stripes go together with
the sea and summertime. This sweater
was inspired by the sweater worn by the
woman at the fore of a large sailboat in
our scrapbook.*

Cast on with Navy Blue and
work 5 rnds in k2, p2 ribbing
for the edges of the sleeves
and body. The neck finishes
with 10 rnds k2, p2 rib.

MARITIME SWEATER
For Basic Pattern, see page 72.

LEVEL OF DIFFICULTY
Intermediate

MATERIALS
Yarn:
CYCA #3 (DK weight)
Schachenmayr Merino Extra-
fine 120 DK, 100% wool (131
yd/120 m / 50 g)
Yarn Colors and Amounts:
Navy Blue 00150, 50 g
White 00101, 50 g
Needles: U.S. sizes 1.5 and 2.5
/ 2.5 and 3 mm: sets of 5 dpn

BLUE SHORTS
For Basic Pattern, see page
145.
LEVEL OF DIFFICULTY
Easy

MATERIALS
Yarn:
CYCA #3 (DK weight)
Schachenmayr Merino Extra-
fine 120 DK, 100% wool (131
yd/120 m / 50 g)
Yarn Color and Amount:
Navy Blue 00150, 50 g
Needles: U.S. sizes 1.5 and 2.5
/ 2.5 and 3 mm: sets of 5 dpn

Milton's surfer outfit.
Did you notice how a little bit of the bathing
suit shows? That's the look you want, to be
truly cool! Salt water and a humid climate are
great for curly hair.

SPOTTED SHORTS

For Basic Pattern, see page 145.

These shorts are not as long as the other
shorts because they're knitted with two
colors and are a bit thicker. If you knit them
as for the basic pattern, they will be too
tight. The chart includes the garter stitch
and ribbed edgings.

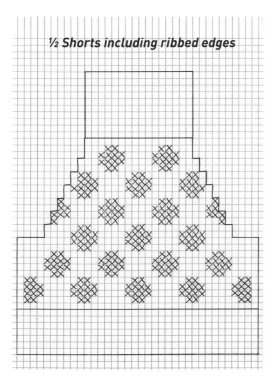

½ Shorts including ribbed edges

Milton

LEVEL OF DIFFICULTY
Intermediate

MATERIALS
Yarn:
CYCA #3 (DK weight)
Schachenmayr Merino
Extrafine 120 DK, 100%
wool (131 yd/120 m / 50 g)
**Yarn Colors and
Amounts:**
Blue 00153, 50 g
White 00101, 50 g
Needles: U.S. sizes 1.5
and 2.5 / 2.5 and 3 mm:
sets of 5 dpn

BOYFRIEND SWEATER

For Basic Pattern, see page 72.

LEVEL OF DIFFICULTY

Advanced

MATERIALS

Yarn:

CYCA #3 (DK weight) Schachenmayr Merino Extrafine 120 DK, 100% wool (131 yd/120 m / 50 g)

Yarn Colors and Amounts:

Navy Blue 00150, 50 g

White 00101, 50 g

Red 00131, small amount

Embroider the heart on the sleeve with duplicate stitch (see page 261).

Needles: U.S. sizes 1.5 and 2.5 / 2.5 and 3 mm: sets of 5 dpn

½ Body

An embroidered heart on the sweater sleeve is as tough-looking as a tattoo, but it hurts less. This sweater is Milton's favorite, knitted for him to wear as autumn approaches.

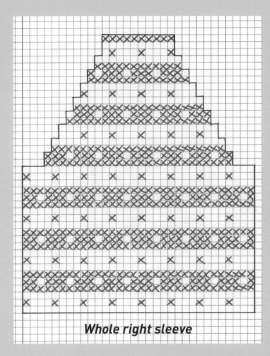

Whole right sleeve

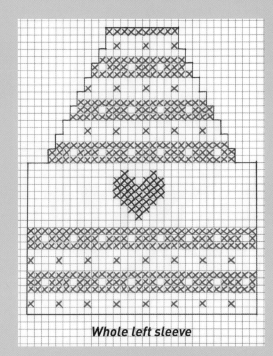

Whole left sleeve

GREEN SHORTS

LEVEL OF DIFFICULTY

Intermediate

MATERIALS

Yarn:

CYCA #3 (DK weight) Schachenmayr Merino Extrafine 120 DK, 100% wool (131 yd/120 m / 50 g)

Yarn Color and Amount:

Green 00170, 50 g

Needles: U.S. sizes 1.5 and 2.5 / 2.5 and 3 mm: sets of 5 dpn

Make each leg the same way:

With smaller needles, CO 36 sts and divide evenly over 4 dpn = 9 sts on each needle. Join, being careful not to twist cast-on row.

Work 7 rnds in garter st as follows:

Rnds 1, 3, 5, 7: Purl.

Rnds 2, 4, 6: Knit.

Change to larger dpn and knit around until leg is desired length. For example, 5¼ in /13 cm for long green trousers, or 3 in / 7½ cm for shorts.

Finish the leg by binding off the first 4 and last 4 sts of the round. Make the other leg the same way and then join them.

Joining Legs:

Begin at center back and the doll's left trouser leg:

Rnd 1: K56.

Shape center front and center back:

Rnd 2: K1, k2tog, k22, k2tog, k2, k2tog, k22, k2tog, k1.

Rnd 3: K52.

Rnd 4: K1, k2tog, k20, k2tog, k2, k2tog, k20, k2tog, k1.

Rnd 5: K48.

Rnd 6: K1, k2tog, k18, k2tog, k2, k2tog, k18, k2tog, k1.

Rnd 7: K44.

Rnd 8: K1, k2tog, k16, k2tog, k2, k2tog, k16, k2tog, k1.

Rnd 9: K40.

Rnd 10: K1, k2tog, k14, k2tog, k2, k2tog, k14, k2tog, k1.

Rnd 11: K36.

Rnd 12: K1, k2tog, k12, k2tog, k2, k2tog, k12, k2tog, k1.

Rnd 13: K32.

Change to smaller needles and work 10 rnds k2, p2 rib.

BO. Sew seam between the legs and weave in all ends on WS. Carefully steam press the shorts except for the ribbing.

We began our careers in the fashion industry and became known for our Norwegian-inspired knitting. Here are some of the most recent patterns we've designed, in this case for a German catalogue. We've added a few items from the dolls' wardrobe and a sweater for our poodle, Freja.

In the Wardrobe

Scarves, Sweaters, and Cardigans

These garments were originally designed for the German company Schachenmayr. They were inspired by some of the items we designed when we produced ready-mades for the fashion industry. We love our rich Nordic cultural heritage, and have always been very much taken with the whole idea of updating the traditional with a modern twist. There are so many pretty patterns to choose from that it's sometimes hard to pick just a few! One solution is to put as many motifs as possible on one garment. You could say that we have a special love for the maximum. For these garments, we tried to use as many motifs and colors as possible. The idea was to create an illusion of fabric similar to "patchwork." They were inspired by a tidying-up project—we cut up squares from old sweaters we didn't wear anymore and sewed them into a cool cardigan.

Scarf

Knitting a scarf in the round makes it twice as thick. The result is a warm and lovely accessory that's perfect for protecting your neck on cold winter days.

With Chocolate and dpn, CO 90 sts. Arrange sts with 22 sts each on Ndls 1 and 4 and 23 sts each on Ndls 2 and 3. Join, being careful not to twist cast-on row. Pm for beginning of rnd. Work in pattern following Chart A and then Chart B. After completing 489 rnds, BO knitwise.

FINISHING
Weave in all ends neatly on WS. Align the scarf as shown on the charts. Pat out scarf to finished measurements, cover it with a damp towel, and leave until completely dry.

LEVEL OF DIFFICULTY
Advanced

FINISHED MEASUREMENTS
Width (= half the circumference; the scarf is doubled): approx. 8 in / 20 cm
Length: approx. 71 in / 180 cm

MATERIALS
Yarn: CYCA #3 (DK weight) Schachenmayr Merino Extrafine 120 DK, 100% wool (131 yd/120 m / 50 g)
Yarn Colors and Amounts:
Color 1: Light Gray Heather 00190, 150 g
Color 2: Chocolate 00111, 150 g
Color 3: Cherry Red 00131, 100 g
Color 4: Royal Blue 00151, 50 g
Color 5: Pink 00136, 50 g
Color 6: Yellow 00121, 50 g
Needles: U.S. size 4 / 3.5 mm: set of 5 dpn
Gauge: 22 sts and 27 rnds in St st pattern = 4 x 4 in / 10 x 10 cm.
Adjust needle size to obtain correct gauge if necessary.

180

170

160

150

140

130

120

110

100

90

80

70

60

50

40

30

20

10

90   80   70   60   50   40   30   20   10

Width

Chart **A**

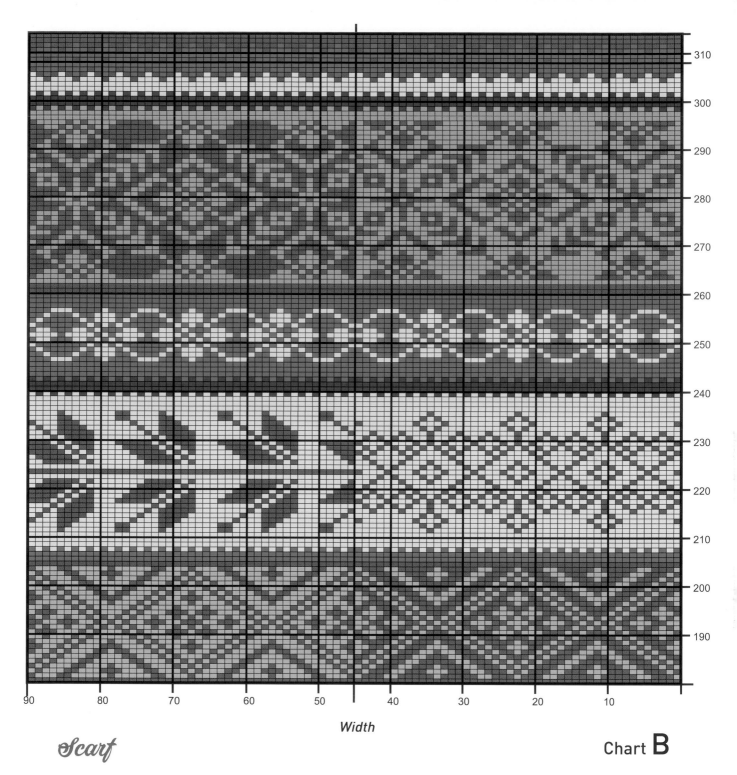

Width

Scarf

Chart **B**

The pattern is worked in St st in the round following the charts.
Chart A shows Rnds 1-180 and Chart B shows Rnds 181-314.

Pattern Sequence:
Work Rnds 1-5 once.
Work Rnds 6-308 once.
Work Rnds 6-180 once.
Work Rnds 309-314 once.
For a total of 489 rnds = approx. 71 in / 180 cm.

☐ **Color 1:** Light Gray Heather 00190
■ **Color 2:** Chocolate 00111
■ **Color 3:** Cherry Red 00131
■ **Color 4:** Royal Blue 00151
☐ **Color 5:** Pink 00136
☐ **Color 6:** Yellow 00121

Women's Cardigan

This is a very sweet and feminine short cardigan with several elements derived from Setesdal patterns. We deconstructed and broke down the pattern motifs and then rearranged the fragments into new combinations. The cardigan is worked with 5 colors.

SIZES: S (M, L) / 36-38 (40-42, 44-46)

LEVEL OF DIFFICULTY
Advanced

FINISHED MEASUREMENTS
Chest: 36¼ (39½, 42½) in / 92 (100, 108) cm
Length to armhole: 11 (11, 11) in / 28 (28, 28) cm
Armhole depth: 8 (8¼, 8¾) in / 20 (21, 22) cm
Shoulder width: 2¾ (3¼, 4) in / 7 (8.5, 10) cm
Neck, width: 9 (9, 9) in / 23 (23, 23) cm
Neck, depth on back: ¾ (¾, ¾) in / 2 (2, 2) cm
Neck, depth on front: 3¼ (3¼, 3¼) in / 8 (8, 8) cm
Total length: 19¾ (20, 20½) in / 50 (51, 52) cm
Sleeves, width at lower edge: 7½ (8, 8¼) in / 19 (20.5, 21) cm
Sleeve length, from underarm: 16½ (16¼, 15¾) in / 42 (41, 40) cm
Sleeve cap length: 6¼ (6¾, 7) in / 16 (17, 18) cm
Sleeves, width at top: 12¾ (13¾, 15) in / 32 (35, 38) cm
Sleeves, total length: 22¾ (22¾, 22¾) in / 58 (58, 58) cm

MATERIALS
Yarn: CYCA #3 (DK weight) Schachenmayr Merino Extrafine 120 DK, 100% wool (131 yd/120 m / 50 g)
Yarn Colors and Amounts:
Color 1: Light Gray Heather 00190, 200 (200, 250) g
Color 2: Cherry Red 00131, 150 (150, 150) g
Color 3: Natural 00102, 150 (150, 200) g
Color 4: Royal Blue 00151, 50 (50, 100) g
Color 5: Navy Blue 00150, 50 (50, 50) g
Other Materials: 5 buttons from Union Knopf, art no. 12227.32, color 04 black-blue or similar buttons
Needles: U.S. size 6 / 4 mm: short and long circulars
Gauge: 21 sts and 27 rows in St st pattern = 4 x 4 in / 10 x 10 cm.
Adjust needle size to obtain correct gauge if necessary.

76
74
72
70
68
66
64
62
60
58
56
54
52
50
48
46
44
42
40
38
36
34
32
30
28
26
24
22
20
18
16
14
12
10
8
6
4
2

75
73
71
69
67
65
63
61
59
57
55
53
51
49
47
45
43
41
39
37
35
33
31
29
27
25
23
21
19
17
15
13
11
9
7
5
3
1

13   5
Repeat = 16 sts

Women's Cardigan

Stitches used:

Ribbing, worked back and forth:
The stitch count is a multiple of 4 sts worked as k2, p2 + 2 edge sts. See pattern for setting up ribbing on each part of sweater.

St st: Knit on RS, purl on WS.

Inc 1 (increase 1): M1 (make 1)—lift strand between two sts and knit into back loop.

☐ **Color 1:** Light Gray Heather 00190
■ **Color 2:** Cherry Red 00131
☐ **Color 3:** Natural 00102
■ **Color 4:** Royal Blue 00151
■ **Color 5:** Navy Blue 00150

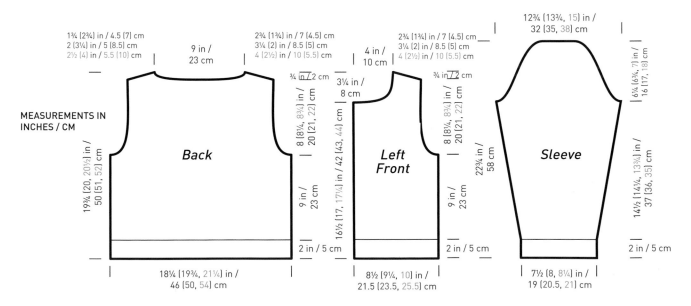

MEASUREMENTS IN INCHES / CM

1¾ (2¾) in / 4.5 (7) cm
2 (3¼) in / 5 (8.5) cm
2½ (4) in / 5.5 (10) cm

9 in / 23 cm

2¾ (1¾) in / 7 (4.5) cm
3¼ (2) in / 8.5 (5) cm
4 (2½) in / 10 (5.5) cm

¾ in / 2 cm

8 (8¼, 8¾) in / 20 (21, 22) cm

Back

19¾ (20, 20½) in / 50 (51, 52) cm

16½ (17, 17¼) in / 42 (43, 44) cm

9 in / 23 cm

2 in / 5 cm

18¼ (19¾, 21¼) in / 46 (50, 54) cm

4 in / 10 cm

2¾ (1¾) in / 7 (4.5) cm
3¼ (2) in / 8.5 (5) cm
4 (2½) in / 10 (5.5) cm

¾ in / 2 cm

3¼ in / 8 cm

8 (8¼, 8¾) in / 20 (21, 22) cm

Left Front

9 in / 23 cm

2 in / 5 cm

8½ (9¼, 10) in / 21.5 (23.5, 25.5) cm

12¾ (13¾, 15) in / 32 (35, 38) cm

6¼ (6¾, 7) in / 16 (17, 18) cm

Sleeve

22¾ in / 58 cm

14¼ (14¼, 13¾) in / 37 (36, 35) cm

2 in / 5 cm

7½ (8, 8¼) in / 19 (20.5, 21) cm

BACK

With Color 1 (Light Gray Heather), CO 98 (106, 114) sts. Work back and forth in k2, p2 ribbing, setting up as follows. The 1st row = WS and is worked as: K1 (edge st), p1, (k2, p2) until 4 sts rem and end k2, p1, k1. Continue with knit over knit, purl over purl, knitting first and last sts on every row for approx. 2 in / 5 cm. On the last WS row, increase 1 st with M1 = 99 (107, 115) sts.

Now work following the charted pattern, setting up as follows: K1 (edge st), work 0 (4, 0) sts before the repeat, work the 16-st repeat 6 (6, 7) times and end with 1 (5, 1) st after rep + k1 (edge st). Work a total of 62 rows from the chart = approx. 9 in / 23 cm above ribbing.

Armhole Shaping: BO 4 (4, 5) sts each at beginning of next 2 rows. Next, on every other row, at each side, BO 3 sts once, 1 (2, 2) sts once, and 1 st 2 times = 79 (85, 91) sts rem. Work another 54 (56, 58) rows following the chart = approx. 8 (8¼, 8¾) in / 20 (21, 22) cm from underarm.

Shape Shoulders and Neck: Begin shoulder and neck shaping on the same row as follows: BO 6 (7, 8) sts for shoulder; BO the center 37 sts for back neck and continue to end of row. Turn and BO 6 (7, 8) sts for shoulder. Now work each side separately. On every other row at side, BO 5 (6, 7) sts 2 times. *At the same time*, at neck edge, on every other row, BO 3 sts once and then 2 sts once. Cut yarn and fasten off in rem st. Work the other side to match, beginning at neck edge.

LEFT FRONT

With Color 1 (Light Gray Heather), CO 46 (50, 54) sts. Work back and forth in k2, p2 ribbing, setting up as follows. The 1st row = WS and is worked as: K1 (edge st), p1, (k2, p2) until 4 sts rem and end k2, p1, k1. Continue with knit over knit, purl over purl, knitting first and last sts on every row for approx. 2 in / 5 cm. On the last WS row, increase 1 st with M1 = 47 (51, 55) sts.

Now work following the charted pattern, setting up as follows:

Size S: K1 (edge st), work the 16-st rep 2 times and then sts 1-13 once, k1 (edge st).

Size M: K1 (edge st), work 4 sts before rep, work 16-st rep 2 times and then sts 1-13 once, k1 (edge st).

Size L: K1 (edge st), work 16-st rep 3 times and then sts 1-5 once, k1 (edge st).

Work a total of 62 rows from the chart = approx. 9 in / 23 cm above ribbing.

Armhole Shaping: At right side, BO 4 (4, 5) sts at beginning of row. Next, on every other row, at right side, BO 3 sts once, 1 (2, 2) sts once, and 1 st 2 times = 37 (40, 43) sts rem. After shaping, continue following the chart until you have 100 (102, 104) rows total = approx. 16½ (17, 17¼) in / 42 (43, 44) cm from cast-on.

Shape Neck and Shoulder: BO 6 sts at left side for front neck. At the same side, on every other row, BO 3 sts 2 times, 2 sts 2 times, and then 1 st 5 times. *At the same time*, after completing 54 (56, 58) rows from underarm [= approx. 8 (8¼, 8¾) in / 20 (21, 22) cm], shape shoulder on right side as for back. Cut yarn and fasten off in rem st.

RIGHT FRONT

Work as for left front, reversing shaping. After completing ribbing, set up charted pattern as follows:

Size S: K1 (edge st), work sts 5-16 once, the 16-st rep 2 times, and then 1 st after rep, k1 (edge st).

Size M: K1 (edge st), work sts 5-16 once, the 16-st rep 2 times, and then 5 sts after rep, k1 edge st).

Size L: K1 (edge st), work sts 13-16 once, work 16-st rep 3 times, and then 1 st after rep, k1 (edge st).

Work a total of 62 rows from the chart = approx. 9 in / 23 cm above ribbing.

SLEEVES

With Color 1 (Light Gray Heather), CO 42 (42, 46) sts. Work back and forth in k2, p2 ribbing, setting up as follows. The 1st row = WS and is worked as: K1 (edge st), p1, (k2, p2) until 4 sts rem and end k2, p1, k1. Continue with knit over knit, purl over purl, and knitting first and last sts on every row for approx. 2 in / 5 cm. On the last WS row, increase 1 (3, 1) sts with M1 = 43 (45, 47) sts.

Now work following the charted pattern, setting up as follows: K1 (edge st), work 4 (5, 6) sts before the repeat, work the 16-st repeat 2 (2, 2) times and end with 5 (6, 7) sts after rep + k1 (edge st).

Shape Sleeve: After completing ribbing, shape sleeve by increasing 1 st with M1 at each side on:
Size S: Every 8th row 8 times and then every 6th row 5 times.
Size M: Every 8th row once and then every 6th row 14 times.
Size L: Every 6th row 11 times and then every 4th row 6 times.
Work new sts into pattern = 69 (75, 81) sts. Work a total of 100 (98, 94) rows after the ribbing = approx. 14½ (14¼, 13¾) in / 37 (36, 35) cm.

Shape Sleeve Cap: BO 4 sts each at beginning of next 2 rows. Next, on every other row, BO 2 sts once, 1 st 14 (16, 17) times, and then 2 sts 5 times. BO rem 9 (11, 15) sts.

Make the second sleeve the same way.

FINISHING

Weave in all ends neatly on WS. Pat out the pieces to finished measurements and cover each with a damp towel; leave until completely dry. Seam the shoulders. Attach sleeves, matching center of sleeve cap with shoulder seam, and sew down on each side of armhole. Seam the sleeves and sides.

Right Buttonhole Band: With RS facing and Color 1 (Light Gray Heather), pick up and knit 83 (87, 87) sts along right front edge. Work back and forth in k2, p2 ribbing, setting up as follows. The 1st row = WS and is worked as: K1 (edge st), p2, (k2, p2) until 4 sts rem and end k2, p1, k1 (edge st). Continue with knit over knit, purl over purl, and knitting first and last sts on every row.
At the same time, work buttonholes on the 6th row (RS) as follows: K1 (edge st), rib 4, BO 2 sts, [rib 16 (17, 17) (rib counts include st from bine-off), BO 2 sts] 4 times total, work 7 sts rib, ending with edge st. On the next row on WS, CO 2 sts over each gap. When ribbing measures approx. 1¼ in / 3 cm, BO in ribbing on RS.

Left Button Band: Work as for buttonhole band, omitting buttonholes.

Neckband: With RS facing and Color 1 (Light Gray Heather), pick up and knit 142 sts around neck. Work back and forth in k2, p2 ribbing, setting up as follows. The 1st row = WS and is worked as: K1 (edge st), p1, (k2, p2) until 4 sts rem and end k2, p1, k1 (edge st). Continue with knit over knit, purl over purl, and knitting first and last sts on every row.
At the same time, on the 6th row (RS), make button-hole: K1 (edge st), BO 2 sts, continue in ribbing to end of row. On the next row, CO 2 sts over gap. When ribbing measures approx. 1¼ in / 3 cm, BO in ribbing on RS.
Sew on buttons.

Men's Sweater

We call this a "patchwork" sweater because it's composed of quite a few different motifs and strong color contrasts. You could tone it down a bit by choosing to work with fewer colors. The possible color combinations are endless, so choose what you like to make this sweater your own. It is a bit difficult to knit, so work slowly and patiently.

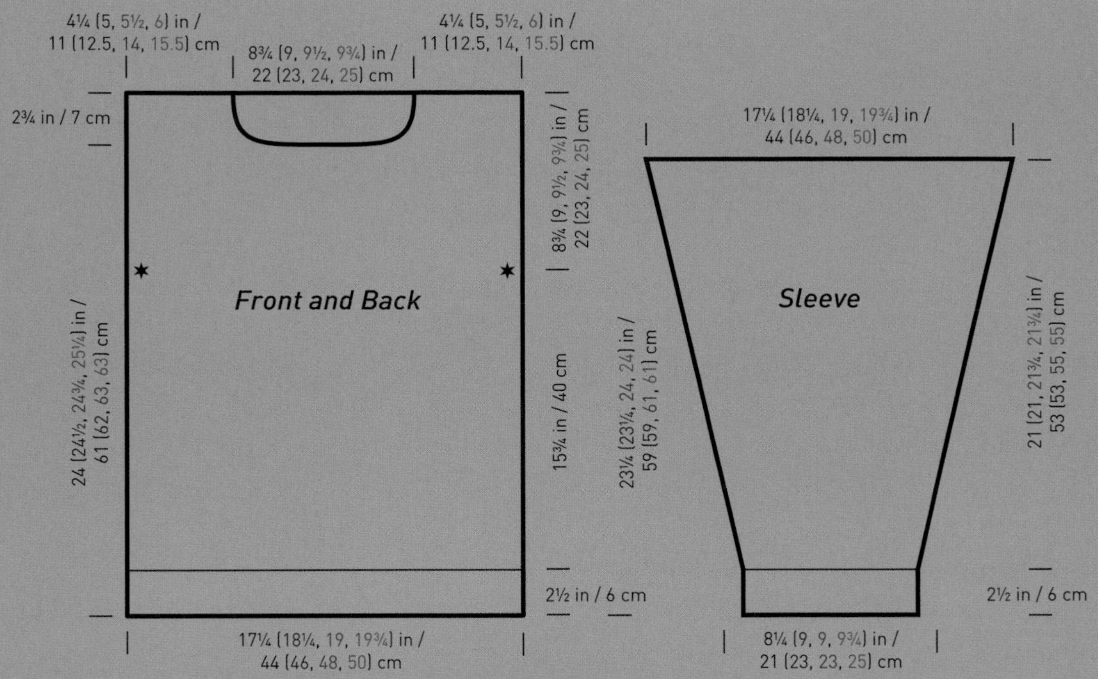

SIZES: XS (S, M, L) / 40-42 (44-46, 48-50, 52-54)

LEVEL OF DIFFICULTY

Advanced

FINISHED MEASUREMENTS

Chest: 34¾ (37¾, 41, 44) in / 88 (96, 104, 112) cm

Length to armhole: 18¼ (18¼, 18¼) in / 46 (46, 46, 46) cm

Armhole depth: 8¾ (9, 9½, 9¾) in / 22 (23, 24, 25) cm

Shoulder width: 4¼ (5, 5½, 6) in / 11 (12.5, 14, 15.5) cm

Neck, width: 8¾ (9, 9½, 9¾) in / 22 (23, 24, 25) cm

Neck, depth on front: 2¾ (2¾, 2¾, 2¾) in / 7 (7, 7, 7) cm

Total length: 26¾ (27¼, 27½, 28) in / 68 (69, 70, 71) cm

Sleeves, width at lower edge: 8¼ (9, 9, 9¾) in / 21 (23, 23, 25) cm

Sleeves, width at top: 17¼ (18¼, 19, 19¾) in / 44 (46, 48, 50) cm

Sleeves, total length: 23¼ (23¼, 24, 24) in / 59 (59, 61, 61) cm

MATERIALS

Yarn: CYCA #3 (DK weight) Schachenmayr Merino Extrafine 120 DK, 100% wool (131 yd/120 m / 50 g)

Yarn Colors and Amounts:

Color 1: Chocolate 00111, 250 (300, 300, 350) g

Color 2: Cherry Red 00131, 150 (150, 150, 200) g

Color 3: Light Gray Heather 00190, 150 (200, 200, 200) g

Color 4: Royal Blue 00151, 50 (50, 50, 100) g

Color 5: Yellow 00121, 150 (150, 200, 200) g

Color 6: Pink 00136, 100 (100, 100, 150) g

Needles: U.S. size 7 / 4.5 mm: short and long circulars

Gauge: 21 sts and 29 rows in St st pattern = 4 x 4 in / 10 x 10 cm.

Adjust needle size to obtain correct gauge if necessary.

Stitches used:

Ribbing, worked back and forth:

The stitch count is a multiple of 4 sts + 2 edge sts. See pattern for setting up ribbing on each part of sweater.

Ribbing worked in the round:

A multiple of 4 sts

Every round: (K2, p2) around.

St st: Knit on RS, purl on WS.

Inc 1 (increase 1): M1 (make 1)—lift strand between two sts and knit into back loop.

BACK

With Color 1 (Chocolate), CO 94 (102, 110, 118) sts. Work back and forth in k2, p2 ribbing, setting up as follows. The 1st row = WS and is worked as: K1 (edge st), p1, (k2, p2) until 4 sts rem and end with k2, p1, k1. Continue in ribbing with knit over knit, purl over purl, knitting first and last sts on every row for approx. 2½ in / 6 cm. On the last WS row, increase as follows with M1: K1 (edge st), 46 (50, 54, 58) sts in ribbing, M1 (= center st), 46 (50, 54, 58) sts in ribbing, k1 (edge st) = 95 (103, 111, 119) sts.

Now work following Chart A, beginning and ending at the arrows for your size.
After completing 180 (182, 186, 188) rows of Chart A, BO all sts. The piece should measure 26¾ (27¼, 27½, 28) in / 68 (69, 70, 71) cm.

FRONT

Work as for back but with a deeper neckline. Work 160 (161, 166, 168) rows following Chart A; piece measures approx. 21¾ (22, 22½, 22¾) in / 55 (56, 57, 58) cm.
Neck Shaping: BO the center 39 (41, 43, 45) sts and work each side separately. At neck edge, on every other row, BO 2 sts once and 1 st 2 times.
When front is same length as back, BO the rem 24 (27, 30, 33) sts for shoulder. Work the other side to correspond.

LEFT SLEEVE

With Color 1 (Chocolate), CO 46 (50, 50, 54) sts. Work back and forth in k2, p2 ribbing, setting up as follows. The 1st row = WS and is worked as: K1 (edge st), p1, (k2, p2) until 4 sts rem and end k2, p1, k1. Continue in ribbing with knit over knit, purl over purl, and knitting first and last sts on every row for approx. 2½ in / 6 cm. On the last WS row, increase as follows with M1: K1 (edge st), 22 (24, 24, 26) sts in ribbing, M1 (= center st), 22 (24, 24, 26) sts in ribbing, k1 (edge st) = 47 (51, 51, 55) sts.
Now work Chart B, beginning and ending at the arrows for your size.
At the same time, shape sleeves. Increase 1 st with M1 at each side on every 6th row 24 (24, 26, 26) times = 95 (99, 103, 107) sts.
After completing a total of 154 (154, 160, 160) rows of charted pattern, BO all sts. Sleeve measures 23¼ (23¼, 24, 24) in / 59 (59, 61, 61) cm.

RIGHT SLEEVE

Work as for left sleeve but follow pattern on Chart C.

FINISHING

Weave in all ends neatly on WS. Pat out the pieces to finished measurements and cover each with a damp towel; leave until completely dry. Seam the shoulders. The asterisk on each side of schematic for front/back indicates armhole depth. Attach sleeves, matching center of sleeve cap with shoulder seam, and sew down on each side of armhole. Seam the sleeves and sides.

Neckband: With RS facing and Color 1 (Chocolate), pick up and knit 112 (116, 120, 124) sts around neck. Join and pm for beginning of rnd. Work around in k2, p2 ribbing for approx. 1 in / 2.5 cm. BO in ribbing.

Fold up the ribbing on the sleeves.

CHARTS A, B, AND C:

The motifs are worked back and forth in St st following the specified chart. All the rows on the chart are as seen on the RS. Work the RS rows and read the chart from right to left and the WS rows from left to right. If working a pattern with two colors, knit the edge st with both colors held together.

See the charts on the following pages.

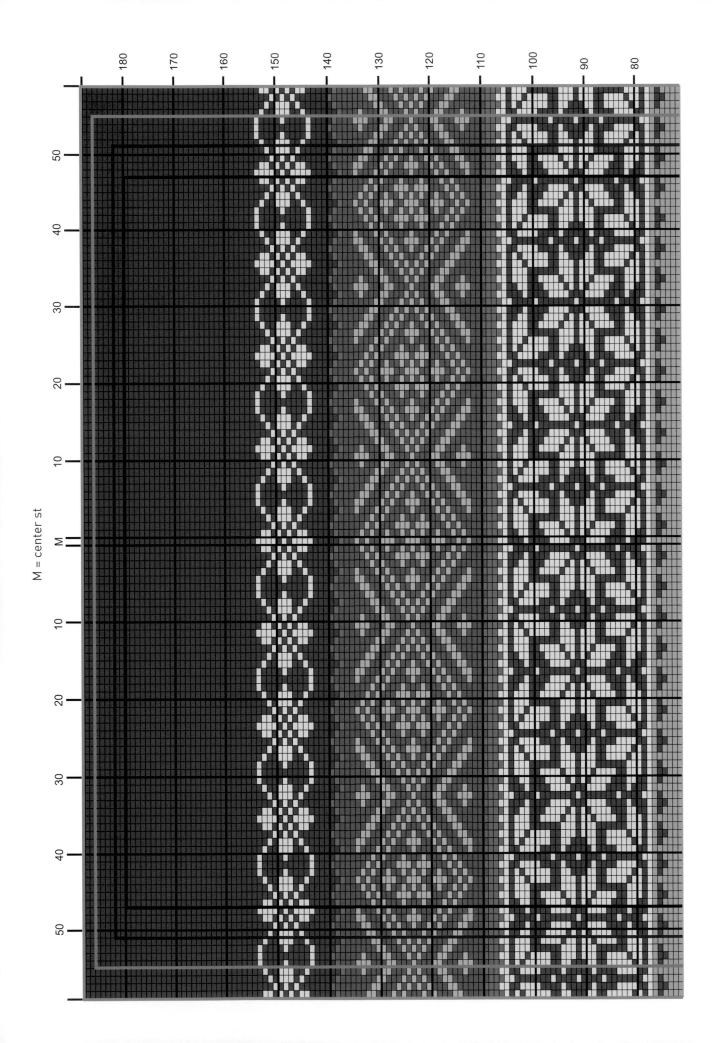

M = center st

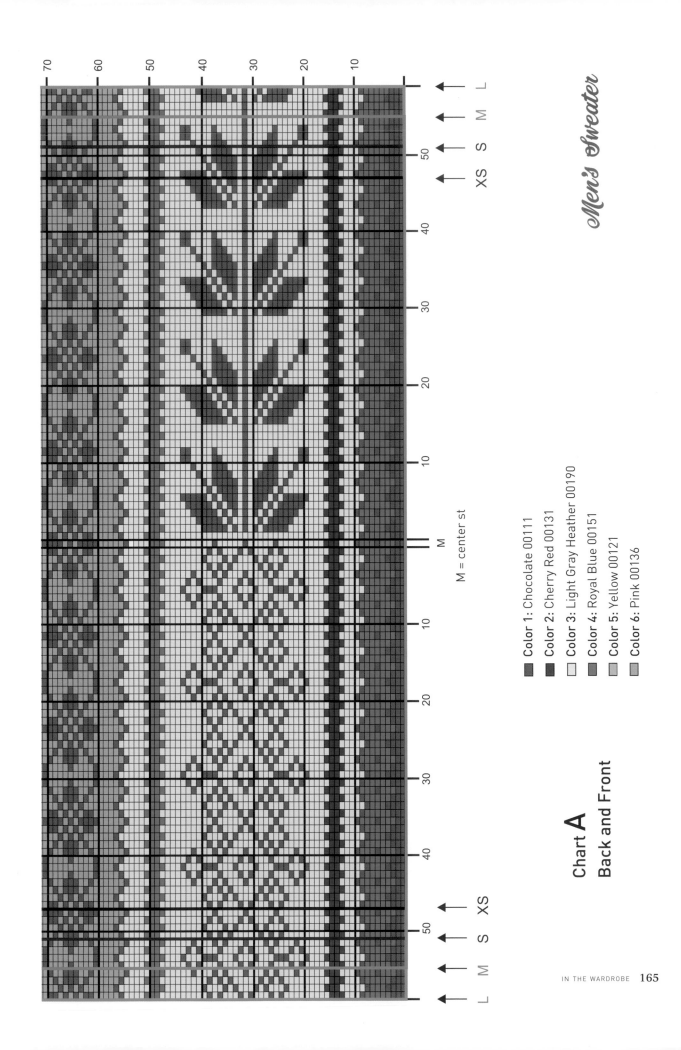

Men's Sweater

Chart A
Back and Front

- ■ **Color 1:** Chocolate 00111
- ■ **Color 2:** Cherry Red 00131
- □ **Color 3:** Light Gray Heather 00190
- ■ **Color 4:** Royal Blue 00151
- □ **Color 5:** Yellow 00121
- ■ **Color 6:** Pink 00136

M = center st

Men's Sweater

Chart B
Left Sleeve

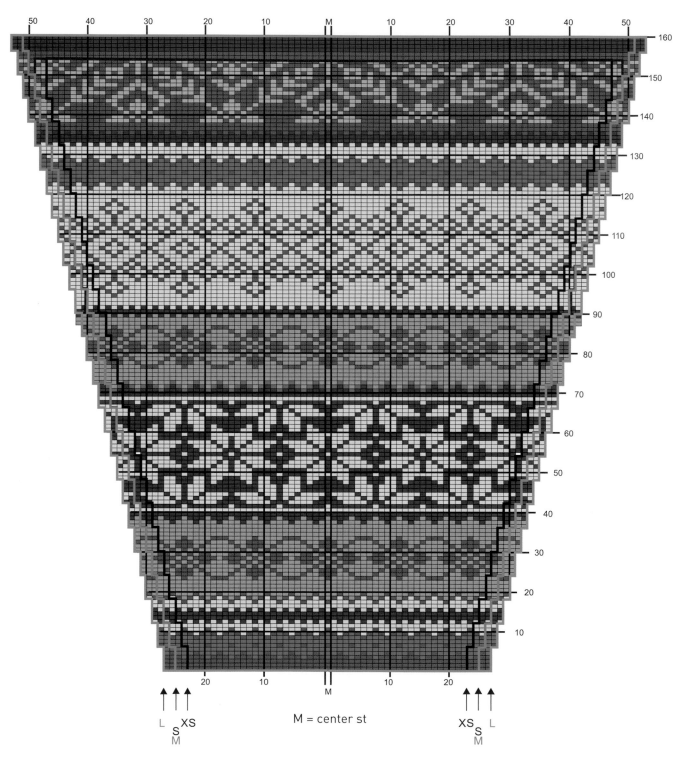

M = center st

Men's Sweater

Chart C
Right Sleeve

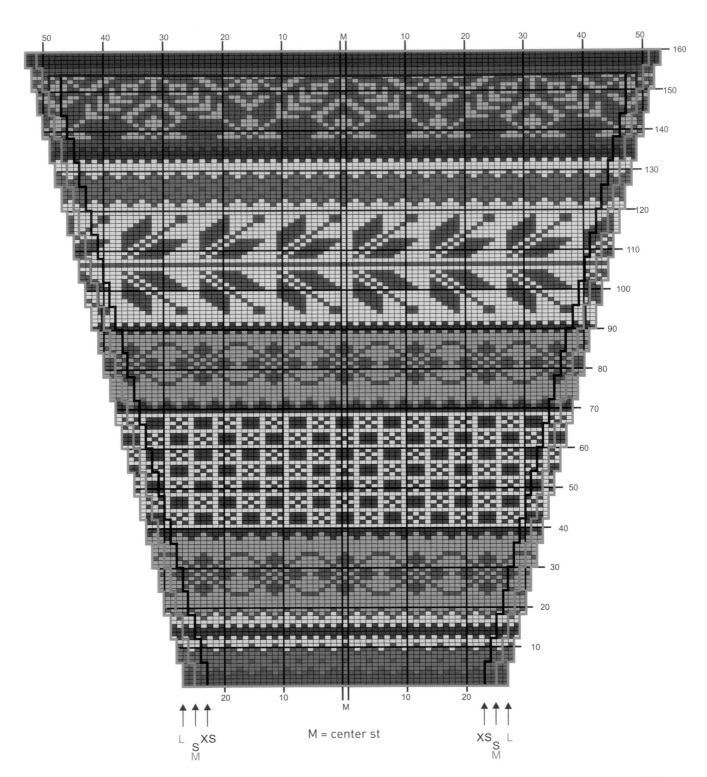

M = center st

The Dolls' Clothing

We've written some basic instructions for the dolls' garments. We have tried to make them as easy as possible and with small variations that can be the basis for many different garments. It can be as simple as knitting a garter stitch edge instead of ribbing to give sweaters and cardigans a totally new look. The basic garments have different patterns for the various themes and, of course, different colors and buttons—all the little things that make it fun to dress up your doll! Once you've learned how to construct the basic garment, following the charts will be easier. The clothes will vary in size from knitter to knitter and depending on what yarn you use. We let you know what yarns we used for all the individual projects, but we knitted some of the garments with leftover yarns whose ball bands were lost a long time ago. We have kept to needles U.S. sizes 1.5 and 2.5 (2.5 and 3 mm) or U.S. 7 and 8 (4.5 and 5 mm). You'll soon realize when you must finish a garment before the pattern ends or make it a little longer. It is impossible to control everything, since we all knit differently. But if you knit the doll yourself, the clothes should fit it. Where we show a number of inches/centimeters of knitting instead of a number of rounds, you should check the length on the doll while you knit so the garment will fit.

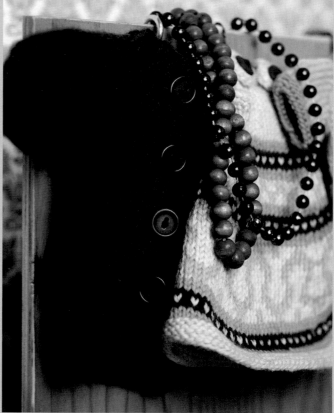

Here's a pretty dress that's just as great to wear in the kitchen as getting coffee with friends. Complete the outfit with heart-shaped buttons and matching red shoes.

Kaja

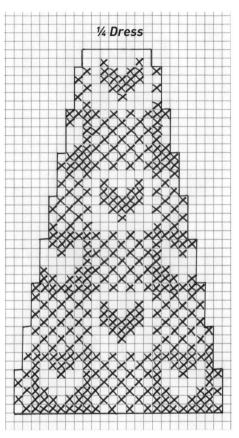

¼ **Dress**

GINGHAM DRESS
LEVEL OF DIFFICULTY
Intermediate

MATERIALS
Yarn:
CYCA #3 (DK weight) Schachenmayr Merino Extrafine 120 DK, 100% wool (131 yd/120 m / 50 g)
Yarn Colors and Amounts:
Red 00140, 50 g
White 00101, 50 g
Other Materials: 2 small (⅜ in / 1 cm in diameter) heart-shaped buttons
Needles: U.S. sizes 1.5 and 2.5 / 2.5 and 3 mm: sets of 5 dpn
Crochet Hook: U.S. size D-3 / 3 mm

With smaller needles, CO 96 sts and divide evenly over 4 dpn = 24 sts on each needle. Join, being careful not to twist cast-on row; pm for beginning of rnd.

Work garter stitch edging for hem:
Rnd 1: Purl.
Rnd 2: Knit.
Rnd 3: Purl.
Rnd 4: Knit.
Rnd 5: Purl.
Rnds 6-10: Change to larger needles and k96, following the chart.
Rnd 11: (K1, k2tog, k18, k2tog, k1) around.
Rnds 12-15: K88.
Rnd 16: (K1, k2tog, k16, k2tog, k1) around.
Rnds 17-20: K80.
Rnd 21: (K1, k2tog, k14, k2tog, k1) around.
Rnds 22-25: K72.
Rnd 26: (K1, k2tog, k12, k2tog, k1) around.
Rnds 27-30: K64.
Rnd 31: (K1, k2tog, k10, k2tog, k1) around.
Rnds 32-35: K56.
Rnd 36: (K1, k2tog, k8, k2tog, k1) around.
Rnds 37-40: K48.
Rnd 41: (K1, k2tog, k6, k2tog, k1) around.
Rnds 42-45: K40.
Rnd 46: (K1, k2tog, k4, k2tog, k1) around.
Rnd 47: K32.
Rnd 48: K2, BO 4, k12 (including last st from bind-off), BO 4, k10 (including last st from bind-off), + the first 2 sts on Ndl 1 = k12.
Going back over the sts of the last row, set aside the sts on each side of the armhole shaping on separate needles = 12 sts on each needle.
Now work the back and front separately.

BACK
Row 1 (WS): Purl.
Row 2: Knit.

Row 3: Purl.
Row 4: Knit.
Row 5: Purl.
Row 6: Knit.
Row 7: P4, BO 4 purlwise, p4 (including the last st from bind-off).
Now make 2 straps separately with 4 sts each:
Work 7 rows back and forth, beginning on RS.
BO purlwise.

FRONT
Row 1 (RS): Knit.
Row 2: Purl.
Row 3: Knit.
Row 4: Purl.
Row 5: Knit.
Row 6: Purl
BO knitwise.

Edge the yoke with single crochet / UK double crochet and then crochet loops at the end of each strap for the buttonholes: Ch 4, sc / UK dc in 1st corner and then work 5 sc / UK dc back across loop.
Weave in all ends on WS. Gently steam press dress under a damp pressing cloth.
Sew buttons on top of front to match button loops on straps.

CAPE
NOTE: The cape is worked from the top down, reading the chart from the bottom up.

With Signal Green 00170 and smaller dpn, CO 64 sts. Divide sts evenly onto 4 dpn with 16 sts on each needle. Join, being careful not to twist cast-on row, and pm for beginning of rnd. Work 30 rnds of k2, p2 ribbing.
Change to larger dpn and work increase rnd: (K1, M1, k14, M1, k1) around = 72 sts. Knit the next 20 rnds following the chart.

A stylish green cape and green ear warmer really set off Siv's red hair.

LEVEL OF DIFFICULTY
Intermediate

MATERIALS
Yarn: CYCA #3 (DK weight) Schachenmayr
Merino Extrafine 120 DK, 100% wool
(131 yd/120 m / 50 g)
Yarn Colors and Amounts:
Signal Green 00170, 50 g
Dark Green 00172, 50 g
Light Green 00175, 50 g
Royal Blue 00151, 50 g
Needles: U.S. sizes 1.5 and 2.5 / 2.5 and 3 mm:
sets of 5 dpn

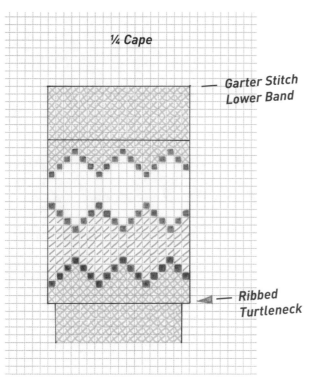

¼ **Cape**

Garter Stitch Lower Band

Ribbed Turtleneck

Finish the bottom of the cape with a garter stitch edging. Change to smaller dpn.

Rnd 1: Purl.
Rnd 2: Knit.
Rnd 3: Purl.
Rnd 4: Knit.
Rnd 5: Purl.
Rnd 6: Knit.
Rnd 7: Purl.
Rnd 8: BO all sts knitwise.

FINISHING

Weave in all end neatly on WS. Gently steam press the cape; do not press ribbing. Make 13 little pompoms and sew them securely to the bottom edge of cape. We used a Norwegian crown coin (¾ in / 2 cm) to measure the diameter of the pompoms.

EAR WARMER WITH POMPOMS

With larger dpn, CO 8 sts. Knit back and forth in garter st for 9½ in / 24 cm. BO. Seam short ends of band. Make 2 small pompoms and place to serve as ear warmers.

Siv

173

Dog Sweater

The ribbing on the body is worked with the same needles as the two-color patterning, because it doesn't have to stretch around the dog's body. It just helps the sweater lie smoothly over the back. We knitted up two sweaters with different needles and different gauges but the same yarn. The small sweater fits Freja, who weighs 13.2 pounds / 6 kilos; the larger sweater fits her mother.

SIZES: Small (Large)

LEVEL OF DIFFICULTY
Intermediate

FINISHED MEASUREMENTS
Measure around your dog's stomach and knit a gauge swatch. Check the gauge measurements against the dog you are knitting for. If your dog is large, you might be able to use the same pattern but with Rauma's Vamse yarn. The small sweater measures 15¾ in / 40 cm around the stomach and is 11 in / 28 cm long, excluding the ribbing around the neck.

MATERIALS
Yarn: CYCA #3 (DK/light worsted), Rauma Mitu (50% superfine alpaca and 50% wool, 109 yd/100 m / 50 g)
Yarn Colors and Amounts:
MC: Gray SFN41, 150 g
CC: Pink 1332, 50 g
Needles:
Small sweater: U.S. size 4 / 3.5 mm: circular; U.S. sizes 2-3 and 4 / 3 and 3.5 mm: sets of 5 dpn.
Large sweater: U.S. size 6 / 4 mm: circular; U.S. sizes 4 and 6 / 3.5 and 4 mm: sets of 5 dpn.
Gauge:
Small sweater: 26 sts and 32 rows in St st on larger needles = 4 x 4 in / 10 x 10 cm.

Large sweater: 20 sts and 25 rows in St st on larger needles = 4 x 4 in / 10 x 10 cm.
Adjust needle sizes to obtain correct gauge if necessary.

SWEATER
With MC and short circular U.S. size 4 (6) / 3.5 (4) mm, CO 86 sts. Work the ribbing back and forth as follows:
Row 1: Work (p2, k2) across to last 2 sts and end with p2.
Row 2: Work (k2, p2 across to last 2 sts and end with k2.
Repeat these 2 rows until you've worked 10 rows total.

Continue back and forth in St st, shaping the lower edge as follows:
Row 1: P43, M1p, p18; turn.
Work back and forth in St st short rows:
Row 2: K37.
Row 3: P38.
Row 4: K39.
Continue in St st, with 1 more stitch on each row until 15 sts rem on WS. Turn work and knit across all sts. Now work in St st, shaping piece as follows:
Row 1: Purl.
Row 2: K1, M1, work until 2 sts rem and end M1, k2.

Dog Sweater

CHART 1—BODY

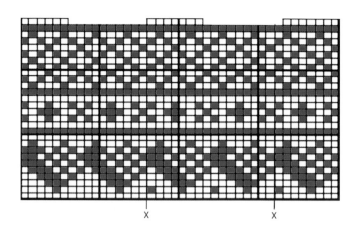

X   X

CHART 2—LEGS

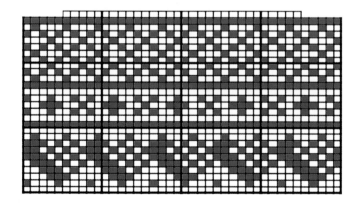

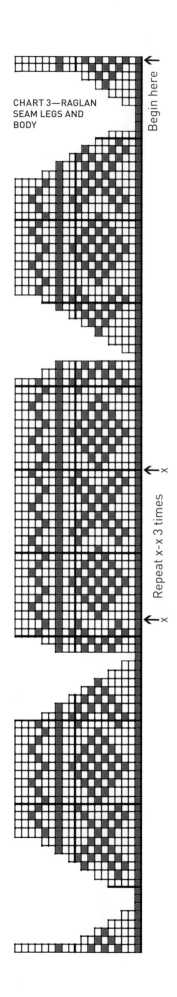

CHART 3—RAGLAN
SEAM LEGS AND
BODY

Begin here

Repeat x-x 3 times

← X

← X

Repeat these 2 rows until there are a total of 103 sts.

Now join the sweater and knit in the round, following Chart 1.

On Rnd 1, inc with M1 inside the 1st st of the row = 104 sts. On the last row of Chart 1, shape leg openings: K7, BO 10 sts loosely, k71 (including last st of bind-off), BO 10 sts loosely, k6 (including last st of bind-off). Place sts on a holder and work the legs.

LEGS

With MC and dpn U.S. size 4 (6) / 3.5 (4) mm, CO 40 sts. Divide sts onto 4 dpn, join and work 5 rnds k2, p2 ribbing. Next, work following Chart 2 and, on the last rnd, BO 5 sts loosely, k30 (including last st of bind-off), BO 5 loosely.

Knit the second leg the same way.

JOINING LEGS AND BODY

Join the legs and body by knitting the pieces in sequence on the same row. *At the same time*, begin Chart 3 as follows:

Rnd 1: Beginning at center front, k7 of body, k30 from first leg, placing it over first gap in body, k71 for back, k30 of second leg, placing it over second gap in body, and then k6 of body = 144 sts total.

Rnd 2: K4, k2tog, k2, k2tog, k11, k2tog, k11, k2tog, k73, k2tog, k11, k2tog, k11, k2tog, k2, k2tog, k3 = 136 sts rem.

Rnd 3: Knit.

Rnd 4: K3, k2tog, k25, k2tog, k73, k2tog, k25, k2tog, k2 = 132 sts rem.

Rnd 5: Knit.

Rnd 6: K2, k2tog, k2, k2tog, k20, k2tog, k73, k2tog, k20, k2tog, k2, k2tog, k1 = 126 sts rem.

Rnd 7: Knit.

Rnd 8: K1, k2tog, k2, k2tog, k18, k2tog, k73, k2tog, k18, k2tog, k2, k2tog = 120 sts rem.

Rnd 9: Knit.

Rnd 10: K2tog, k2, k2tog, k16, k2tog, k73, k2tog, k16, k2tog, k1, k2tog = 114 sts rem.

Rnd 11: Knit.

Rnd 12: K3, k2tog, k14, k2tog, k73, k2tog, k14, k2tog, k2 = 110 sts rem.

Rnd 13: Knit.

Rnd 14: K3, k2tog, k12, k2tog, k2, k2tog, k65, k2tog, k2, k2tog, k12, k2tog, k2 = 104 sts rem.

Rnd 15: Knit.

Rnd 16: K3, k2tog, k10, k2tog, k2, k2tog, k63, k2tog, k2, k2tog, k10, k2tog, k2 = 98 sts rem.

Rnd 17: Knit = last row of chart.

Rnd 18: K1, k2tog, knit to last 3 sts and end k2tog, k1 = 96 sts rem.

Change to smaller dpn, and work in k2 p2 ribbing for 6 in / 15 cm.

FINISHING

Seam gap under legs and then weave in all ends neatly on WS.

Lightly steam press sweater under a damp pressing cloth, but do not press ribbing.

The Easiest and Second-Easiest Socks in the World

Socks have become one of our specialties. It all began with an invitation to collaborate with the German company Regia.

After we had knitted a few pairs of socks, we decided that these two patterns were our favorites. We call them the "easiest socks in the world" but they are also referred to as "socks with Russian (or 'afterthought') heels." On the second-easiest socks, the heel is knitted back and forth over two double-pointed needles. To tighten the holes created when working knit and purl rows, we knit two together, balanced by an increase.

Both of these sock designs can be worked from the toe up if you aren't sure how many stitches to cast on for your size on top-down socks. If you're working with our color designs for Regia Pairfect yarn, you should knit from the ribbed cuff down, since that's how the yarn is designed to be worked. Make a pair of "toe up" socks first so you can calculate the stitch count for the next pair of socks.

LEVEL OF DIFFICULTY
Advanced

MATERIALS
Yarn:
CYCA #1 (fingering), Regia Design Line by ARNE & CARLOS, 4 ply (75% wool, 25% nylon, 459 yd/420 m / 100 g)
Yarn Colors
We designed a total of 21 colorways, so there is a color choice for every taste. You can also use a 50 g ball of single-color yarn or Regia 4-ply for the heels, or work the entire pair of socks with the same yarn.
Needles: U.S. sizes 1.5 and 2.5 / 2.5 and 3: sets of 5 dpn

The Easiest Socks in the World

We learned to knit sock heels with reinforcing thread. We cut the thread, knitted it in, and then continued the round with the sock yarn. That left us with two ends that we could use to sew up any holes or loose stitches. However, after knitting a few pairs of socks, we stopped cutting off the yarn and kept it "on hold." We knitted in the reinforcing thread and then continued on with the sock yarn over the stitches with the reinforcing thread, so as to keep working without cutting the sock yarn. That way, the reinforcing thread disappears into the fabric—and since the stitches are knitted on the next round, why not just let them be on this round?

KNITTING SOCKS FROM THE TOE UP

With larger dpn, CO 16 sts and divide sts evenly onto 4 dpn = 4 sts per needle. Join and pm for beginning of rnd.

Rnd 1: K16.

Now begin increasing at the sides on every other rnd:

Rnd 2: K1, M1, k6, M1, k2, M1, k6, M1, k1.

Rnd 3: K20.

Rnd 4: K1, M1, k8, M1, k2, M1, k8, M1, k1.

Rnd 5: K24.

Rep Rnds 4-5, increasing as set, adding 4 more sts on each alternate rnd. Increase until the toe section fits around your foot. We increase to 48 sts = 16 sts per needle because that fits our feet well.

Knit in the round, without increasing, to the beginning of the heel; try on the sock occasionally. The heel adds length to the foot, so stop when you are about 1¾-2 in / 4.5-5 cm before the back of your heel. When you reach the rnd for beginning the heel, knit across Ndls 1 and 2 with smooth waste yarn. Slide the sts back and knit them with working yarn. Make sure that the heel stitches align with the sides of the toe shaping. Continue knitting around until the leg is desired length before the cuff. Work the cuff in k2, p2 ribbing, using smaller dpn. BO loosely in ribbing.

HEEL

Insert a dpn into the row below the waste yarn and another dpn into the row above the waste yarn. Carefully remove waste yarn and divide sts onto 4 dpn with, for example, 16 sts per needle. Work in the round, decreasing 4 sts on every other rnd. Make sure that the decreases align with the toe shaping. The heel shaping for the socks described here begins with 64 sts.

Rnd 1: K64.

Rnd 2: K1, k2tog, k26, k2tog, k2, k2tog, k26, k2tog, k1.

Rnd 3: K60.

Rnd 4: K1, k2tog, k24, k2tog, k2, k2tog, k24, k2tog, k1.

Rnd 5: K56.

Rnd 6: K1, k2tog, k22, k2tog, k2, k2tog, k22, k2tog, k1.

Rnd 7: K52.

Rep Rnds 6-7, decreasing as set, with 4 fewer sts on each alternate rnd. When 16 sts rem (= 4 sts per needle), join the two sets of sts with Kitchener st. Weave in all ends neatly on WS. Gently steam press socks, except on ribbing.

If you are knitting with Arne & Carlos yarn from Regia, begin at an obvious place in the yarn color sequence. Note where you started the first sock and then find the same place in the color sequence to start the second sock. It's easiest to begin where the yarn changes color.

LEVEL OF DIFFICULTY
Advanced

MATERIALS
Yarn:
CYCA #1 (fingering), Regia Pairfect,
4 ply (75% wool, 25% nylon, 459 yd/
420 m / 100 g)
Needles: U.S. sizes 1.5 and 2.5 /
2.5 and 3: sets of 5 dpn.

This pair of socks is worked from
the cuff down, with 64 sts divided
onto 4 dpn = 16 sts per needle.

The Second-Easiest Socks in the World "Short Rows"

These instructions guide you through knitting a heel with short rows. You can knit this heel either for top-down or toe-up socks. The sock is worked in the round to the heel, and then the stitches from two needles are worked back and forth in St st. Our basic socks have 64 stitches around, but you can have more or fewer stitches. The heel is worked on two needles no matter the stitch count.

With smaller dpn, CO 64 sts; divide sts onto 4 dpn = 16 sts per needle. Join, being careful not to twist cast-on row; pm for beginning of rnd. Work around in k2, p2 ribbing for desired length of cuff. Change to larger dpn. Work around in St st for desired length to start of heel (about 1¾-2 in / 4.5-5 cm before base of your heel).

HEEL SHAPING

With 16 sts per needle, work the heel over a total of 32 sts as follows:
Row 1 (RS): K31; do not work last st; turn.
Row 2: Sl 1 purlwise wyf, p29; do not work last st; turn.
Row 3: Sl 1 purlwise wyb, k28 = to last st before gap before next-to-last st; turn.
Row 4: Sl 1 purlwise wyf, p27; turn.
Row 5: Sl 1 purlwise wyb, k26 = to last st before gap; turn.
Row 6: Sl 1 purlwise wyf, p25; turn.
Row 7: Sl 1 purlwise wyb, k24 = to last st before gap; turn.
Row 8: Sl 1 purlwise wyf, p23; turn.
Rep Rows 7-8 with 1 st less before gap on each row. When you've worked a row with 1 sl st + k12, begin knitting back (you will add 1 more st to each row). You will join heel sts to those left on holder until 12 sts rem at center of row, between gaps. For a smaller sock, you might want to knit a couple of rows before working longer rows. On a larger sock, you might want to begin working out sooner. Here's how to work back:
Row 1: Sl 1 purlwise wyf, p11, p2tog, LLI (left-lifted increase) into left side of st below the last st you worked together (called the "grandmother" stitch or second loop below loop on needle); turn.

Row 2: Sl 1 purlwise wyb, k12, k2tog, LLI into st below the last st you worked together; turn.
Row 3: Sl 1 purlwise wyf, p13, p2tog, LLI into st below the last st you worked together; turn.
Row 4: Sl 1 purlwise wyb, k14, k2tog, LLI into st below the last st you worked together; turn.
You should now see that the st before the gap is worked together with the stitch after the gap, so you shouldn't need to continue counting stitches. Continue with knit and purl rows until all the sts have been worked across. If there are any loose stitches at the "corners," after the heel is complete, pick up the st with the needle and work it together with a st from the St st. See page 62 for the same technique used on the bird's stomach. Continue around in St st until you are ready to shape the toe.

TOE SHAPING

Rnd 1: K64.
Rnd 2: K1, k2tog, k26, k2tog, k2, k2tog, k26, k2tog, k1.
Rnd 3: K60.
Rnd 4: K1, k2tog, k24, k2tog, k2, k2tog, k24, k2tog, k1.
Rnd 5: K56.
Rnd 6: K1, k2tog, k22, k2tog, k2, k2tog, k22, k2tog, k1.
Rnd 7: K52.
Rep Rnds 6-7, decreasing as set, with 4 fewer sts on each alternate rnd. When 16 sts rem (= 4 sts per needle), join the two sets of sts with Kitchener st. Weave in all ends neatly on WS. Gently steam press socks, except on ribbing.

Long Stockings

Cozy stockings for long cold winter days. These are good for wearing with cold ski boots and will protect you from cold floors.

STOCKINGS 1

LEVEL OF DIFFICULTY
Advanced

FINISHED MEASUREMENTS
Total length leg to heel: 20 in / 51 cm
From heel to toe: 10¼ in / 26 cm
Measure your foot and add or omit single color rnds if necessary for fit.

MATERIALS
Yarn:
CYCA #2 (sport/baby), Rauma PT5 (80% wool, 20% nylon, 140 yd/ 128 m / 50 g)
Yarn Colors and Amounts:
Color 1: Royal Blue 572, 100 g
Color 2: Green 588, 50 g
Color 3: Red 543, 50 g
Color 4: Mustard 516, 50 g
Color 5: White 503, 50 g
Color 6: Light Gray 504, 50 g
Color 7: Dark Gray 510, 50 g
Needles: U.S. sizes 1.5 and 2.5 / 2.5 and 3 mm: sets of 5 dpn
Gauge: 26 sts and 33 rnds in St st on larger needles = 4 x 4 in / 10 x 10 cm.
Adjust needle sizes to obtain correct gauge if necessary.

Charts: See page 186.

STOCKINGS

With smaller dpn and Color 1, CO 92 sts. Divide sts over 4 dpn (= 23 sts per dpn). Join, being careful not to twist cast-on row; pm for beginning of rnd. Work around in k2, p2 ribbing for 2½ in / 6 cm. Change to larger dpn and Color 2. Work 8 rnds in St st and, *at the same time*, decrease 2 sts evenly spaced on first rnd = 90 sts rem. The round begins at center back. Now work in pattern following Chart 1. The patterning is reversed at center front so read the chart from left to right for the second half of the round; do not repeat center front stitch.

At A on the chart, decrease as follows: (K5, k2tog) 3 times; work until 21 sts rem and then (k2tog, k5) 3 times = 6 sts decreased and 84 sts rem.
At B, C, and D, decrease as follows: (K4, k2tog) 3 times; work until 18 sts rem and then (K2tog, k4) 3 times = 66 sts rem after last dec rnd.

After completing charted rows, divide the sts with 16 sts each on Ndls 1 and 3 and 17 sts each on Ndls 2 and 4. Work in St st with Color 1 for 1½ in / 4 cm, but, at ¾ in / 2 cm, decrease 4 sts around:
Ndls 1 and 2: Dec 1 st at beginning of needle.
Ndls 3 and 4: Dec 1 st at end of needle.
After dec rnd, 62 sts rem.

HEEL

With Color 3, work heel over sts on Ndls 1 and 4 = 31 sts. Work back and forth in St st for 2¼ in / 5.5 cm. Slip the 1st st of each row purlwise for an edge st. The last row = RS.
Heel Turn: Begin on WS: Work until 1 st past center st, p2tog, p1; turn. Work until 1 st past center st, ssk, k1; turn.
Now work until 1 st before gap, join (p2tog on WS, ssk on RS) the st before the gap with the st after gap, k1; turn. Continue the same way until all the sts outside the gap at each side have been used up = 17 sts rem. Divide heel sts onto 2 dpn with 9 sts on Ndl 1 and 8 sts on Ndl 4. The round now begins at center of sole.

Stockings 1

FOOT

Change to Color 1 and knit 1 rnd St st, picking up and knitting 9 sts along edge sts on each side of heel = 35 sts on sole. Knit 2 more rnds. On 4th rnd, dec 1 st at end of Ndl 1 and 1 st at beginning of Ndl 4. Work in pattern following Chart 2, reversing the pattern from center front so the second side of the stocking matches the first. Repeat the decreases on, alternately, the 4th and 14th rnds until 60 sts rem. When pattern is complete, continue in toe color (Color 2) until foot, as measured from back of heel, is approx. 9 in / 23 cm long. If you need to shorten the foot, omit the last pattern panel on the chart.

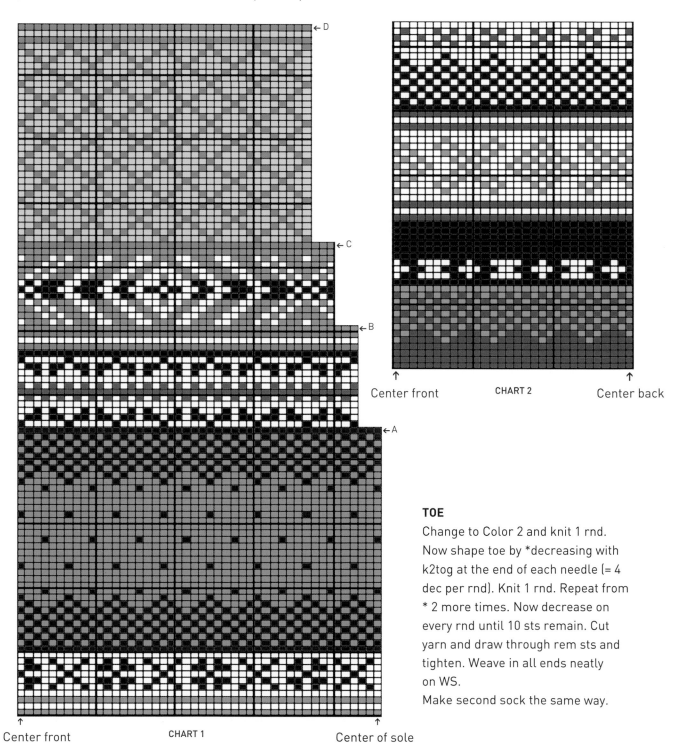

← D

← C

← B

← A

Center front   CHART 2   Center back

Center front   CHART 1   Center of sole

TOE

Change to Color 2 and knit 1 rnd. Now shape toe by *decreasing with k2tog at the end of each needle (= 4 dec per rnd). Knit 1 rnd. Repeat from * 2 more times. Now decrease on every rnd until 10 sts remain. Cut yarn and draw through rem sts and tighten. Weave in all ends neatly on WS.
Make second sock the same way.

STOCKINGS 2

LEVEL OF DIFFICULTY
Advanced

FINISHED MEASUREMENTS
Total length leg to heel: 19 in / 48 cm
From heel to toe: 10¼ in / 26 cm
Measure your foot and add or omit single color rnds if necessary for fit.

MATERIALS
Yarn:
CYCA #2 (sport/baby), Rauma PT5 (80% wool, 20% nylon, 140 yd/128 m / 50 g)
Yarn Colors and Amounts:
Color 1: Blue 572, 100 g
Color 2: White 502, 50 g
Color 3: Red 543, 50 g
Color 4: Green 588, 50 g
Color 5: Pink 548, 50 g
Color 6: Mustard 516, 50 g
Color 7: Gray 510, 50 g
Needles: U.S. sizes 1.5 and 2.5 / 2.5 and 3 mm: sets of 5 dpn
Gauge: 26 sts and 33 rows in St st on larger needles = 4 x 4 in / 10 x 10 cm.
Adjust needle sizes to obtain correct gauge if necessary.

STOCKINGS
With smaller dpn and Color 1, CO 92 sts. Divide sts over 4 dpn (= 23 sts per dpn). Join, being careful not to twist cast-on row; pm for beginning of rnd. Work around in k2, p2 ribbing for 2½ in / 6 cm. Change to larger dpn and begin Chart 1 (page 189). On the 1st rnd, decrease 2 sts evenly spaced around = 90 sts. The round begins at center back. The patterning is reversed at center front so read the chart from left to right for the second half of the round; do not repeat center front stitch.

At A on the chart, decrease as follows: (K5, k2tog) 3 times; work until 21 sts rem and then (k2tog, k5) 3 times = 6 sts decreased and 84 sts rem. At B, C, and D, decrease as follows: (K4, k2tog) 3 times; work until 18 sts rem and then (K2tog, k4) 3 times = 66 sts rem after last dec rnd.

Change to Color 7 and knit 8 rnds. On the next rnd, decrease: (K4, k2tog) 3 times. Work until 18 sts rem and work (k2tog, k4) 3 times = 60 sts rem.

HEEL
With Color 3, work heel over sts on Ndls 1 and 4 = 29 sts. Work back and forth in St st for 2¼ in / 5.5 cm. Slip the 1st st of each row purlwise for an edge st. The last row = RS.

Heel Turn: Begin on WS: Work until 1 st past center st, p2tog, p1; turn. Work until 1 st past center st, ssk, k1; turn.
Now work until 1 st before gap, join (p2tog on WS, ssk on RS) the st before the gap with the st after gap, k1; turn. Continue the same way until all the sts outside the gap at each side have been used up = 17 sts rem. Divide heel sts onto 2 dpn = 9 sts on Ndl 1 and 8 sts on Ndl 4. The round now begins at center of sole.

FOOT
Change to Color 7 and knit 1 rnd St st, picking up and knitting 9 sts along edge sts on each side of heel = 35 sts on sole. Knit 6 more rnds, decreasing 1 st at each side of sole on Rnds 1, 4, and 7 = 60 sts rem. Work in pattern following Chart 2 (page 189), reversing the pattern from center front so the second side of the stocking will match the first. At A on the chart, dec 1 st on each side of the sole. When pattern is complete, foot, as measured from back of heel, is approx. 8¾ in / 22 cm long. Divide sts so 2 ndls have 15 sts each and 2 ndls have 14 sts each.

TOE
Change to Color 3 and knit 1 rnd. Now shape toe by *decreasing with k2tog at the end of each needle (= 4 dec per rnd). Knit 1 rnd. Repeat from * 2 more times. Now decrease on every rnd until 10 sts remain. Cut yarn and draw through rem sts and tighten. Weave in all ends neatly on WS. Make second sock the same way.

Stockings 2

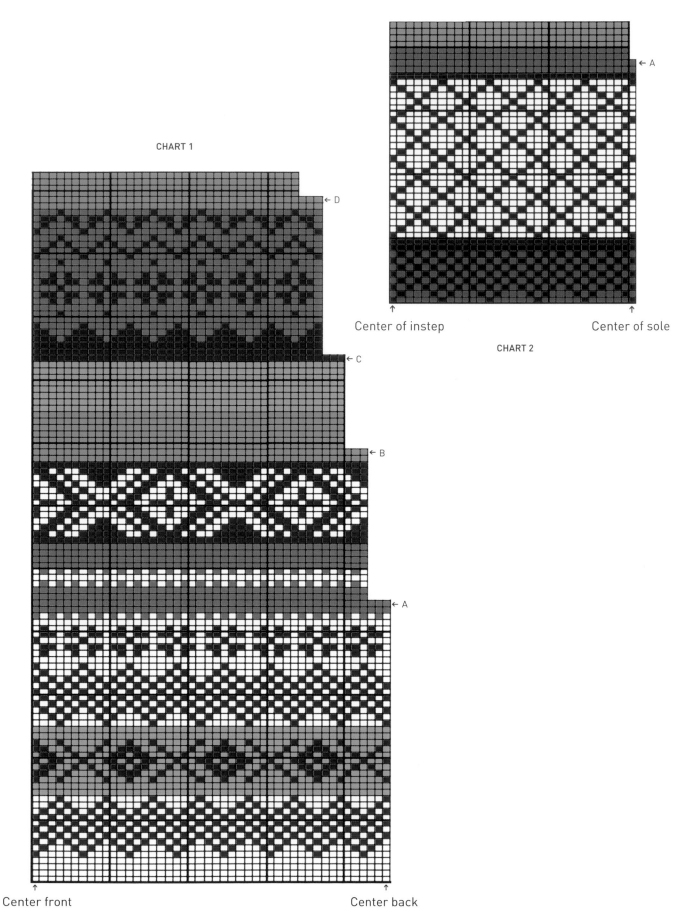

CHART 1

← D

← C

← B

← A

CHART 2

← A

Center of instep   Center of sole

↑   ↑

↑   ↑
Center front   Center back

Wrist Warmers

with *Klo* (5 Wise Virgins) Panels

It was quite common in the old days for people to wear wrist warmers, so why not revive the tradition? Knit a pair in bright colors and spiff up that suit! Knitting the wise virgins motif is easier and faster than embroidering it.

WRIST WARMERS

With smaller dpn and Color 1, CO 48 sts. Divide sts evenly over 4 dpn = 12 sts per dpn. Join, being careful not to twist cast-on row; pm for beginning of rnd. Work around in k2, p2 ribbing for 1¼ in / 3 cm.

Change to larger dpn and work in pattern following the chart. Work chart repeat twice around and once in length. Finish by changing to smaller dpn and working in k2, p2 ribbing for 1¼ in / 3 cm. BO loosely in ribbing.

Weave in all ends neatly on WS. Lightly steam press the cuffs (except for ribbing) under a damp pressing cloth.

LEVEL OF DIFFICULTY
Advanced

FINISHED MEASUREMENTS
Circumference: 9 in / 23 cm
Length: 6¼ in / 16 cm

MATERIALS
Yarn:
CYCA #3 (DK/light worsted), Rauma Mitu (50% superfine alpaca and 50% wool, 109 yd/100 m / 50 g)
Yarn Colors and Amounts:
Color 1: Black SFN50, 50 g
Color 2: Red 4932, 50 g
Color 3: Yellow 0184, 50 g
Color 4: Blue 4922, 50 g
Color 5: Green 6315, 50 g
Color 6: Pink 1832, 50 g
Needles: U.S. sizes 2.5 and 4 / 3 and 3.5: sets of 5 dpn
Gauge: 22 sts and 28 rnds in St st on larger needles = 4 x 4 in /10 x 10 cm after blocking. Adjust needle sizes to obtain correct gauge if necessary.

NOTE: All the white squares on the chart are knitted with Black.

Doubled Hat

Our hat was inspired by a stocking cap from Setesdal. The stocking cap was a long cap knitted in red and black yarn with a crown shaped like a sock heel. It's mentioned in Johannes Skar's book, *Gamalt or Sætesdal II*. The cap shown in the book is red, green, and white, with the white part folded in as a lining.

LEVEL OF DIFFICULTY
Advanced

SIZE
Women's Medium

MATERIALS
Yarn:
CYCA #4 (worsted/afghan/aran), Rauma Vamse (100% wool, 91 yd/83 m / 50 g)
Yarn Colors and Amounts:
Color 1: White V01, 100 g
Color 2: Red V35, 50 g

Color 3: Green V80, 50 g
Needles: U.S. size 8 / 5 mm: 16 in / 40 cm circular and set of 5 dpn
Gauge: 16 sts and 22 rnds in St st = 4 x 4 in / 10 x 10 cm.
Adjust needle size to obtain correct gauge if necessary.

HAT

Begin with top of hat lining. With Color 1 and dpn, CO 12 sts. Divide sts onto 4 dpn = 3 sts per needle. Join, being careful not to twist cast-on row; pm for beginning of rnd.

Shape the hat as explained below. Begin on dpn and change to short circular when dpn become too full.

Rnd 1: K12.
Rnd 2: (K1, M1, k2) around.
Rnd 3: K16.
Rnd 4: (K1, M1, k2, M1, k1) around.
Rnd 5: K24.
Rnd 6: (K1, M1, k4, M1, k1) around.
Rnd 7: K32.
Rnd 8: (K1, M1, k6, M1, k1) around.
Rnd 9: K40.
Rnd 10: (K1, M1, k8, M1, k1) around.
Rnd 11: K48.
Rnd 12: (K1, M1, k10, M1, k1) around.
Rnd 13: K56.
Rnd 14: (K1, M1, k12, M1, k1) around.
Rnd 15: K64.
Rnd 16: (K1, M1, k14, M1, k1) around.
Rnd 17: K72.
Rnd 18: (K1, M1, k16, M1, k1) around.
Rnd 19: K80.
Rnd 20: (K1, M1, k18, M1, k1) around.
Rnd 21: K88.
Rnd 22: (K1, M1, k20, M1, k1) around.
Rnds 23-41: K96.
Rnd 42: (K2tog, yo) around = eyelet fold row.
Rnd 43: K96.

Outside of hat

Change to Color 2 and work pattern following the chart through chart Row 42 (= Rnds 44-84), with the motif worked 4 times around and once in length.

The crown shaping shown at the top of the chart is worked as follows:

Rnd 85: (K1, k2tog, k18, k2tog, k1) around.
Rnd 86: K88.
Rnd 87: (K1, k2tog, k16, k2tog, k1) around.
Rnd 88: K80.
Rnd 89: (K1, k2tog, k14, k2tog, k1) around.
Rnd 90: K72.
Rnd 91: (K1, k2tog, k12, k2tog, k1) around.
Rnd 92: K64.
Rnd 93: (K1, k2tog, k10, k2tog, k1) around.
Rnd 94: K56.
Rnd 95: (K1, k2tog, k8, k2tog, k1) around.
Rnd 96: K48.
Rnd 97: (K1, k2tog, k6, k2tog, k1) around.
Rnd 98: K40.
Rnd 99: (K1, k2tog, k4, k2tog, k1) around.
Rnd 100: K32.
Rnd 101: (K1, k2tog, k2, k2tog, k1) around.
Rnd 102: K24.
Rnd 103: (K1, k2tog, k2tog, k1) around.
Rnd 104: K16.
Rnd 105: (K1, k2tog, k1) around.

Cut yarn and draw through rem 12 sts. Weave in all ends neatly on WS. Lightly steam press hat under damp pressing cloth. Fold in lining at eyelet round.

TOP WITH CAT

Yarn:

CYCA #3 (DK/light worsted)
Schachenmayr Merino
Extrafine 120 (100% wool,
131 yd/120 m / 50 g)

Yarn Colors and Amounts:

Turquoise 00167, 50 g

Dark Red 00140, 50 g

Needles: U.S. sizes 1.5 and 2.5 /
2.5 and 3 mm: sets of 5 dpn

Crochet Hook: U.S. size D-3 / 3 mm

WHITE TROUSERS

See page 145 for instructions.

Yarn:

CYCA #3 (DK/light worsted)
Schachenmayr Merino Extrafine
120 (100% wool, 131 yd/120 m /
50 g)

Yarn Colors and Amounts:

White 00101, 50 g

Needles: U.S. sizes 1.5 and
2.5 / 2.5 and 3 mm: sets of
5 dpn

Kaja

½ Body, Whole Sleeve

BODY

With smaller dpn and Turquoise, CO 48 sts. Divide sts evenly onto 4 dpn = 12 sts per needle. Join and pm for beginning of rnd.

Rnds 1-5: Work around in k2, p2 ribbing.

Rnd 6: Change to larger dpn. Work (k3, M1) around = 64 sts.

Rnds 7-27 (7-15): Now knit 21 rnds for a long sweater or (9) rnds for a short version.

Rnd 28 (16): BO 3 sts, k26 (including last st from bind-off), BO 6, k26 (including last st from bind-off), BO 3 sts = 52 sts rem. Divide sts for front and back onto 2 dpn = 26 sts per needle.

SLEEVES (MAKE BOTH ALIKE)

With smaller dpn and Turquoise, CO 24 sts. Divide sts evenly onto 4 dpn = 6 sts per needle. Join and pm for beginning of rnd.

Rnd 6: Change to larger dpn. Work (k3, M1) around = 32 sts.

Rnds 7-27 (7-15): Now knit 21 rnds for long sleeves or (9) rnds for short sleeves.

Rnd 28 (16): BO 3 sts, k26 (including last st from bind-off), BO 3 sts = 26 sts rem.

Join body and sleeves:

Rnd 29: K26 for back, k26 for sleeve, k26 for front, k26 for sleeve = 104 sts.

Rnd 30: (K1, k2tog, k20, k2tog, k1) around.

Rnd 31: K96.

Rnd 32: (K1, k2tog, k18, k2tog, k1) around.

Rnd 33: K88.

Rnd 34: (K1, k2tog, k16, k2tog, k1) around.

Rnd 35: K80.

Rnd 36: (K1, k2tog, k14, k2tog, k1) around.

Rnd 37: K72.

Rnd 38: (K1, k2tog, k12, k2tog, k1) around.

Rnd 39: K64.

Rnd 40: (K1, k2tog, k10, k2tog, k1) around.

Rnd 41: K56.

Rnd 42: (K1, k2tog, k8, k2tog, k1) around.

Rnd 43: K48.

Rnd 44: (K1, k2tog, k6, k2tog, k1) around.

Rnd 45: K40.

Rnd 46, Eyelets: (K2tog, yo, p2) around.

Neckband: Work 8 rnds of k2, p2 ribbing. BO.

With Red, crochet a chain long enough to draw through the eyelets on neckband and tie into a bow. Make 2 small pompoms to sew securely to each end of the cord.

FINISHING

Seam the underarms and weave in all ends neatly on WS. Carefully steam press all but the ribbing. Crochet a chain stitch cord and thread through the eyelet row.

Embroider the cat with duplicate stitch (see chart on opposite page) and steam press garment again.

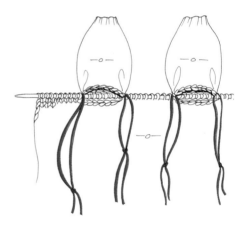

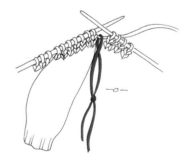

Knitting Tip

Place a marker or marker thread at each intersection of sleeve and body to make it easy to see where to decrease for the raglan shaping.

Christmas is a special time for everyone living in the Nordic countries. Winters are so dark here; it always feels cozy to sit inside doing handcrafts surrounded by candlelight. It's only natural that we'd have a whole chapter about Christmas and Christmas decorations, because we are both especially fond of this time of year. Our Christmas workshop at home is an important place during November and December. It is a peak time for creativity and the joy of handcrafting. Arne, in particular, is so enraptured by Christmas that he starts planning new Christmas projects at the beginning of January.

Christmas at the Cabin

LEVEL OF DIFFICULTY
Advanced

MATERIALS
Yarn:
CYCA #4 (worsted/afghan/aran), Rauma
Vamsegarn (100% wool, 91 yd/83 m / 50 g)
Yarn Colors and Amounts:
Lime Green V80, 150-200 g
Red V18, 50 g
Light Gray Heather V03, 50 g
small amounts of Pale Pink V66, Dark
Brown Heather V64 (or Black), Medium
Blue V50, and White, V00
Needles: U.S. size 8-10 / 5-6 mm: circular
and set of 5 dpn
Recommended Gauge: 14-16 sts = 4 in /
10 cm
NOTE: Alternate two strands of yarn on
every stitch throughout (as for two-end or
Fair Isle knitting).

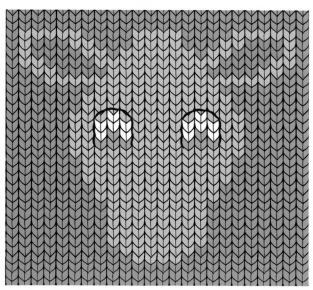

EMBROIDERY CHART

Rudolph's antlers

Find the center of the I-cord for the antlers and
pin it to the center of the head. Pin the antlers the
same way on each side of the head and sew them
down as invisibly as possible.

Rudolph Slippers

These fun slippers were inspired by Robert Lewis May's Christmas story, with a little felted pompom for the red nose. You can form reindeer antlers with an I-cord.

With one strand of Lime Green and circular, CO 56 (60, 64) sts; join, being careful not to twist cast-on row. Join second strand of Lime Green and knit 15 rnds, alternating strands on every stitch.

HEEL
Row 1: K14 (15, 16), knitting last st with both strands; turn.
Row 2: Sl 1, p27 (29, 31), purling last st with both strands; turn.
Work another 11 rows back and forth in St st over the 28 (30, 32) heel sts, always slipping the first st.

Heel Turn
Row 14: P13 (15, 17), p2tog, p1 with both strands; turn.
Row 15: K3 (5, 7), k2tog, k1 with both strands; turn.
Rows 16-23: Continue the same way, working back and forth in St st and shaping, with 1 more st before the decrease on each row (the decrease joins the sts before/after the gap).
Row 24: P12 (14, 16), p2tog, p1 with both strands; turn.
Row 25: K13 (15, 17), k2tog with both strands; turn. (This row ends with k2tog and not k1 as previously).
Row 26: P13 (15, 17), p2tog, p1 with both strands; turn.

FOOT
Set-up Rnd: Ssk, k6 (7, 8). Pm at center of sole, k7 (8, 9), pick up and knit 7 sts evenly spaced across one side of the heel flap, k28 (30, 32) across instep, pick up and knit 7 sts evenly spaced across other side of heel flap and k7 (8, 9) on sole. The beginning of the rnd is at center of sole.
Foot: Knit 33 (36, 39) rnds on the 56 (60, 64) sts of foot.

Toe Shaping
Divide the sts onto 4 dpn with 14 (15, 16) sts on each needle. Shape toe as follows, with 8 sts decreased on each decrease rnd.
Rnd 1 (decrease rnd): At beginning of each needle: K1, k2tog. At end of each needle: K2tog, k1.
Rnd 2: Knit.
Repeat Rnds 1-2 until 16 (20, 16) sts rem. Cut yarn and draw end through remaining sts. Pull tight and weave in all ends neatly on WS.

FINISHING
Steam press slippers.
Embroider the charted motif with duplicate stitch, using Gray, Pink, Light Blue, and White yarn. Edge the eyes between the white and gray areas, using Black and backstitch.
Steam press the embroidery.

Antlers: Knit 2 I-cords each about 27½ in / 70 cm long. Shape and attach the antlers as described on previous page. Use a knitting mill for the cords or handknit them.
I-cord: With White and dpn, CO 5 sts. Knit across and then *slide sts to front of dpn. Bring yarn around back and k5*. Rep from * to * until cord is desired length. Cut yarn and bring end through sts; tighten and weave in end to WS.

Make two Red pompoms 2¼ in / 5.5 cm in diameter.

Felt the slippers and pompoms at the same time. Sew on pompoms for the red nose after felting is complete.

Felting
Use a wool-safe liquid soap. For 2.2 lb / 1 kg knitted fabric, you should use about 6 tablespoons / 100 ml soap. Set the water temperature for the machine at 104-140°F / 40-60°C (the temperature options vary from machine to machine). Start at the lower temperature and check the degree of felting occasionally.

Christmas Balls

Basic Pattern

This pattern is used for all the Christmas balls. Follow the charted motif for each individual ball.

Each chart shows the motif, which is worked four times around, with the stitches divided over four double-pointed needles. The first row of 3 stitches on the chart represents the 3 cast-on stitches and is not knitted. The top 3 stitches are not worked either. On the last round, cut the yarn and pull the tail through the remaining 12 stitches; pull tight and weave in tail on WS. Most of the patterns are divided over four double-pointed needles, but some of the balls have patterns over only two needles. In that case, the chart shows two repeats side-by-side.

Work as follows:

Rnd 1: This is the bottom row on the chart with 3 blocks. With dpn, cast on 12 sts over US 2.5 / 3 mm. Divide these 12 sts over 4 dpn = 3 sts per ndl.
Rnd 2: Knit 12.
Rnd 3: (K2, inc 1, k1) on each ndl. (See page 259 for increase method.)
Rnd 4: Knit 16.
Rnd 5: (K1, inc 1, k2, inc 1, k1) on each ndl.
Rnd 6: Knit 24.
Rnd 7: (K1, inc 1, k4, inc 1, k1) on each ndl.
Rnd 8: Knit 32.
Rnd 9: (K1, inc 1, k6, inc 1, k1) on each ndl.
Rnd 10: Knit 40.
Rnd 11: (K1, inc 1, k8, inc 1, k1) on each ndl.
Rnd 12: Knit 48.
Rnd 13: (K1, inc 1, k10, inc 1, k1) on each ndl.
Rnd 14: Knit 56.
Rnd 15: (K1, inc 1, k12, inc 1, k1) on each ndl.
Rnds 16-27: Knit 64.
Rnd 28: (K1, k2tog, k10, k2tog, k1) on each ndl.
Rnd 29: Knit 56.
Rnd 30: (K1, k2tog, k8, k2tog, k1) on each ndl.
Rnd 31: Knit 48.
Rnd 32: (K1, k2tog, k6, k2tog, k1) on each ndl.
Rnd 33: Knit 40.
Rnd 34: (K1, k2tog, k4, k2tog, k1) on each ndl.
Rnd 35: Knit 32.
Rnd 36: (K1, k2tog, k2, k2tog, k1) on each ndl.
Rnd 37: Knit 24.
Rnd 38: (K1, k2tog, k2tog, k1) on each ndl.
Rnd 39: Knit 16.
Rnd 40: (K1, k2tog, k1) on each ndl.
Rnd 41: This is the top round with 3 blocks on the chart; do not knit. Cut yarn, leaving an end about 8 in / 20 cm long. Pull through the last 12 sts.

LEVEL OF DIFFICULTY
Advanced

MATERIALS
Yarn:
CYCA #3 (DK/light worsted)
Schachenmayr Merino Extrafine 120 (100% wool, 131 yd/120 m / 50 g)
Yarn Colors and Amounts:
Red 00131, 50 g
White 00102, 50 g
Other Materials: ¾ oz / 20 g clean wool roving per ball
Needles: U.S. size 2.5 / 3 mm: set of 5 dpn
Gauge: 22 sts = 4 in / 10 cm. Adjust needle size to obtain correct gauge if necessary.

Finishing the ball: Use the tip of your index finger to push the 12 stitches at the top smoothly together and under at the top of the ball. Thread the yarn once more through all the stitches at the top. Bring the needle and yarn through the hole at the top, secure the yarn by pressing the top towards the hole at the base of the ball and sewing it down securely. Steam the ball and fill with wool batting.

Thread the yarn through the stitches at the base, tighten, and tie off yarn. When you fill the ball with wool batting, loosen the wool first so the filling is lofty, and then spread it out well inside the ball. Use the index finger to press in fine layers of wool batting. Don't wad the batting when you are stuffing it in the ball because it will clump up.

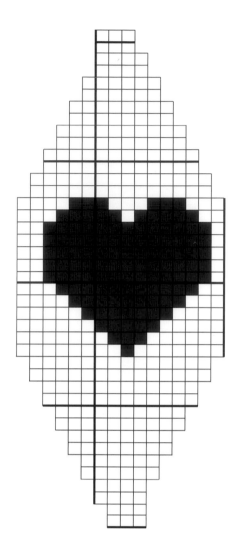

Heart

A simple heart, embellished with 16 crystals artfully arranged over the knitted heart.

We attached the crystals with textile glue, which worked quite well. If you are unsure about what kind of glue to use, ask at the store.

You can probably buy these crystals at your local craft or hobby shop, in mixed colors or colorless.

Angel

Harp

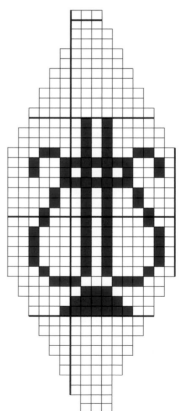

★ *Angel with Candle* ★

★ *Christmas Lights* ★

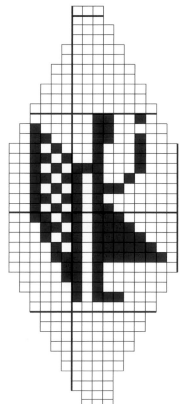

Magnus the Garden Mouse on a Christmas Ball

It's always fun to knit a new garden mouse in the days before Christmas. Although we first placed a mouse on an ornament a few years ago, we still aren't completely finished with the idea. The mouse on an ornament has become one of our prettiest Christmas decorations. We hang them up under the veranda roof so they can sway in the breeze. It takes a while to knit a mouse, a sweater, and a Christmas ball, but a mouse with an ornament has never been left lying around unfinished. That's because it's always exciting to see which mouse ends up on which ball. There are quite a few ways to attach a mouse to an ornament, and that's what compels us to keep knitting. The cord for the ball is attached as usual, but it can vary in length, all depending on where you want the mouse to be attached. In any case, the cord should always be long enough over the highest point so it can be hung. The highest point will either be over the mouse's head (if the mouse is sitting on the ball) or higher than the ball (if the mouse is hanging below the ball).

We have knitted large and small mice, large and small Christmas balls. Everything is made with the same pattern and we just change the yarn and needles. When knitting a mouse, it's best to have a firmer gauge than that recommended on the yarn-ball band, no matter what yarn you're using. If you usually knit loosely, check your gauge to see how far down in needle sizes you need to go. You want to knit firmly enough so the filling won't show through; this will produce a smooth surface. We've knitted the largest ornaments with Merino Extrafine 45 and needles U.S. size 8 / 5 mm. If you can't find this yarn, you can work with two strands of Rauma's Vamse-garn held together or Troll from Hifa and needles U.S. size 8 / 5 mm. This makes a large enough ball relative to the size of Magnus the Garden Mouse.

How to Knit
Magnus the Garden Mouse

All gardens have at least one mouse! Here's the pattern for our own Magnus the Garden Mouse.

BEGIN WITH THE LEFT FOOT

With smaller dpn, CO 6 sts and divide evenly over 3 dpn = 2 sts on each needle. Join, being careful not to twist cast-on row.

NOTE: See page 259 for increase method.

Rnd 1: K6.

Rnd 2: (K1, inc 1, k1) around.

Rnd 3: K9.

Rnd 4: (K1, inc 1, k1, inc 1, k1) around.

Rnd 5: K15.

Rnd 6: (K1, inc 1, k3, inc 1, k1) around = 21 sts. Knit 9 rnds without increasing.

Sew the tip of the foot together, weave the yarn end inside the foot and then use it as a marking thread.

HEEL AND LEG

Work back and forth only over the sts on the first dpn.

Row 1: K7.

Row 2: P7.

Row 3: K7.

Row 4: P7.

Row 5: K7.

Row 6: P7.

Row 7: K7. Using a second dpn, pick up and knit 4 sts on the side of the heel and k7 from dpn. K7 across 3rd dpn; with another dpn, pick up and knit 4 sts along side of heel. Move marking thread so it is between the 1st and 4th dpn.

Now work in the round in St st, shaping leg as follows:

Rnd 7: Divide the sts onto 4 dpn as you knit around:

    Ndl 1: K7.

    Ndl 2: K8.

    Ndl 3: K6.

    Ndl 4: K8.

Rnd 8:   **Ndl 1:** K7.

    Ndl 2: K2tog, k6.

    Ndl 3: K6.

    Ndl 4: K6, k2tog.

Rnd 9:   Knit around.

Rnd 10: **Ndl 1:** K7.

    Ndl 2: K2tog, k5.

    Ndl 3: K6.

    Ndl 4: K5, k2tog.

Rnd 11: Knit around.

Rnd 12: **Ndl 1:** K2tog, k3, k2tog.

    Ndl 2: K2tog, k4.

    Ndl 3: K2, k2tog, k2.

    Ndl 4: K4, k2tog.

Rnd 13: Knit around = 20 sts rem.

Rnd 14: (K1, k2tog, k2) around.

Rnd 15: Knit.

Rnd 16: (K1, k2tog, k1) around = 12 sts rem.

LEVEL OF DIFFICULTY
Intermediate

MATERIALS
Yarn:
CYCA #3 (DK/light worsted) Schachen-mayr Merino Extrafine 120 (100% wool, 131 yd/120 m / 50 g)
Yarn Colors and Amounts Suggested for Head and Body:
Light Gray 00190, 50 g
Dark Gray 00192, 50 g
Medium Gray 00198 or Camel 00105, 50 g
Pale Pink 00135, 50 g (for the nose and inside of ears)
Black, 00199, 50 g for eyes
Other Materials: 1¾ oz / 50 g clean wool roving per ball
Needles: U.S. size 2.5 / 3 mm: set of 5 dpn
Crochet Hook: U.S. size C-2 / 2.5 mm
Gauge: 22 sts = 4 in / 10 cm. Adjust needle size to obtain correct gauge if necessary.

Fill the foot and leg with wool batting.

Continue in St st, dividing the sts onto 3 dpn with 4 sts on each needle.

Rnds 17-46: K12 (total of 30 rnds).

Rnd 47: K1, inc 1, k10, inc 1, k1.

Rnd 48: Knit.

Rnd 49: K1, inc 1, k12, inc 1, k1.

Rnd 50: Knit.

Rnd 51: BO 2 sts knitwise, k12 (including last st from bind-off); BO 2 knitwise.

Divide the leg sts onto 2 dpn with 6 sts on each needle. Fill leg with wool.

Right Leg

Work as for the left leg through Rnd 46.

Rnd 47: K5, inc 1, k2, inc 1, k5.

Rnd 48: Knit.

Rnd 49: K6, inc 1, k2, inc 1, k6 = 16 sts.

Rnd 50: Knit.

Rnd 51: K6, BO 4 sts knitwise, k6 (including last st from bind-off).

Divide the leg sts onto 2 dpn with 6 sts on each needle. Fill leg with wool.

JOIN THE LEGS AND KNIT THE BODY

Rnd 1: Begin where the yarn is hanging at the right leg:

> **Ndl 1:** K6 from right leg.
>
> **Ndls 2-3:** K6 sts each needle from left leg.
>
> **Ndl 4:** K6 from right leg.

Move marker up the side.

The 4 bound-off sts on each leg should be facing each other between the legs.

Rnd 2: K13, inc 1, k10, inc 1, k1.

Rnd 3: K26.

Rnd 4: K13, inc 1, k12, inc 1, k1.

Rnd 5: K28.

Rnd 6: K13, inc 1, k14, inc 1, k1.

Rnd 7: K30.

Rnd 8: K13, inc 1, k16, inc 1, k1.

Rnd 9: K32.

Seam the crotch.

Rnd 10: K13, inc 1, k18, inc 1, k1.

Rnd 11: K34.

Rnd 12: K13, inc 1, k20, inc 1, k1.

Rnd 13: K36.

Rnd 14: K13, inc 1, k22, inc 1, k1.

Rnd 15: K38.

Rnd 16: K13, ssk, k7, k2tog, k2, ssk, k7, k2tog, k1.

Rnd 17: K34.

Rnd 18: K13, ssk, k5, k2tog, k2, ssk, k5, k2tog, k1.

Rnd 19: K30.

Rnd 20: K13, ssk, k3, k2tog, k2, ssk, k3, k2tog, k1.

Rnd 21: K26.

Rnd 22: K13, ssk, k8, k2tog, k1.

Rnd 23: K24.

Rnd 24: BO 2 knitwise, k8 (including last st from bind-off), BO 4 knitwise, k8 (including last st from bind-off), BO 2 knitwise.

Place the sts for back on 1 dpn and the sts for front on another dpn.

ARMS

With smaller dpn, CO 6 sts. Divide sts onto 3 dpn and join to work in the round.

Rnd 1: K6.

Rnd 2: (K1, inc 1, k1) around.

Rnd 3: K9.

Rnd 4: (K1, inc 1, k1, inc 1, k1) around.

Rnd 5: K15.

Rnd 6: (K1, inc 1, k3, inc 1, k1) around.

Secure yarn tail at tip of hand and use the tail as a marker.

Rnds 7-13: K21.

Rnd 14: (K1, k2tog, k1, k2tog, k1) around.

Rnd 15: K15.

Rnd 16: (K1, k2tog, k2) around.

Rnd 17: K12.

Rnd 18: (K1, k2tog, k1) around.

Fill the hand with wool. Fill the arm with wool every now and then as you work up the arm.

Rnds 19-40: K9 (total of 22 rnds).

Rnd 41: BO 2 knitwise, k5 (including last st of bind-off), BO 2 knitwise.

Place the sts from the arm on a holder and make another arm the same way.

JOIN THE BODY AND ARMS
Rnd 1: Divide the sts onto 4 dpn as follows:

> Back: K8.
> Left arm: K5.
> Front: K8.
> Right arm: K5.

Rnd 2: Back: K1, k2tog, k2, k2tog, k1.
> Left arm: K5.
> Front: K1, k2tog, k2, k2tog, k1.
> Right arm: K5.

Rnd 3: Knit.
Rnd 4: Back: K2, k2tog, k2.
> Left arm: K5.
> Front: K2, k2tog, k2.
> Right arm: K5.

Rnd 5: Knit.
Rnd 6: (K1, k2tog, k2) around.
Rnd 7: Knit.
Rnd 8: (K1, k2tog, k1) around.

Seam the underarms and fill the arms and body with wool.

Rnds 9–12: Knit.

BEGIN HEAD
Rnd 13: (K1, inc 1, k1, inc 1, k1) around.
Rnd 14: K20.
Rnd 15: (K1, inc 1, k3, inc 1, k1) around.
Rnd 16: K28.
Rnd 17: (K1, inc 1, k5, inc 1 k1) around.
Rnd 18: K36.

MAKE THE OPENING FOR THE SNOUT
Place the sts on Ndl 3 on a waste yarn holder while you work the next 9 rows over Ndls 1, 2, and 4.
Row 19: K across Ndls 1 and 2.
Row 20: Purl across Ndls 2, 1, and 4.
Row 21: Knit across Ndls 4, 1, and 2.
Row 22: Purl across Ndls 2, 1, and 4.
Row 23: Knit across Ndls 4, 1, and 2.
Row 24: Purl across Ndls 2, 1, and 4.
Row 25: Knit across Ndls 4, 1, and 2.
Row 26: Purl across Ndls 2, 1, and 4.
Row 27: Knit across Ndls 4, 1, and 2.

CO 9 sts onto a new dpn, over the ones on a holder from Ndl 3. Knit around all 4 dpn.

The opening for the snout is now complete.

Continue working in the round over all 4 dpn.

Rnd 28: K36.
Rnd 29: (K1, k2tog, k3, k2tog, k1) around.
Rnd 30: K28.
Rnd 31: (K1, k2tog, k1, k2tog, k1) around.
Rnd 32: K20.
Rnd 33: (K1, k2tog, k2) around.
Rnd 34: K16.
Rnd 35: (K1, k2tog, k1) around.
Rnd 36: K12.

Cut yarn and draw through remaining 12 sts.

Seam the opening and weave in end on WS.

MAKE THE SNOUT
Pick up and knit 9 sts on each of the sides and over the hole for the snout; divide the sts over 4 dpn.
Rnds 1–3: K36.
Rnd 4: (K1, k2tog, k3, k2tog, k1) around.
Rnds 5–7: K28.
Rnd 8: (K1, k2tog, k1, k2tog, k1) around.
Rnds 9–11: K20.
Rnd 12: (K1, k2tog, k2) around.
Rnds 13–15: K16.
Rnd 16: (K1, k2tog, k1) around.
Change to Pink.
Rnds 17–19: K12.

Cut yarn and draw through remaining 12 sts.

Fill with wool and seam the opening on the snout.

Weave in ends.

EARS FOR THE GARDEN MOUSE
Make 2 triangles with Gray and 2 triangles with Pink as follows:

With U.S. size 1.5 / 2.5 mm needles, CO 10 sts.

Row 1: Purl.

Row 2: Knit.

Row 3: Purl.

Row 4: Knit.

Row 5: Purl.

Row 6: K1, k2tog, k4, k2tog, k1.

Row 7: Purl.

Row 8: Knit.

Row 9: Purl.

Row 10: K1, k2tog, k2, k2tog, k1.

Row 11: Purl.

Row 12: K1, k2tog, k2tog, k1.

Row 13: P4.

Row 14: K1, k2tog, k1.

BO purlwise.

Place a pink triangle with WS facing WS against a gray triangle and crochet them together with sc / UK dc on the long sides, using gray yarn on the pink side.

Crochet to join the other ear the same way. Use your index finger to curve each ear and sew ears to the head.

With Black, embroider eyes on each side of head (see photo, page 215).

Tail

With 2 dpn U.S. size 1.5 / 2.5 mm, CO 4 sts; join to work in the round. Work around in St st until tail is desired length—the tail on our mouse is 8 in / 20 cm long.

BO and sew the tail to the center back of the body, about ⅝ in / 1.5 cm from the crotch seam. Weave in the yarn tail at the end of the mouse tail.

LARGE MAGNUS ON A PIG ORNAMENT

CHRISTMAS BALL
LEVEL OF DIFFICULTY
Advanced

MATERIALS
Yarn:
CYCA #6 (super bulky) Schachenmayr Merino
Extrafine 40 (100% wool, 43 yd/39 m / 50 g)
Yarn Colors and Amounts
Red 00331, 50 g
White 00302, 100 g
Other Materials: clean wool roving for filling
Needles: U.S. size 8 / 5 mm: set of 5 dpn

MAGNUS
LEVEL OF DIFFICULTY
Intermediate

MATERIALS
Yarn:
CYCA #3 (DK/light worsted) Schachenmayr Merino
Extrafine 120 (100% wool, 131 yd/120 m / 50 g)
Yarn Colors and Amounts:
Violet 00147, 50 g
Gray 00192, 50 g
Pink 00136, 50 g
Small amount of Black 00199 for eyes
Other Materials: clean wool
roving for filling
Needles: U.S. size 1.5 /
2.5 mm: set of 5 dpn

SWEATER
LEVEL OF DIFFICULTY
Intermediate

MATERIALS
Yarn: CYCA #3 (DK/light
worsted) Schachenmayr
Merino Extrafine 120 (100%
wool, 131 yd/120 m / 50 g)
Yarn Colors and Amounts:
Color 1: Burgundy 00132, 50 g
Color 2: White 00101, 50 g
Needles: U.S. sizes sizes 1.5 and
2.5 / 2.5 and 3 mm

CHRISTMAS BALL
LEVEL OF DIFFICULTY
Intermediate

MATERIALS
Yarn:
CYCA #6 (super bulky) Schachen-
mayr Merino Extrafine 40 (100%
wool, 43 yd/39 m / 50 g)
Yarn Colors and Amounts
Red 00331, 50 g
White 00302, 100 g

Other Materials: clean wool roving
for filling
Needles: U.S. size 8 / 5 mm: set of
5 dpn

MAGNUS
LEVEL OF DIFFICULTY
Intermediate

MATERIALS
Yarn:
CYCA #3 (DK/light worsted)
Schachenmayr Merino Extrafine
120 (100% wool, 131 yd/120 m /
50 g)
Yarn Colors and Amounts:

Burgundy 00132, 50 g
Gray 00192, 50 g
Pink 00136, 50 g
Small amount of Black 00199 for
eyes

Other Materials: clean wool roving
for filling
Needles: U.S. size 1.5 / 2.5 mm:
set of 5 dpn

SWEATER
LEVEL OF DIFFICULTY
Intermediate

MATERIALS
Yarn:
CYCA #3 (DK/light worsted)
Schachenmayr Merino Extrafine
120 (100% wool, 131 yd/120 m /
50 g)
Yarn Colors and Amounts:
Color 1: Denim 00154, 50 g
Color 2: Light Blue 00152, 50 g
Needles: U.S. sizes 1.5 and 2.5 /
2.5 and 3 mm

For Basic Patterns, see page 203 for a Christmas Ball, page 221 for the sweater, and page 214 for Magnus.

Sweater for Magnus
Basic Pattern

BODY

With smaller dpn and Color 1, CO 40 sts and divide evenly onto dpn (10 sts on each needle). Join, being careful not to twist cast-on row. Pm for beginning of rnd.

Work 7 rnds in k2, p2 ribbing.

Change to larger dpn and continue in stripe pattern:

Rnd 1: Adding Color 2, knit around, increasing 2 sts evenly spaced around = 42 sts.

Rnds 2-13: Knit following the chart.

Rnd 14: BO 2 knitwise, k17 (including the last st from bind-off), BO 4 knitwise, k17 (including last st from bind-off), BO 2 knitwise = 34 sts rem.

Divide the sts for front and back onto 2 dpn with 17 sts on each needle.

SLEEVES

With smaller dpn and Color 1, CO 20 sts and divide evenly onto 4 dpn (5 sts on each needle).

Work 4 rnds in k2, p2 ribbing.

Change to larger dpn and continue in stripe pattern:

Rnd 1: Knit, increasing 1 st = 21 sts.

Rnds 2-13: Knit following the chart.

Rnd 14: BO 2 knitwise, k17 (including last st from bind-off), BO 2 knitwise = 17 sts rem.

Place sts on a holder and make the other sleeve the same way.

JOIN BODY AND SLEEVES

Divide the 68 sts onto 4 dpn (= 17 sts per needle), arranging body and sleeves; pm at each intersection of body and sleeve; slip markers as you come to them.

Rnd 1: K68.

Rnd 2: Work (k1, k2tog, k11, k2tog, k1) around = 8 sts decreased, 60 sts rem.

Rnd 3: K60.

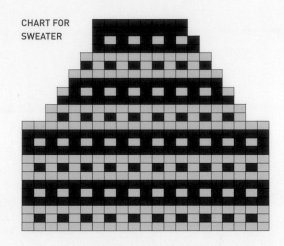

CHART FOR SWEATER

For the body, repeat the chart twice around; for sleeves, work across chart once.

Rnd 4: Work (k1, k2tog, k9, k2tog, k1) around = 52 sts rem.

Rnd 5: K52.

Rnd 6: Work (k1, k2tog, k7, k2tog, k1) around = 44 sts rem.

Rnd 7: K44.

Rnd 8: Work (k1, k2tog, k5, k2tog, k1) around = 36 sts rem.

Rnd 9: K36.

Rnd 10: (K1, k2tog, k6) around = 32 sts rem.

Rnd 11: K32.

Divide the remaining 32 sts onto 4 smaller dpn (8 sts on each needle). With Color 1, work 6 rnds of k2, p2 ribbing. BO in ribbing.

Seam the underarms and weave in all ends neatly on WS.

Gently steam press the sweater on the St st areas (do not press ribbing).

SWEATER
LEVEL OF DIFFICULTY
Intermediate

MATERIALS
Yarn:
CYCA #3 (DK/light worsted) Schachen-
mayr Merino Extrafine 120 (100% wool,
131 yd/120 m / 50 g)
Yarn Colors and Amounts:
Color 1: Red 00131, 50 g
Color 2: Green 00175, 50 g
Needles: U.S. sizes 1.5 and 2.5 /
2.5 and 3 mm
Gauge: 22 sts and 30 rnds = 4 x 4 in /
10 x 10 cm

LARGE MAGNUS ON A CHRISTMAS BALL

MATERIALS
Yarn:
CYCA #3 (DK/light worsted) Schachenmayr
Merino Extrafine 120 (100% wool, 131 yd/
120 m / 50 g)
Needles: U.S. Size 0 / 2 mm

Follow the Basic Pattern for Magnus but
choose a color you like for the legs, which will
shift to gray on the 10th round of the body.
The recommended gauge of 28 sts and 36 rnds
in 4 x 4 in / 10 x 10 cm with recommended
needles U. S. sizes 2.5-4 / 3-3.5 mm is too
loose for the mouse, so we went down to U.S.
size 0 / 2 mm, knitting at a gauge of 35 sts in 4
in / 10 cm.
The most important factor to remember about
the gauge is that for a project like this, the
point isn't the exact number of stitches in 4 in /
10 cm, but rather to make sure the fabric is
tight enough that the filling won't show through
once Magnus has been knitted and filled.

MAGNUS
LEVEL OF DIFFICULTY
Intermediate

MATERIALS
Yarn:
CYCA #1 (fingering), Schachenmayr
Merino Extrafine 170 (100% Merino wool,
185 yd/169 m / 50 g)
Yarn Colors and Amounts:
Legs: Royal Blue 00051, 50 g
Arms, Body, Tail, and Head:
Gray 00090, 50 g
Ears and Snout: Pink 00035, small
amount
Eyes: Black, small amount
Needles: U.S. size 0 / 2 mm: sets of 5 dpn

SWEATER
LEVEL OF DIFFICULTY
Intermediate

MATERIALS
Yarn:
CYCA #3 (DK/light worsted) Schachen-
mayr Merino Extrafine 120 (100% wool,
131 yd/120 m / 50 g)
Yarn Colors and Amounts:
Color 1: Chocolate 00111, 50 g
Color 2: Light Blue 00152, 50 g
Needles: U.S. sizes 2.5 and
4 / 3 and 3.5 mm: sets of 5 dpn

CHRISTMAS BALL
LEVEL OF DIFFICULTY
Intermediate

MATERIALS
Yarn:
CYCA #4 (worsted, Afghan, Aran),
Schachenmayr Merino Extrafine 85
(100% Merino wool, 93 yd/85 m / 50 g)
Yarn Colors and Amount:
Red 00231, 50 g
White 00201, 50 g
Needles: U.S. sizes 7 and 8 /
4.5 and 5 mm: sets of 5 dpn

Sweater for Little Magnus
Basic Pattern

BODY

With Color 1 and smaller dpn, CO 32 sts. Divide sts evenly onto 4 dpn. Join and pm for beginning of rnd. Work 5 rnds k2, p2 ribbing.

Change to larger dpn and work following the chart. On the first rnd, increase as follows (see page 259 for increase method):

Rnd 1: (K1, inc 1, k15) 2 times.

Rnds 2-9: K34 following the chart.

Rnd 10: BO 2 sts, k13 (including last st of bind-off), BO 4 sts, k13 (including last st of bind-off), B) 2 sts. Divide sts for body onto 2 dpn: 13 sts each for front and back.

SLEEVES

With Color 1 and smaller dpn, CO 16 sts. Divide sts evenly onto 4 dpn. Join and pm for beginning of rnd. Work 5 rnds k2, p2 ribbing.

Rnd 1: Inc 1: K1, inc 1, k15.

Rnds 2-9: K17 following the chart.

Rnd 10: BO 2 sts, k13, BO 2 sts. Place sleeve sts on 1 dpn = 13 sts. Make the second sleeve the same way.

JOIN THE BODY AND SLEEVES

Divide the 52 sts onto 4 dpn (= 13 sts per needle), arranging body and sleeves; pm at each intersection of body and sleeve; slip markers as you come to them.

Rnd 1: K52.

Rnd 2: Work (K1, k2tog, k7, k2tog, k1) around = 44 sts rem.

Rnd 3: K44.

Rnd 4: Work (K1, k2tog, k5, k2tog, k1) around = 36 sts rem.

Rnd 5: K36.

Rnd 6: Work (K1, k2tog, k3, k2tog, k1) around = 28 sts rem.

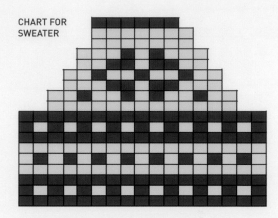

CHART FOR SWEATER

For the body, repeat the chart twice around; for sleeves work across chart once.

Rnd 7: K28.

Rnd 8: Work (K1, k2tog, k4) around = 24 sts rem.

Divide the remaining 24 sts onto 4 smaller dpn (6 sts on each needle). With Color 1, work 15 rnds of k2, p2 ribbing. BO loosely in ribbing. Seam the underarms and weave in all ends neatly on WS.

Gently steam press the sweater on the St st areas (do not press ribbing).

LEVEL OF DIFFICULTY

Intermediate

MATERIALS

CYCA #3 (DK/light worsted) Schachenmayr Merino Extrafine 120 (100% wool, 131 yd/120 m / 50 g)

Needles: U.S. sizes 1.5 and 2.5 / 2.5 and 3 mm: sets of 5 dpn

Gauge: 22 sts = 4 in / 10 cm

★ *Christmas Pig* ★

★ *Peppermint Pig* ★

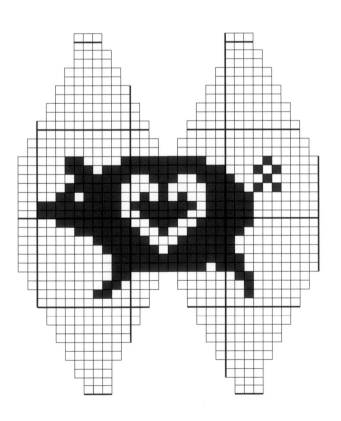

Squirrel

This Christmas ball has rather large blocks of color, so you should twist the yarns around each other frequently to prevent long floats that could draw the ball in and make it lumpy.

MAGNUS

MATERIALS

Yarn:

CYCA #1 (fingering), Schachenmayr Merino Extrafine 170 (100% Merino wool, 185 yd/169 m / 50 g)

Yarn Colors and Amounts:

Legs: Red 00035, 50 g

Arms, Body, Tail, and Head: Gray 00090, 50 g

Ears and Snout: Pink 00035, small amount

Eyes: small amount Black

Needles: U.S. size 0 / 2 mm: sets of 5 dpn

SWEATER

MATERIALS

CYCA #3 (DK/light worsted) Schachenmayr Merino Extrafine 120 (100% wool, 131 yd/120 m / 50 g)

Yarn Colors and Amounts:

Color 1: Green 00172, 50 g

Color 2: Blue 00165, 50 g

Needles: U.S. sizes 1.5 and 2.5 / 2.5 and 3 mm: sets of 5 dpn

CHRISTMAS BALL

MATERIALS

Yarn:

CYCA #4 (worsted, Afghan, Aran), Schachenmayr Merino Extrafine 85 (100% Merino wool, 93 yd/ 85 m / 50 g)

Yarn Colors and Amount:

Gray 00090, 50 g

Red 00231, 50 g

Needles: U.S. sizes 7 and 8 / 4.5 and 5 mm: sets of 5 dpn

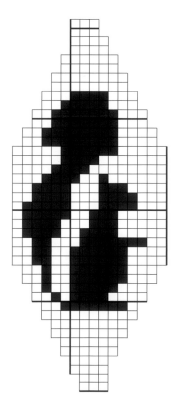

MAGNUS

MATERIALS

Yarn:

CYCA #1 (fingering), Schachenmayr Merino Extrafine 170 (100% Merino wool, 185 yd/ 169 m / 50 g)

Yarn Colors and Amounts:

Legs: Green 00074, 50 g

Arms, Body, Tail, and Head: Gray 00090, 50 g

Ears and Snout: Pink 00035, small amount

Eyes: Black, small amount

Needles: U.S. size 0 / 2 mm: sets of 5 dpn

SWEATER

MATERIALS

Yarn:

CYCA #3 (DK/light worsted) Schachenmayr Merino Extrafine 120 (100% wool, 131 yd/ 120 m / 50 g)

Yarn Colors and Amounts:

Color 1: Purple 00147, 50 g

Color 2: White 00102, 50 g

Needles: U.S. sizes 1.5 and 2.5 / 2.5 and 3 mm: sets of 5 dpn

CHRISTMAS BALL

MATERIALS

Yarn:

CYCA #4 (worsted, Afghan, Aran), Schachenmayr Merino Extrafine 85 (100% Merino wool, 93 yd/85 m / 50 g)

Yarn Colors and Amounts:

Red 00231, 50 g

White 00201, 50 g

Needles: U.S. sizes 7 and 8 / 4.5 and 5 mm: sets of 5 dpn

★ *Dancing Around the Tree* ★

This traditional panel for dancing couples goes around our tree at Christmas.

There are many ways to attach a mouse to a Christmas ball!

This mouse is struggling to hold onto the ball.

MAGNUS

MATERIALS

Yarn: CYCA #1 (fingering), Schachenmayr Merino Extrafine 170 (100% Merino wool, 185 yd/169 m / 50 g)

Yarn Colors and Amounts:

Legs: Burgundy 00033, 50 g

Arms, Body, Tail, and Head: Gray 00090, 50 g

Ears and Snout: Pink 00035, small amount

Eyes: small amount Black

Needles: U.S. size 0 / 2 mm: sets of 5 dpn

SWEATER

MATERIALS

CYCA #3 (DK/light worsted) Schachenmayr Merino Extrafine 120 (100% wool, 131 yd/120 m / 50 g)

Yarn Colors and Amounts:

Color 1: Red 00131, 50 g

Color 2: Lime-Green 00175, 50 g

Needles: U.S. sizes 1.5 and 2.5 / 2.5 and 3 mm: sets of 5 dpn

CHRISTMAS BALL

MATERIALS

Yarn:

CYCA #4 (worsted, Afghan, Aran), Schachenmayr Merino Extrafine 85 (100% Merino wool, 93 yd/85 m / 50 g)

Yarn Colors and Amount:

Blue 00251, 50 g

White 00201, 50 g

Needles: U.S. sizes 7 and 8 / 4.5 and 5 mm: sets of 5 dpn

This little
Christmas tree,
only 23½ in /
60 cm high, is
decorated with
6 miniature
Christmas balls.

Miniature Christmas Balls

A few years ago, we received an inquiry from Japan asking whether we could design some smaller Christmas balls for Japanese knitters. They wanted small Christmas balls for their small Christmas trees in their small Japanese apartments. We downsized the balls and knitted 24 new ones. Most of the motifs we used were taken from the larger balls, but we also designed a few new motifs. Later, the smaller Christmas balls also landed in Europe and the United States as part of our work with Schachenmayr. We have plans to knit more Christmas balls, so you can expect even more Christmas ball designs in the coming years!

Rnd 1: The bottom row of 3 squares on all charts: With dpn, CO 12 sts. Divide the sts onto 4 dpn, with 3 sts per needle.

Rnd 2: K12.

Rnd 3: (K2, inc 1, k1) around. (See page 259 for increase method.)

Rnd 4: K16.

Rnd 5: (K1, inc 1, k2, inc 1, k1) around.

Rnd 6: K24.

Rnd 7: (K1, inc 1, k4, inc 1, k1) around.

Rnd 8: K32.

Rnd 9: (K1, inc 1, k6, inc 1, k1) around.

Rnd 10: K40.

Rnd 11: (K1, inc 1, k8, inc 1, k1) around.

Rnds 12-21: K48.

Rnd 22: (K1, k2tog, k6, k2tog, k1) around.

Rnd 23: K40.

Rnd 24: (K1, k2tog, k4, k2tog, k1) around.

Rnd 25: K32.

Rnd 26: (K1, k2tog, k2, k2tog, k1) around.

Rnd 27: K24.

Rnd 28: (K1, k2tog, k2tog, k1) around.

Rnd 29: K16.

Rnd 30: (K1, k2tog, k1) around.

Rnd 31: K12 (the 3 squares at top of chart).

Cut yarn, leaving an end of about 8 in / 20 cm. Draw end through rem 12 sts but do not tighten. Fill ball as for Easter eggs (see page 55).

If you want even smaller balls, you can knit with CYCA #1 (fingering), Schachenmayr Merino Extrafine 170 (100% Merino wool, 185 yd/169 m / 50 g) and needles U.S. size 0 / 2 mm: set of 5 dpn for a gauge of 28 sts in 4 in / 10 cm.

LEVEL OF DIFFICULTY
Advanced

MATERIALS FOR MINIATURE CHRISTMAS BALLS
Yarn:
CYCA #3 (DK/light worsted) Schachenmayr Merino Extrafine 120 (100% wool, 131 yd/120 m / 50 g)
Yarn Colors and Amounts:
Red 00131, 50 g
White 00102, 50 g
Other Materials: ¾ oz / 20 g clean wool roving for filling
Needles: U.S. size 2.5 / 3 mm: set of 5 dpn
Gauge: 22 sts = 4 in / 10 cm.
The balls we made are 2½ in / 6 cm high and the cord is 2¾ in / 7 cm long when attached to the ball.

Knitting Tips

The most important factor to remember about the gauge is that it's not a matter of exactly the right number of stitches in 4 in / 10 cm, but rather of making the fabric tight enough that the filling won't show through once the ornament has been knitted and filled.

★ *Christmas Basket* ★

★ *Halling Panel* ★

This motif was inspired by the old plaited Christmas baskets that one, in theory, filled with sweets and hung on the tree. In reality, the sweets never got that far.

In our book *55 Christmas Balls to Knit*, we had one Christmas ball with a similar panel. It was called the Halling Panel. On the original ball, the panel was halved, but we feature the whole motif here.

★ Eight-Petal Panel ★

★ Selbu ★

For this Christmas ball, the eight-petaled roses peek out from the red sections at the top and bottom of the ball. This will look like two different designs depending on which color you focus on.

A smaller version of the Selbu ball from our book, *55 Christmas Balls to Knit*. It's a classic design that is often used for panels on mittens, hats, and garments.

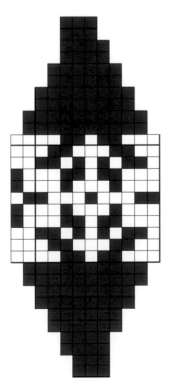

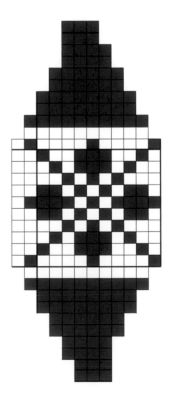

Acanthus

Doodling inspired by acanthus featured on wood carvings and rosemaling.

Christmas Gift

A little present under the tree. Everyone knows the smallest gifts are the best, and should be opened last!

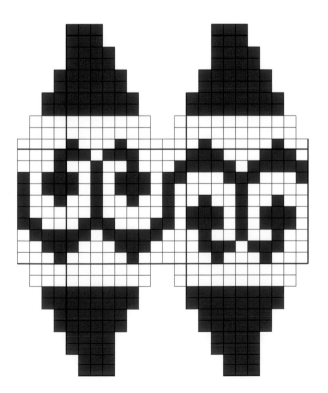

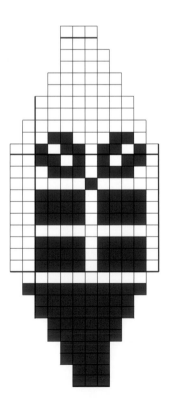

The bullfinch is knitted in three colors following the basic pattern. There's no stranded patterning and no embroidery. We decided to make this bird as easy as possible. With the single-color head, it can look out in any direction no matter where you place the beak and eyes.

LEVEL OF DIFFICULTY
Intermediate

MATERIALS
Yarn: CYCA #3 (DK weight) Schachenmayr Merino Extrafine 120 DK, 100% wool (131 yd/120 m / 50 g)
Yarn Colors and Amounts:
Black 00199, 50 g
White 00102, 50 g
Red 00131, 50 g
Needles: U.S. size 0-2.5 / 2-3 mm: set of 5 dpn
Crochet Hook: U.S. size C-2 / 2.5 mm
Gauge: 30 sts and 40 rnds in 4 x 4 in / 10 x 10 cm. Adjust needle size to obtain correct gauge if necessary.

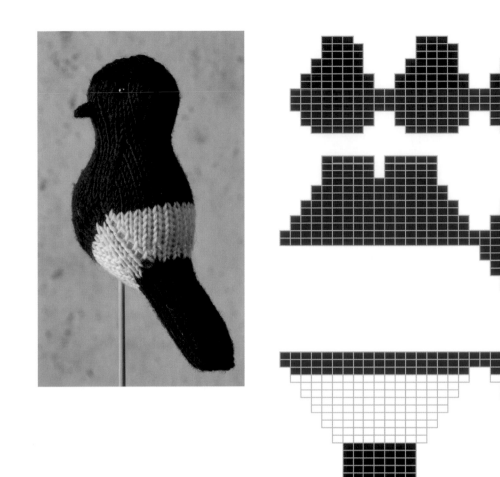

Bullfinch

Pyrrhula Pyrrhula

With Black, CO 14 sts and divide onto 4 dpn: 4 + 3 + 4 + 3. Join to work in the round.

Work following the Basic Pattern on page 62 and the chart on this page.

Flatten the tail and sew the end at the cast-on row, making sure that the top and bottom sides are correctly oriented. Stretch the body well and tighten any stitches that are too loose. Birds without any stranded patterning are more flexible than those knitted in pattern, so you can shape them as you like when you fill them.
Block by gently steam pressing under a damp pressing cloth. Fill the bird and sew the hole at top of head to close.
Crochet the beak and sew on the eyes. This bird has a black beak and dark gray eyes.

MATERIALS
Yarn:
CYCA #3 (DK weight) Schachenmayr Merino Extrafine
120 DK, 100% wool (131 yd/120 m / 50 g)
Yarn Colors and Amounts:
Red 00131, 50 g
Gray 00192, 50 g
Burgundy 00133, 50 g
Black 00199, 50 g
Needles: U.S. size 0-2.5 / 2-3 mm: set of 5 dpn
Crochet Hook: U.S. size C-2 / 2.5 mm
Gauge: 30 sts and 40 rnds in 4 x 4 in / 10 x 10 cm.
Adjust needle size to obtain correct gauge if necessary.

Redtail

Phoenicurus Phoenicurus

With Red, CO 14 sts and divide onto 4 dpn: 4 + 3 + 4 + 3. Join to work in the round.

TAIL
Knit 21 rnds.
Continue with the body following the Basic Pattern on page 62 and the chart on this page.

Cut yarn and draw end through rem 12 sts.
Flatten the tail and sew the end at the cast-on row, making sure that the top and bottom sides are correctly oriented. Stretch the body well and tighten any stitches that are too loose.
Block by gently steam pressing under a damp pressing cloth. Fill the bird and sew the hole at top of head to close.
Crochet the beak and sew on the eyes. This bird has a gray beak and blue eyes.

See chart for the embroidery.

Use duplicate stitch to embroider the Burgundy on the back and Black to outline the wings. The bird has blue eyes and a gray crocheted beak.

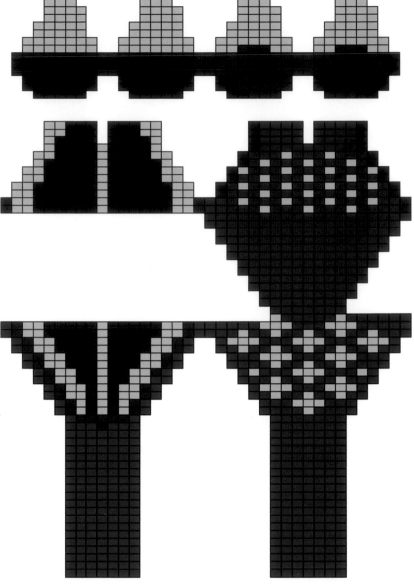

Christmas Stockings

These slippers feature a Christmas tree with ornaments embroidered on with red duplicate stitch, while the presents have white embroidery.

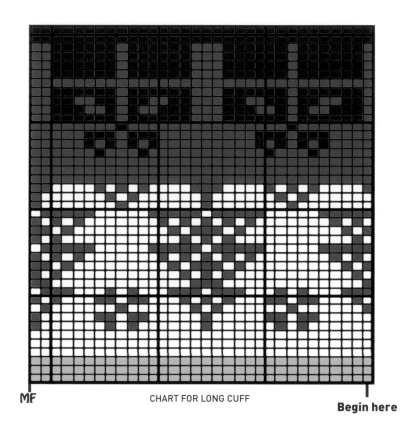

MF   CHART FOR LONG CUFF   **Begin here**

LEVEL OF DIFFICULTY
Advanced

MATERIALS
Yarn:
CYCA #4 (worsted, afghan, aran),
Rauma Vamsegarn (100% wool,
91 yd/83 m / 50 g)

Yarn Colors and Amounts:
Dark Brown Heather V64,
150-200 g
Warm Yellow V25, 50 g
White V01, 50 g
Dark Green V34, 50 g
Needles: U.S. size 8-10 / 5-6 mm:
circular and set of 5 dpn
Recommended Gauge: 14-16 sts =
4 in / 10 cm

NOTES:
All sizes begin with the same
stitch count so the cuff will be
large enough for you to get the
slippers on your feet after felting.
Alternate two strands of yarn on
every stitch throughout (as for
two-end or Fair Isle knitting).

With one strand of Yellow and circular, CO 64 sts; join, being careful not to twist cast-on row. Join second strand of Yellow and knit around following chart on page 243 (chart Row 1 = cast-on row) until 2 rnds remain. Alternate 2 strands of the same color on single-color rnds. If there is a long float between colors, twist the colors around each other every 3 or 4 sts.

On second-to-last rnd, knit, alternating the 2 strands of Brown. On last rnd, decrease evenly spaced around as follows:

Size S: decrease 8 sts = 56 sts rem
Size M: decrease 4 sts = 60 sts rem
Size L: decrease 0 sts = 64 sts rem

HEEL

Continue working with two strands of Brown as follows:

Row 1: K14 (15, 16), knitting last st with both strands; turn.
Row 2: Sl 1, p27 (29, 31), purling last st with both strands; turn.

Work another 11 rows back and forth in St st over the 28 (30, 32) heel sts, always slipping the first st.

Heel Turn

Row 14: P13 (15, 17), p2tog, p1 with both strands; turn.
Row 15: K3 (5, 7), k2tog, k1 with both strands; turn.
Rows 16-23: Continue the same way, working back and forth in St st and shaping, with 1 more st before the decrease on each row (the decrease joins the sts before/after the gap).
Row 24: P12 (14, 16), p2tog, p1 with both strands; turn.
Row 25: K13 (15, 17), k2tog with both strands; turn. (This row ends with k2tog and not k1 as previously).
Row 26: P13 (15, 17), p2tog, p1 with both strands; turn.

FOOT

Set-up Rnd: Ssk, k6 (7, 8). Pm at center of sole, k7 (8, 9), pick up and knit 7 sts evenly spaced across one side of the heel flap, k28 (30, 32) across instep, pick up and knit 7 sts evenly spaced across other side of heel flap and k7 (8, 9) on sole. The beginning of the rnd is at center of sole.

Foot: Knit 33 (36, 39) rnds on the 56 (60, 64) sts of foot.

Toe Shaping:

Divide the sts onto 4 dpn with 14 (15, 16) sts on each needle. Shape toe as follows, with 8 sts decreased on each decrease rnd.
Rnd 1 (decrease rnd): At beginning of each needle: K1, k2tog. At end of each needle: K2tog, k1.
Rnd 2: Knit.
Repeat Rnds 1-2 until 16 (20, 16) sts rem. Cut yarn and draw end through remaining sts. Pull tight and weave in all ends neatly on WS.

FINISHING

Steam press slippers.
With white and red yarns, follow charts below to embroider the tree decoration and gifts onto slippers.
Steam press embroidery and then felt slippers.

Felt slippers

Use a wool-safe liquid soap. For 2.2 lb / 1 kg knitted fabric, you should use about 6 tablespoons / 100 ml soap. Set the water temperature for the machine at 104-140°F / 40-60°C (the temperature options vary from machine to machine). Start at the lower temperature and check the degree of felting occasionally.

EMBROIDERY CHART FOR CHRISTMAS TREE

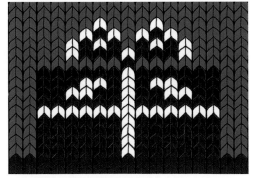

EMBROIDERY CHART FOR GIFTS

Mittens with Åkle Tapestry Motifs

Girls' and Women's Mittens with *Åkle* Motifs

These mittens feature solid-color rhomboids on the back of the hand and a netting pattern on the palm. We sized the mittens for both girls and women. An *åkle* is a woven tapestry, often hung on the walls in old Norwegian homes.

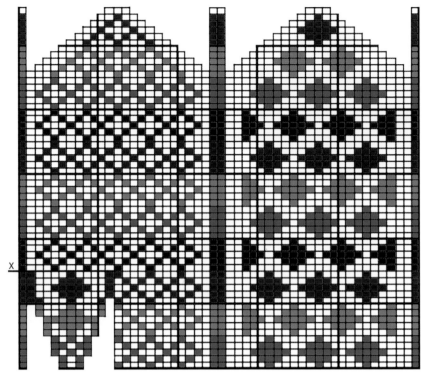

X

GIRLS' MITTEN

WOMEN'S MITTEN

THUMB: GIRLS' MITTEN

THUMB: WOMEN'S MITTEN

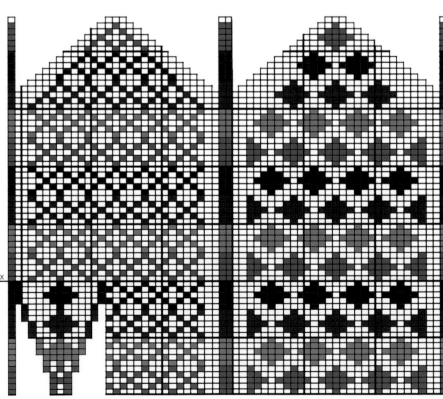

X

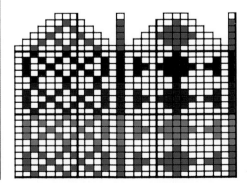

MITTENS

With smaller needles and Color 1, CO 42 (52) sts; divide sts as evenly as possible over 4 dpn. Join, being careful not to twist cast-on row. Work around in k1, p1 rib for 2½ in / 6 cm.

Change to larger dpn and work in pattern following the chart. Increase for the thumb gusset as indicated on the chart. Increase with M1R before and M1L after the center set of sts for thumb gusset. When you reach the row marked with X at the left side of the chart, place the 11 (13) thumb sts on a holder. CO 11 (13) sts over the gap = 50 (62) sts.

Now divide the sts with 12 (16) sts each on Ndls 1 and 3 and 13 (15) sts each on Ndls 2 and 4. Continue, following the chart. Shape the top with decreases on each side of the 2-st bands at sides of hand.

Top Shaping: At the beginning of Ndls 1 and 3: Ssk (or sl 1, k1, psso); knit to end of needle. At the end of Ndls 2 and 4: K2tog.
End by cutting yarn and drawing through remaining 10 sts; tighten.

THUMB

Slip sts on holder to larger dpn; knit across in pattern and then pick up and knit 11 (13) sts above thumbhole + 1 st at each side = 24 (28) sts total. Work in pattern following the thumb chart. Shape top of thumb as shown on chart. End by cutting yarn and drawing through remaining 8 sts; tighten. Weave in all ends neatly on WS.

Make the other mitten the same way, placing thumb on opposite side of palm.

FINISHING

Weave in all ends neatly on WS. Gently steam press mittens, except for ribbing, under a damp pressing cloth.

LEVEL OF DIFFICULTY
Advanced

SIZES: Girl's (Women's)

FINISHED MEASUREMENTS:
Total length 9¾ (11½) in / 25 (29) cm; circumference 8 (9½) in / 20 (24) cm

MATERIALS
Yarn:
CYCA # 2 (sport /baby), Rauma PT5, 80% wool, 20% nylon (140 yd/128 m / 50 g)
Yarn Colors and Amounts:
Color 1: White 503, 50 g
Color 2: Green 588, 50 g
Color 3: Blue 571, 50 g
Color 4: Purple 562, 50 g
Color 5: Red 543, 50 g
Needles: U.S. sizes 2.5 and 4 / 3 and 3.5 mm: sets of 5 dpn
Gauge: 25 sts and 30 rnds in St st on larger needles = 4 x 4 in / 10 x 10 cm.
Adjust needle sizes to obtain correct gauge if necessary.

Draft Stopper

A draft stopper modeled on those found in Paris.
This one is knitted with five colors.

LEVEL OF DIFFICULTY
Advanced

FINISHED MEASUREMENTS
8¾ in / 22 cm wide x 37 in / 94 cm long. Work the
panels as many times as needed for the draft
stopper to be the right length for your window or door.

MATERIALS
Yarn:
CYCA #4 (worsted/afghan/aran), Rauma Vamsegarn
(100% wool, 91 yd/83 m / 50 g)
Yarn Colors and Amounts:
Color 1: Mustard V63, 100 g
Color 2: Brown V64, 100 g
Color 3: Red V23, 50 g
Color 4: Light Blue V50, 50 g
Color 5: White V01, 50 g
Needles: U.S. size 8 / 5 mm: 16 in / 40 cm circular
Other Materials: Fiber Fill from Coats
Gauge: 19 sts and 23 rnds = 4 x 4 in / 10 x 10 cm.
Adjust needle size to obtain correct gauge if necessary.

NOTE: The pattern repeat at each end of the draft stopper
measures approx. 14¼ in / 36 cm. Measure your gauge and
the space where the draft stopper will be used and then use
that length to determine the number of pattern repeats
needed. Work the lice in the center until the draft stopper is
long enough. The first row of the lice pattern at the bottom of
the chart = cast-on row.

DRAFT STOPPER

With short circular and Color 1, CO 72 sts; join, being careful not to twist cast-on row. Pm for beginning of round. Work around following the chart.
NOTE: The first row of the chart = cast-on row.

Continue in lice pattern to desired length (see Note above) and then work chart from the top down until 1 row remains. BO with Color 1.

FINISHING

Weave in all ends neatly on WS. Gently steam press under a damp pressing cloth. Join seam at one end.
Make a pillow form to fit the cover or stuff the draft stopper with fiber fill. Seam other opening.

The bright colors of these slippers should put you in a good mood, so save them to wear on cold gray days!

LEVEL OF DIFFICULTY
Intermediate

MATERIALS
Yarn: CYCA #4 (worsted, afghan, aran), Rauma Vamsegarn
(100% wool, 91 yd/83 m / 50 g)
Yarn Colors and Amounts:
Brown V64, 50-100 g
Warm Yellow V25, 50 g
Bright Pink V56, 50 g
Needles: U.S. size 8-10 / 5-6 mm: circular and set of 5 dpn
Recommended Gauge: 14-16 sts = 4 in / 10 cm

FELT SLIPPERS
Use a wool-safe liquid soap. For 2.2 lb / 1 kg knitted fabric, you should use about 6 tablespoons / 100 ml soap. Set the water temperature for the machine at 104-140°F / 40-60°C (the temperature options vary from machine to machine). Start at the lower temperature and check the degree of felting occasionally.

Chevron Pattern Slippers

These slippers were inspired by the bands used to decorate Sami costumes.

NOTES:

If there are more than 4 sts between color changes, twist the yarns around each other every 3 to 4 stitches to avoid long floats.
Alternate two strands of yarn on every stitch throughout (as for two-end or Fair Isle knitting).

With one strand of Yellow and circular, CO 55 (59, 63) sts. Join, being careful not to twist cast-on row; pm for beginning of rnd. Join second strand of Yellow and work following the chart (the first row of the chart = cast-on row), alternating two strands of yarn on each stitch. On last rnd from chart, increase 1 st at end of rnd = 56 (60, 64) sts
Continue with two strands of Brown, working heel as follows:

HEEL

Row 1: K14 (15, 16), knitting last st with both strands; turn.
Row 2: Sl 1, p27 (29, 31), purling last st with both strands; turn.
Work another 11 rows back and forth in St st over the 28 (30, 32) heel sts, always slipping the first st.

Heel Turn

Row 14: P13 (15, 17), p2tog, p1 with both strands; turn.
Row 15: K3 (5, 7), k2tog, k1 with both strands; turn.
Rows 16-23: Continue the same way, working back and forth in St st and shaping, with 1 more st before the decrease on each row (the decrease joins the sts before/after the gap).
Row 24: P12 (14, 16), p2tog, p1 with both strands; turn.
Row 25: K13 (15, 17), k2tog with both strands; turn. (This row ends with k2tog and not k1 as previously).
Row 26: P13 (15, 17), p2tog, p1 with both strands; turn.

FOOT

Set-up Rnd, with Brown: Ssk, k6 (7, 8). Pm at center of sole, k7 (8, 9), pick up and knit 7 sts evenly spaced across one side of the heel flap, k28 (30, 32) across instep, pick up and knit 7 sts evenly spaced across other side of heel flap and k7 (8, 9) on sole. The beginning of the rnd is at center of sole.
Foot: Working in charted pattern for foot, knit 33 (36, 39) rnds on the 56 (60, 64) sts of foot.

Toe Shaping

Divide the sts onto 4 dpn with 14 (15, 16) sts on each needle. With Bright Pink only, shape toe as follows, with 8 sts decreased on each decrease rnd.
Rnd 1 (decrease rnd): At beginning of each needle: K1, k2tog. At end of each needle: K2tog, k1.
Rnd 2: Knit.
Repeat Rnds 1-2 until 16 (20, 16) sts rem. Cut yarn and draw end through remaining sts. Pull tight and weave in all ends neatly on WS.

FINISHING
Steam press and then felt slippers.

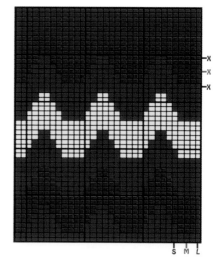

CHART FOR CUFF

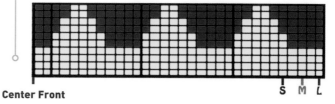

Center Front

Kautokeino Slippers

The pattern for these slippers was inspired by a woven band from 1944, the *skalle* band for men from Kautokeino. The long cuffs of the slippers make them cozy and very warm.

NOTES:

All sizes begin with the same stitch count so the leg will be large enough for you to get the slippers on your feet after felting.

If there are more than 4 sts between color changes, twist the yarns around each other every 3 to 4 stitches to avoid long floats.

Alternate two strands of yarn on every stitch throughout (as for two-end or Fair Isle knitting).

With circular and one strand of Blue, CO 72 sts. Join, being careful not to twist cast-on row; pm for beginning of rnd. Join second strand of Blue and work following the chart until 1 row remains; the first row of chart = cast-on row.

On the last rnd of the charted pattern (the Blue round), decrease evenly spaced around as follows:

Size S: decrease 16 sts to 56 sts total

Size M: decrease 12 sts to 60 sts total

Size L: decrease 8 sts to 64 sts total.

Continue to the heel and heel shaping with Blue, alternating the two strands on every stitch.

HEEL

Row 1: K14 (15, 16), knitting last st with both strands; turn.

Row 2: Sl 1, p27 (29, 31), purling last st with both strands; turn.

Work another 11 rows in St st over the 28 (30, 32) heel sts, always slipping the first st.

Heel Turn

Row 14: P13 (15, 17), p2tog, p1 with both strands; turn.

Row 15: K3 (5, 7), k2tog, k1 with both strands; turn.

Rows 16-23: Continue in St st and shaping, with 1 more st before the decrease on each row (the decrease joins the sts before/after the gap).

Row 24: P12 (14, 16), p2tog, p1 with both strands; turn.

Row 25: K13 (15, 17), k2tog with both strands; turn. (This row ends with k2tog and not k1 as previously).

Row 26: P13 (15, 17), p2tog, p1 with both strands; turn.

FOOT

Set-up Rnd: Ssk, k6 (7, 8). Pm at center of sole, k7 (8, 9), pick up and knit 7 sts evenly spaced across one side of the heel flap, k28 (30, 32) across instep, pick up and knit 7 sts evenly spaced across other side of heel flap and k7 (8, 9) on sole. The beginning of the rnd is at center of sole.

Foot: Knit 33 (36, 39) rnds on the 56 (60, 64) sts of foot.

Toe Shaping

Divide the sts onto 4 dpn with 14 (15, 16) sts on each needle. Shape toe as follows, with 8 sts decreased on each decrease rnd.

Rnd 1 (decrease rnd): At beginning of each needle: K1, k2tog. At end of each needle: K2tog, k1.

Rnd 2: Knit.

Repeat Rnds 1-2 until 16 (20, 16) sts rem. Cut yarn and draw end through remaining sts. Pull tight and weave in all ends neatly on WS. Steam press and then felt slippers.

LEVEL OF DIFFICULTY
Advanced

MATERIALS
Yarn:
CYCA #4 (worsted, afghan, aran), Rauma Vamsegarn
(100% wool, 91 yd/83 m / 50 g)
Yarn Colors and Amounts:
Blue V82, 150 g
Red V24, 50 g
White V00, 50 g
3 balls Blue V82
Needles: U.S. size 8-10 / 5-6 mm: circular and set of
5 dpn
Recommended Gauge: 14-16 sts = 4 in / 10 cm

FELT SLIPPERS
Use a wool-safe liquid soap. For 2.2 lb / 1 kg knitted
fabric, you should use about 6 tablespoons / 100 ml
soap. Set the water temperature for the machine at
104-140°F / 40-60°C (the temperature options vary from
machine to machine). Start at the lower temperature
and check the degree of felting occasionally.

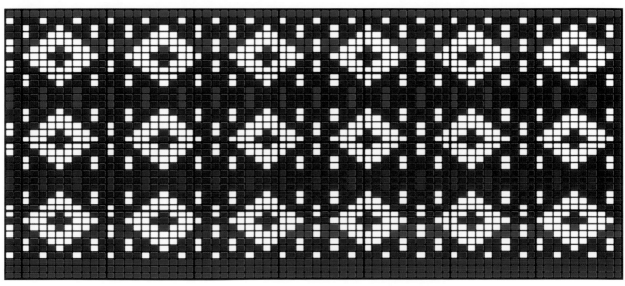

LEVEL OF DIFFICULTY
Advanced

FINISHED MEASUREMENTS
Approx. 4¾ x 4¾ in / 12 x 12 cm after blocking.

MATERIALS
Yarn: CYCA #3 (DK weight/light worsted),
Rauma 3-ply Strikkegarn, 100% wool
(115 yd/105 m / 50 g)
Yarn Colors and Amounts:
Color 1: Red 144, 50 g
Color 2: White 101, 50 g
Needles: U.S. size 4 / 3.5 mm: straight
needles
Gauge: 20 sts and 28 rows = 4 x 4 in /
10 x 10 cm.
Adjust needle size to obtain correct gauge
if necessary.

Coasters with Hearts and Crosses for Christmas

These decorative coasters were inspired by motifs from Setesdal sweaters. Because the coasters are double-knitted, you can choose whichever side best suits your table, the white or the red.

CO 25 sts with each color in double knitting cast-on (see page 256 for basic double knitting instructions). Work back and forth in double knitting following the chart. The first row of the chart = cast-on row.

Before binding off, see instructions on page 257. BO with red on the red side and white on the white side so the colors will match those of the cast-on row.

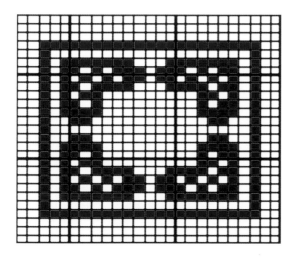

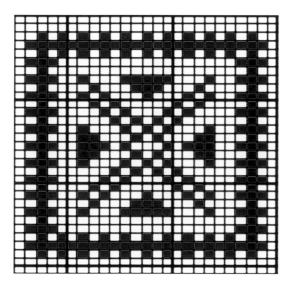

Double Knitting

We have to admit that we have been bewitched by double knitting! Everyone knows that you can easily get hooked by knitting, and this is so much fun that it is difficult to stop.

We learned double knitting by experimentation. Later on we found instructions for how it should be worked, which were a bit different from our method; we didn't think they worked quite as well. So here is how we work double knitting.

CO with alternating colors, 1 white, 1 blue. As you cast on, hold the two strands of each color on the same side of the needle throughout. In this case, the blue yarn is held at the front of the needle while you make each white stitch and vice versa. Begin with a slip knot each of blue and white (photo 2). Make sure there is enough of the loose hanging strand of each color for the number of stitches you need. CO 1 st with white, using long-tail cast-on and

leave strands behind needle. CO 1 st with blue and leave strands in front of needle (photos 3 and 4).

When you turn the work to knit the first row (photo 5), the white strand will be facing you at the front of the work while the blue yarn will be at the back. This means that the blue yarn will be purled and the white yarn knitted.

There's is how to work solid-color double knitting: On the first row, slip the 1st two sts while you hold the strands you are knitting with between the 2 sts (photo 6). Place the blue strand (purl) on your finger (photo 7) and *bring the white towards you, between the sts, to the front of the work and purl

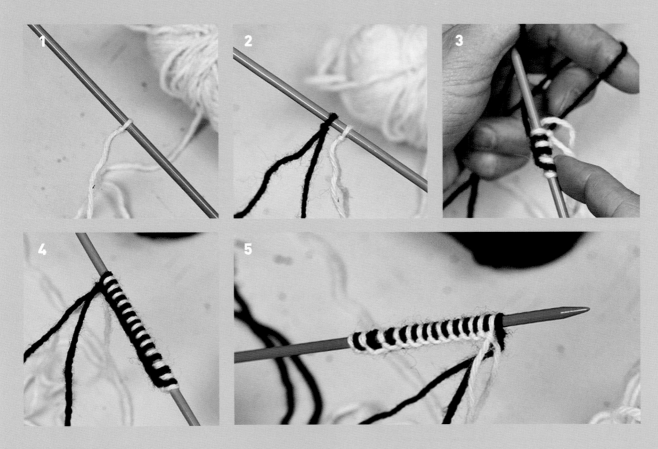

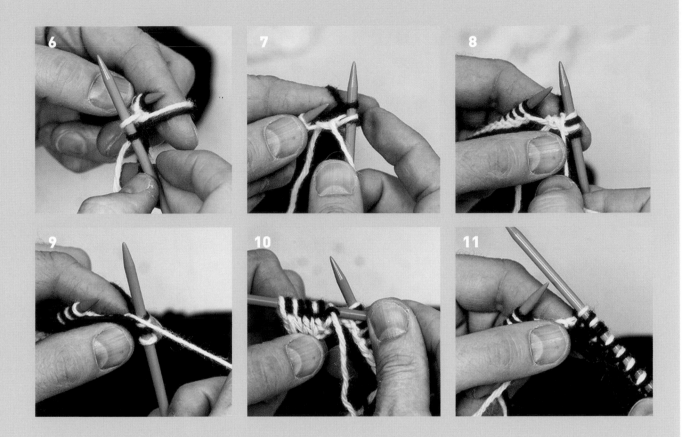

the 1st blue st; take the white yarn to back of work and knit the 1st white st*. Repeat from * to * across. When you come to the end of the row, twist the strands and work back the same way, noting that now the white sts are purled and blue ones knitted.

DOUBLE KNIT PATTERNS

When you work patterns in double knitting, always think in pairs. The knit st is always the opposite color of the purl st. If you want to knit a blue st next to a white knit st and the white sts are on the facing RS and the blue sts on facing WS, change positions of the colors (photos 9–11).

Here's how to double knit a pattern: Place the white yarn on your finger, *bring the blue towards you, between the sts, to front of work, and purl the 1st blue st with white; take blue strand to back of work and knit the 1st white st with blue yarn*. If you cast on without crossing the colors, you will soon notice whether the lower edge was worked with blue or white. Continue working in pattern

following the chart and don't forget that the knit st is always the opposite color of the purl st so that the pattern on one side is the reverse image of that on the other side.

In other descriptions of double knitting, the first two sts are always knitted together with the 2 colors held together. This makes a somewhat sloppy barber pole edge. We prefer to slip both sts, leaving the edge open between the layers. It is actually rather nice to see that you have knitted double. When the pattern begins, the layers will be bound together.

BINDING OFF

We bind off by switching the first two sts so they can be bound off with the same color. We twist the needle so each color can be bound off with the same color, thus binding off every other stitch across. Double knitting is usually looser than regular knitting, so go down a needle size or two if you notice the piece is too loosely knitted.

Knitting Techniques

CASTING ON WITH LONG-TAIL CAST-ON

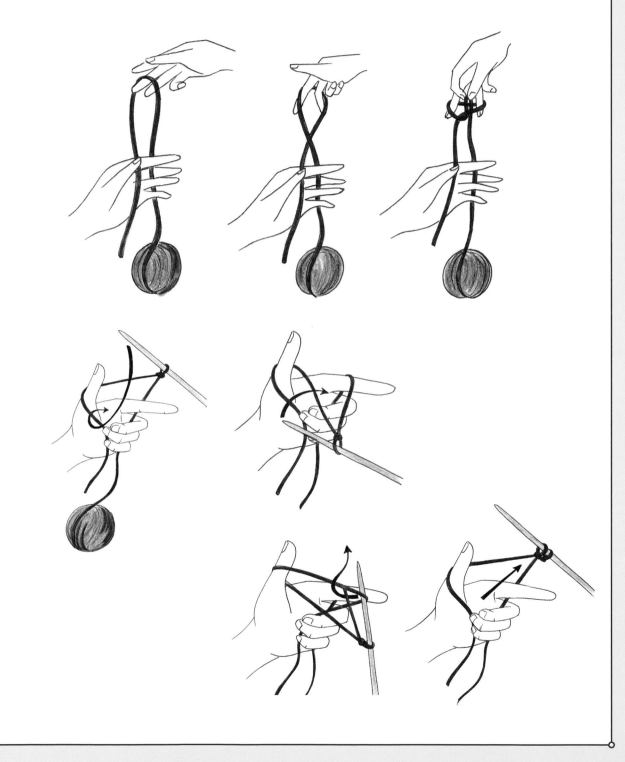

INCREASING

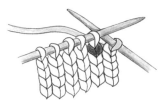 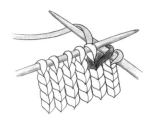 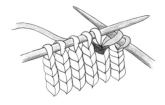

Increase at the beginning of a row with a right-lifted increase (RLI): Knit the 1st stitch and then knit into the right side of the stitch below the 2nd stitch; knit the second stitch and continue across.

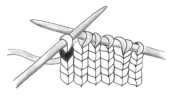 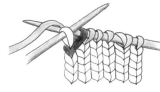 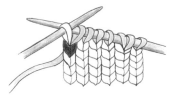

Increase at the end of a row also with a right-lifted increase (RLI): Knit into the right side of the loop of the stitch below the last stitch and then knit the last stitch.

DECREASING WHEN ONE STITCH IS A PATTERN COLOR

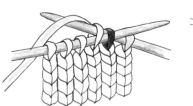 

When you need to knit two stitches together and the first of them is a pattern color, insert the right needle through the back of the first stitch and then the back of the second stitch and knit the two stitches together (=k2tog tbl). This way, the pattern color will lie on top of the background color.

If the pattern color is the second stitch of the pair to be knitted together, work a knit two together (k2tog) as usual. Insert the right needle into the front of 2nd stitch and then into the front of 1st stitch, and then bring the yarn through both stitches.

Crochet Techniques

HANGING LOOPS

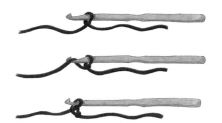

1. Begin with a slip knot over the crochet hook. Make sure the loop is not too tight. Leave a tail long enough to sew through the ball for fastening. Use the hook to catch the yarn from the yarn ball and bring it through the loop on the hook. Now you've made a chain stitch.

2. Continue bringing one loop through after the other until you have made 40 chain stitches.

3. Insert the hook into the first stitch of the chain.

4. Catch the yarn from the ball and bring it through the two loops on the hook.

5. Cut the yarn, leaving a long tail. Draw both ends though the loop on the hook and tighten. Now the hanging loop is ready to sew onto the ball. Thread the ends on a tapestry needle and bring ends though the ball, from top to bottom. Sew the ends separately through the ball on each side of the holes on the top and bottom. Draw the yarn firmly through the ball so the loop sits well at the top, but not too hard or you'll have an apple instead of a Christmas ball! Tie the ends together and weave them into the ball. Trim the ends and the ball is finished!

Embroidery Techniques

EMBROIDERY INSTEAD OF PATTERN KNITTING

If you think that some of the pattern knitting would be a bit difficult with a seldom-used color and/or long floats between the colors, you can work those stitches in the background color instead. After completing the knitting, add the omitted colors with duplicate stitch embroidery. Mark the center of the motif/pattern repeat and then work the stitches in duplicate stitch.

FLOWER EMBROIDERY

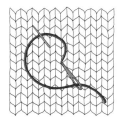 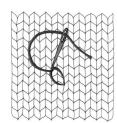 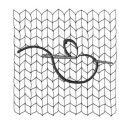 

Embroider flower petals with equal-size large loops, beginning at the center of the flower. On our flower cardigan, we added a few extra stitches in another color over the innermost flower petals.

BACK STITCH

1. Determine the length of each stitch when you work the first stitch.

2. For the second stitch, insert the needle down a half-stitch length from the end of the first stitch and then bring the needle up in the center of the first stitch. Continue the same way until the stitching is completed.

3. When we work with this method, the stitches are all the same length. It is important that the stitches look smooth, even, and aligned.

Making Pompoms

Draw two circles on card stock or cardboard. You can use an egg cup for sizing. Cut out a small hole at the center.

Lay the two circles together and wind the yarn around them. Thread the yarn on a tapestry needle to make the work easier. Insert sharp-pointed scissors between the disks and cut yarn.

Firmly tie a doubled strand of thread between the two disks.

Remove the paper circles and trim the pompom before you sew it on. To make the pompom fluffier, carefully steam it over a tea kettle of boiling water (protect your hands!).

Materials

We used a variety of different types of yarn and other materials in this book—and not all of them may be easily available where you live! Here's a little more information about some places to start your search.

YARN

Rauma yarns are available in the US and Canada through the Yarn Guys (www.theyarnguys.com); visit their website to find a retailer they serve near you.

Rowan, Schachenmayr, and Regia yarns may be available at large yarn stores, and many of their yarns can also be ordered online through Webs®—America's Yarn Store (www.yarn.com). Wash + Filz-it! (a yarn specifically for felting) can be ordered online through LoveKnitting.com (www.loveknitting.com/us). Anchor and DMC Mouliné 6-strand embroidery floss and wool embroidery yarn (for the horse motif pillow) are likely to be available at your local craft or hobby shop, and are also available to order online from retailers such as JoAnn (www.joann.com) and 123Stitch (www.123stitch.com).

DECORATIVE ELEMENTS

Check your local craft or hobby shop for decorative elements such as feathers, sequins, beads, and anti-slip slipper soles, or for materials like glue, wire, and dowels (as for the knitted birds).

Some of these materials may also be available to order online from larger craft retailers such as Michaels (www.michaels.com).

FILLING (STUFFING)

Use acrylic fiberfill or pillow filling; either can be purchased at any craft or hobby shop. You can also use 100% carded wool batting. Use wool filling for Christmas balls, Easter eggs, birds, dolls, rabbits, and mice. We particularly like using natural materials because they're very easy to work with and don't typically clump—but acrylic filling may be cheaper and easier for you to find. Either will work!

NEEDLES

When it comes to needle choice, bamboo or wood needles are easy on the hands—but for knitted dolls and birds, we recommend metal needles, which usually produce the tighter knitting needed for a fabric dense enough to keep the filling from showing through.

WASTE CANVAS

We use Permin waste canvas, which can be hard to find outside Scandinavia! Your local craft or hobby shop may have canvas (and sewing tools and buttons, for that matter). Michaels (www.michaels.com) also stocks waste canvas—which typically can't be ordered online, but you can check to see whether it's available in the store nearest you using their website.

Abbreviations

BO	bind off (= British cast off)	m	meter(s)	sl	slip st without knitting it
CC	contrast color	M1	make 1 = lift strand between 2 sts and knit into back loop	sl m	slip marker
ch	chain st			ssk	(slip 1 st knitwise) 2 times; knit the 2 sts together through back loops = 1 st decreased; left-leaning decrease
cm	centimeter(s)				
CO	cast on	M1p	make 1 purlwise = lift strand between 2 sts and purl into back loop		
dc	double crochet (= treble crochet)				
dec	decrease	MC	main color	St st	stockinette st (UK stocking st)
dpn	double-pointed needles	mm	millimeter(s)		
in	inch(es)	ndl	needle(s)	tbl	through back loop(s)
inc 1	increase 1 st with RLI (right-lifted increase): see page 259 for increase method	p	purl	tr	treble crochet (= UK double treble)
		p2tog	purl 2 together		
		pm	place marker	WS	wrong side
k	knit	psso	pass slipped st over	wyb	with yarn held in back
k2tog	knit 2 sts together = 1 st decreased; right-leaning decrease	rem	remain(s)(ing)	wyf	with yarn held in front
		rep	repeat(s)	yd	yard(s)
		rnd(s)	round(s)	yo	yarnover
		RS	right side